CYBER SECURITY AND RESILIENCY POLICY FRAMEWORK

May 2016

To My Marketing mentor: Jim Rogers

Philip A

NATO Science for Peace and Security Series

This Series presents the results of scientific meetings supported under the NATO Programme: Science for Peace and Security (SPS).

The NATO SPS Programme supports meetings in the following Key Priority areas: (1) Defence Against Terrorism; (2) Countering other Threats to Security and (3) NATO, Partner and Mediterranean Dialogue Country Priorities. The types of meeting supported are generally "Advanced Study Institutes" and "Advanced Research Workshops". The NATO SPS Series collects together the results of these meetings. The meetings are co-organized by scientists from NATO countries and scientists from NATO's "Partner" or "Mediterranean Dialogue" countries. The observations and recommendations made at the meetings, as well as the contents of the volumes in the Series, reflect those of participants and contributors only; they should not necessarily be regarded as reflecting NATO views or policy.

Advanced Study Institutes (ASI) are high-level tutorial courses to convey the latest developments in a subject to an advanced-level audience.

Advanced Research Workshops (ARW) are expert meetings where an intense but informal exchange of views at the frontiers of a subject aims at identifying directions for future action.

Following a transformation of the programme in 2006 the Series has been re-named and re-organised. Recent volumes on topics not related to security, which result from meetings supported under the programme earlier, may be found in the NATO Science Series.

The Series is published by IOS Press, Amsterdam, and Springer Science and Business Media, Dordrecht, in conjunction with the NATO Emerging Security Challenges Division.

Sub-Series

A.	Chemistry and Biology	Springer Science and Business Media
B.	Physics and Biophysics	Springer Science and Business Media
C.	Environmental Security	Springer Science and Business Media
D.	Information and Communication Security	IOS Press
E.	Human and Societal Dynamics	IOS Press

http://www.nato.int/science
http://www.springer.com
http://www.iospress.nl

Sub-Series D: Information and Communication Security – Vol. 38
ISSN 1874-6268 (print)
ISSN 1879-8292 (online)

Cyber Security and Resiliency Policy Framework

Edited by

Ashok Vaseashta

Institute for Advanced Sciences Convergence & Int'l Clean Water Institute
Norwich University Applied Research Institutes
13873 Park Center Rd, Suite 500
Herndon, VA 20112, USA

Philip Susmann

Norwich University Applied Research Institutes
57 Old Freight Way
Northfield, VT 05663, USA

and

Eric Braman

Norwich University Applied Research Institutes
57 Old Freight Way
Northfield, VT 05663, USA

IOS
Press

Amsterdam • Berlin • Tokyo • Washington, DC
Published in cooperation with NATO Emerging Security Challenges Division

Proceedings of the NATO Advanced Research Workshop on
Best Practices and Innovative Approaches to Develop Cyber Security and
Resiliency Policy Framework
Ohrid, Former Yugoslav Republic of Macedonia
June 10-12, 2013

ISBN 978-1-61499-445-9 (print)
ISBN 978-1-61499-446-6 (online)
Library of Congress Control Number: 2014 949 223

Publisher
IOS Press BV
Nieuwe Hemweg 6B
1013 BG Amsterdam
Netherlands
fax: +31 20 687 0019
e-mail: order@iospress.nl

Distributor in the USA and Canada
IOS Press, Inc.
4502 Rachael Manor Drive
Fairfax, VA 22032
USA
fax: +1 703 323 3668
e-mail: iosbooks@iospress.com

PRINTED IN THE NETHERLANDS

Cyber Security and Resiliency Policy Framework
A. Vaseashta et al. (Eds.)
IOS Press, 2014

Preface

The primary objective of the NATO Advanced Research Workshop (ARW) titled "Best Practices and Innovative Approaches to Develop Cyber Security and Resiliency Policy Framework" was to gather specialists who are well versed with the technical problems, case studies, legal and policy development issues related to securing critical cyber infrastructures and enhancing resilience. All aspects of research involving hardening systems, attack prevention, response and recovery, and maximizing resources was included in the ARW. Cyberspace touches nearly every part of our daily lives. It's the broadband networks beneath us and the wireless signals around us, the local networks in our schools and hospitals and businesses, and the massive grids that power almost all nations. It is critical that we secure our cyberspace to ensure that we can continue to grow the economy and protect our way of life. Due to the significance and overarching impact of securing cyber infrastructures, a diverse range of scientific and technological disciplines must be tactically integrated to achieve effective solutions to various scientific, commercial, and operational requirements.

Cyber warfare has become a major concern for international governments, military and civil agencies. Uniform enforcement within organizationally or territorially-defined jurisdictions is nearly impossible given the global architecture of networks and significant number of system administrators, as addressed in the drafting of the 2001 Council of Europe Convention on Cybercrime. A recent wave of cyber-attacks against NATO member Estonia in 2007 and Georgia in 2008 highlighted the crippling impact cyber warfare can have against a nation's critical national infrastructure. The difficulties in responding to these events for a nation state are exacerbated by ownership, operation, and associated national legal systems. Cyber critical infrastructure and its telecommunication networks are owned by the private sector. Gaining situational awareness to an emerging attack is difficult, as organizations must independently determine when to engage law enforcement or governmental agencies. The construction of these systems is dictated by competitive advantage and profit motive, not national security. All of these factors require a public-private partnership in a coordinated national policy framework.

The devastating attacks in Estonia were distributed denial of service events, primarily focused on the financial system. The trend over the last decade to network previously isolated industrial control and monitoring systems has placed national assets, including critical infrastructure, at a much higher risk. Industrial control and monitoring systems are a subset of computer systems that are subject to cyber exploitation. Furthermore, organizations increasingly share information between business systems and local and geographically remote control systems. Security breaches can cause the loss of trade secrets and/or interrupt information flow, resulting in the loss or destruction of services or products. Even more devastating consequences include potential loss of life, damage to the environment, violations of regulatory statutes, and compromises to operational safety. Effective responses to these events requires a logical escalation method through information sharing based on a decision-making model. Threats to these systems can come in many forms such as terrorist, clandestine organizations, and even trusted insiders who misuse authority. Actions in the cyber eco-system outpace the ability of human decision making. Motives and attribution in cyber-attacks are difficult to ascertain. An understanding of the impacts for diverse stakeholders is required and must be fed into the situational awareness of the cyber event which warrants engaging national security apparatus for significant events.

Cyber infrastructures are typically secured by defending the perimeter of the information system. The grand challenges of information security thus cannot be addressed by advanced science or technology alone, but needs to be layered with a national policy context and with engagement of law enforcement, judicial, legislative, and national security agencies. Design of future technologies must enhance both system security and resiliency, and allow swift restoration to full operational capacity to minimize disruption of services. This will require an organized cyber policy framework that defines situational awareness, escalation, and national or super-national decision making for continuity of critical infrastructure and government.

This workshop aimed to develop a governing policy framework to enhance the cyber security of a nation state's critical infrastructure through a process of defining the problem, followed by engaging the participants in interactive "exercises" to illustrate the issues as listed below that provided understanding of the framework.

- Establish a national cyber risk governance model that defines risks and levels of risk tolerance under varying circumstances, assigns responsibility among various stakeholders for defining and managing assigned risks, sets risk management goals and metrics, and determines the conditions for evaluating and refining the model as circumstances warrant;
- Identify and allocate resources necessary to meet risk management goals; and
- Be codified in appropriate policy-setting mechanisms, chosen from those that are constitutionally available, including national or regional legislation, executive order, and non-binding coordinating framework.

The workshop aimed to address views of the conflicting elements of a cyber policy and to initiate a dialogue across key stakeholders in the following areas, such as identifying who is responsible for actions needed to protect government, critical infrastructure, and the civilian population from the effects of a cyber-attack; engaging members of the legislature and judicial systems in developing cyber policy; and understanding what is possible and who is responsible for protecting networks and infrastructure. Furthermore the technical operators must anticipate what the next attack type may be, its severity, and what additional resources might be necessary to help defend, in addition to enhancing prevention of cyber-attacks against the government, military, critical infrastructure and the nation's civilians.

In all, approximately 15 countries participated to experience rich technical contents at a venue with significant historical importance. The ARW site - Hotel Inex Gorica by Ohrid Lake offered an air-conditioned auditorium, sound system, internet connection, adjustable terrace seats, and space suitable for conferences, workshops and congresses. The facility supported formal and informal settings for structured and spontaneous learning and sharing of ideas. Lake Ohrid - the largest and most beautiful of Macedonia's three tectonic lakes, provided a serene mountain setting. With its unique flora and fauna characteristic of the tertiary period, Ohrid is one of Europe's great biological preserves. Most of the lake's plant and animal species are endemic and unique to Ohrid. In 1980, UNESCO proclaimed Lake Ohrid a location of world natural and cultural heritage.

The meeting lasted 3 days. The agenda was packed with sessions. The meals were arranged either in the city or at a walking distance from the hotel. This provided a much needed break from the conference room environment and most everyone stayed engaged despite the inevitable post-lunch slowdown. The unique balance of technical and social interactions materialized in alliances among participants, which have been evidenced by continued correspondence in the months following the ARW. The co-directors interpret the ongoing interaction and positive feedback from participants as an affirmation of a successful ARW. Such a constructive ARW is the outcome of efforts by participants, speakers, and co-directors in addition to a host of caring individuals who supported their work.

Much appreciation is extended to the management of staff at the Hotel Inex Gorica for their gracious hospitality to all participants. Logistics help from Dr. Anka Trajkovska and timely publication of abstract help from Dr. Anita Grozdanov is much appreciated. We offer our gratitude to Dr. Deniz Beten, the director of the NATO Emerging Security Challenges Division and Ms. Alison Trapp for their resolute encouragement and support of the ARW. The co-directors are confident that ARW participants will continue research collaborations that began in Ohrid, Republic of Macedonia to enhance safety and security for all mankind in Support of NATO mission. The ARW was supported by NATO – Emerging Security Challenges division of Science for Peace and Security program.

Organizational Support
Eric Braman, Ashok Vaseashta, Anka Trajkovska, Anita Grozdanov, Ernest Drew, Petar Dimovski, Vilma Petkovska, Aleksander Risteski and Philip Susmann

Editorial Team
Ashok Vaseashta, Philip Susmann, and Eric Braman

Meet the Authors

Sabina BARAKOVIĆ is employed as a professional associate in the Sector for Informatics and Telecommunication Systems of the Ministry of Security of Bosnia and Herzegovina, Sarajevo, Bosnia and Herzegovina since 2009. She received her Dipl.-Ing degree in electrical engineering from the University of Tuzla, Bosnia and Herzegovina in 2009. Currently she is working toward her Ph.D. at the Faculty of Electrical Engineering and Computing, University of Zagreb, Croatia. Her main research interests include Cyber security, Quality of Experience and Quality of Service management in wireless and mobile environments, with a focus on Web services and applications. She has published 20 papers in international journals and conference proceedings. She is currently involved in EU COST Action IC1003 (European Network on Quality of Experience in Multimedia Systems and Services, QUALINET) as a management committee member for Bosnia and Herzegovina and the coordinator of the Qualinet online training school.

Nazife BAYKAL completed her undergraduate studies at the Mathematics Department of the Middle East Technical University in 1987 and got an MS degree from the Computer Engineering Department at METU in 1991. She studied at the Computer Science Department at University of Maryland, College Park as a NATO science scholar between the years 1993 and 1994 for thesis research and other research projects. She received her PhD Degree from the Computer Engineering Department of the METU. After working as an academic staff at the Computer Engineering Department of METU between 1996 and 1999, she was appointed as an academic staff at the Informatics Institute at METU. In 2000, she received the title of Associate Professor of Computer Science. Between January 2002 and January 2003, Dr. Baykal studied Health Informatics at the "School of Health Information Sciences" at the University of Texas. Upon her return, Dr. Baykal contributed to the foundation of the Health Informatics Department at the Informatics Institute, METU, much earlier than most of the prominent colleges around the world did. In 2004, Dr. Baykal was appointed as the director of the Informatics Institute at METU, where she is currently working. She then opened up the Cyber Security graduate program within the same institute, together with a research center - Cyber Defense and Security Center. Her main research interests are: cyber security, cyber defense, computer networks, artificial intelligence, fuzzy logic. Furthermore, she is an active instructor of data mining, medical informatics and computer network graduate courses offered by the Informatics Institute. She provides consultancy services to many governmental and industrial organizations. She has more than 150 Refereed Publications and 7 text books.

Galit M. BEN-ISRAEL (Fixler) is the Head of the Project of Identity, Terror and CyberSpace, in the Institute of Identity Research (IDmap). Dr. Galit Ben-Israel is also a Terrorism analyst and counter-terrorism training consultant & senior lecturer of political science at the Public Administration and Policy, The Faculty of Society and Culture, Beit-Berl Academic College. She teaches courses of: World Politics and Globalization; Terror on the Digital Era and Virtual Communities and Cyber-

Terrorism. Her research field covers themes of: Hostage-Barricade Terrorism (HBT); Suicide Terrorism; Disaster Management via Social Media (Web 2.0) and Diaspora and Internet networks.

Mitko BOGDANOSKI received his B.Sc. degree from the Military Academy, Skopje, Macedonia, and M.Sc. and Ph.D. degree from the Faculty of Electrical Engineering and Information Technologies, Ss Cyril and Methodius University, Skopje, Macedonia, in 2000, 2006 and 2012 respectively. He is currently an assistant professor at the Military Academy "General Mihailo Apostolski" in Skopje. He is an author of more than 50 international/national conference/journal publications. Dr. Bogdanoski was a project leader and participant of several national international projects sponsored. He is a Senior Member of the IEEE Organization and Member of the Organization Committees of several national and international conferences. He is also a reviewer for several journals, magazines and conferences (IJCS (Wiley) (ISI), KSII-TIIS (ISI), IJNS (SCImago), Defence Science Journal (ISI), IMACST, ETAI, etc.). His research interests include cyber security, wireless and mobile networks, MANET, WSN, energy efficiency and communication theory.

Luben BOYANOV graduated from Sofia Technical University in 1985 as a computer science engineer. He defended MSc thesis (1989) and PhD thesis (1996) at the University of Manchester, UK. He became an Associate Professor at the Institute of Parallel Processing at the Bulgarian Academy of Sciences in 2006. His major is in computer science, and the topics of his research activities were LANs, computer architectures, telecommunications. His early research and interests were on LAN interfaces and transputers where he built a shared-memory model and working prototype of transputer link communications. Later work and research was on computer architectures for distributed logic simulation. During the last decade he has been teaching, consulting and working on scientific and research projects on computer networks, GRID computing, e-infrastructure, information and human behavior, smart homes and human behavior. For 8 months he was director of the first Bulgarian supercomputing center. He participated in 10 international projects, on two of which he was project manager. He is also working on two national projects, for one of which he is project manager. Since 2001 he works at the department of Computer Architectures and Networks at the Institute of Information and Communication Technologies at the Bulgarian Academy of Sciences (formerly Institute for Parallel Processing). For more than 15 year he has lectured Computing Machines, Computer Architectures and Computer Networks at Sofia Technical University, University of National and World Economy (Sofia), New Bulgarian University (Sofia), International University College (Dobrich) and European Polytechnical University (Pernik). He has more than 35 publications, including 6 books.

Eric BRAMAN is the Vice President of the NUARI and serves as the Director of the Defense Technologies Research Institute. As a former Deputy Chief of Staff for Operations in the National Guard Bureau for the Pentagon, COL. Braman's expertise lies in leadership, planning, and organization for projects involving experts from military, scientific, academic, and government domains. COL. Braman has served as the principal investigator and director for many government projects and contracts with a successful record of ensuring that all stakeholders and resources remain committed to achieving their overarching goals.

Amir HUSIĆ is employed as a head of Department for Computer Networks in the Sector for Informatics and Telecommunication Systems of the Ministry of Security of Bosnia and Herzegovina, Sarajevo, Bosnia and Herzegovina since 2009. He received his Dipl.-Ing degree in electrical engineering from the University of Tuzla, Bosnia and Herzegovina, in 2003. His main research interests include Cyber security management in public sector and VPN security.

Jasmina Baraković HUSIĆ is employed by BH Telecom, Joint Stock Company, Sarajevo since 2005. She has been working as a professional associate in the Directorate BH Mobile. She graduated from the University of Tuzla, Faculty of Electrical Engineering in 2004. She spent six months at the Munich University of Technology as a scientific researcher during the same year. She has defended doctoral thesis in the field of signaling information transmission at the University of Zagreb, Faculty of Electrical Engineering and Computing in 2009. She joined the University of Sarajevo, Faculty of Electrical Engineering in 2011, where she works as Assistant Professor at the Department for Telecommunications. She also teaches at the Department of Communications of the Faculty of Traffic and Communication. Her research concerns a variety of topics in quality of service and signaling in next generation networks. She has published more than 30 science and professional papers based on her research interests. She is member of IEEE Communication Society and Bosnian-Herzegovinian Society for Telecommunications–BHTEL.

Adnan KULOVAC is employed as head of the CIS Security Department in the Sector for Protection of Classified Information of the Ministry of Security of Bosnia and Herzegovina, Sarajevo, Bosnia and Herzegovina since 2008, after working as a head of IT department in Coal mines “Kreka” and Central Election Commission. He received his Dipl.-Ing and M. Sc. degree in electrical engineering from the University of Tuzla, Bosnia and Herzegovina, in 2002 and 2008, respectively. His main research interests include security management of Web applications and Web services.

Miroslav JOVANOVIC is an expert in the sphere of information technologies with an engineer’s degree in computer science and IT. In the course of his engagement at various managerial positions both in Macedonia and in Serbia, he was dedicated to the IT management and implementation of large ICT systems in the public sector, while in the position of IT Director at the Ministry of Finance he was meritorious for the successful implementation of several projects, including the e-budget project. Prior to his appointment as the Chief Technical Director of Makedonski Telekom in 2009, Mr. Jovanovic worked as a Key Long-Term Expert - Financial Management Information Systems in Serbia. He was appointed to the position of Chief IT Officer of T-Mobile Macedonia on 15 March 2010 and as of 15th October 2011 he assumed the position of Chief IT Officer of Makedonski Telekom.

Gevorg MARGAROV is the head of Information Security and Software Development Department at the State Engineering University of Armenia (Polytechnic), Yerevan, Armenia. The scope of his current scientific interests includes Architecture of Computer Systems and Complexes, Organization and Management of Information Security Systems, Digital Steganography, Applied Cryptography, E-learning and Knowledge Assessment Tools. Gevorg has over 180 scientific publications. He has supervised 10 theses for Candidate of Sciences (PhD) degrees in Armenia and a thesis for the degree of Doctor of Philosophy (PhD) in computer science in France. Gevorg is a member of the Governing Board of National Centre for Professional Education Quality Assurance Foundation (ANQA, Yerevan, Armenia), a professional member of the Association for Computing Machinery (ACM, New York, USA) and a member of the Computer Science Teachers Association (CSTA, New York, USA).

Zlatogor MINCHEV is an 'Associate Professor' on 'Automation and Control' at the Institute of Information and Communication Technologies (IICT), Bulgarian Academy of Sciences (BAS), IT for Security Department (2010); collaborator of the 'Cognitive Psychophysiology' department, Institute of Neurobiology, BAS (since 2003); part-time Associate Professor at the Institute of Mathematics and Informatics – BAS, Operations Research, Probability & Statistics department (2010); B.Sc. degree on 'Informatics & Mathematics' from 'St. St. Cyril and Methodius', University of Veliko Tarnovo (2001); PhD on 'Cybernetics & Robotics' (2006) from Center for Biomedical Engineering 'Prof. Ivan Daskalov', BAS. Since 2001 he is working in the areas of: Computer Science, Robotics and Psychophysiology and since 2005, he is with the applied Operations Research, Planning, Modelling & Simulation for Crisis Management. In 2007 he was appointed as a Director of Joint Training Simulation & Analysis Center, IICT-BAS. During his ten years scientific career he took part in more than 25 scientific projects funded by: Bulgarian government, EU, NATO, USA and the non-governmental sector. Since 2006 Dr. Minchev works with young Bulgarian talents in the fields of mathematics and informatics in cooperation with the non-governmental sector. Since 2010 he participated in a European Network of Excellence in the field of cybersecurity – SysSec where his achievements are marked by UN, EU and NATO. He is also participating in a number of national and international project and initiative in the cyber security area. He has authored and co-authored more than 60 scientific publications, including: nine books and two patents.

Mladen MRKAJA is employed as an assistant minister of security in the Sector for Informatics and Telecommunication Systems of the Ministry of Security of Bosnia and Herzegovina, Sarajevo, Bosnia and Herzegovina since 2010. He received his Dipl.-Ing degree in electrical engineering from the University of East Sarajevo, Bosnia and Herzegovina, in 2003. Currently he is working toward his M.Sc. at the Faculty of Electrical Engineering, University of East Sarajevo, Bosnia and Herzegovina. His main research interests include spectral efficiency of mobile WiMAX, and he is an author of two papers in conference proceedings.

Constantine PAPATHEODOROU is Assistant Professor in the Geomatics & Surveying Department of the Technological Educational Institute of Serres, Greece. He obtained PhD in Engineering Geology from the Civil Engineering Department of the University of Thessaloniki, Greece. He has over 17 years teaching experience in subjects including "Engineering Geologic applications in Civil Engineering", "Chartographic applications in Geology", "Remote Sensing Applications", "Geomatics & Data analysis" (post graduate course in Natural Hazard Prevention & Management), "Geographical Information Systems applications in Natural Hazard Prevention and Management" (post graduate course in Natural Hazard Prevention & Management), "Geographic Information Systems" Post- graduate course "The environment & New Technologies"). His research interests include natural Hazard prevention and management, Geographic Information Systems applications (especially in Natural Hazard Mitigation and in Environmental Protection), Groundwater protection and management, Remote Sensing applications in Geology and the Environment, Applied geophysical research using Ground Penetrating Radar and Seismic Refraction. He is editorial board member of many professional magazines including Geoinformatics.

Predrag PALE was the first one to chase hackers in Croatia as early as 1994 and ever since is present in the information security (IS). He is leading the Information security group within the Laboratory for systems and signals at Faculty of Electrical Engineering at University of Zagreb. The group is intensely involved in technical aspects of information security, is assisting their clients in detecting vulnerability of their systems and designing their protection. He is also active in theoretical research in subfields of IS attack taxonomies, knowledge based authentication, untamperable monitoring of operating systems, and anonymity in electronic voting systems. He established Croatian national CERT and was a member of governmental task force designing National program for information security, the predecessor of the Law on information security. Ever since 1993 he is frequent invited speaker on topic of information security and information warfare at worldwide conferences, NATO & RACVIAC workshops and NATO open road conference. He regularly speaks, teaches and leads workshops for managers, IT specialists, parents, teachers and general public. He is the founder and head of the Center for information security at the Faculty of Electrical Engineering and Computing of Zagreb University aimed at raising awareness about information security in general public and especially to work with youth attracted to the field of information security.

Aleksandar RISTESKI received his B.Sc., M.Sc. and Ph.D. degrees in telecommunications at the University Sts. Cyril and Methodius, Skopje, Macedonia in 1996, 2000 and 2004, respectively. He is currently a professor and a vice-dean for research and international cooperation at the same university, in the Faculty of Electrical Engineering and Information Technologies. In 2001, 2003 and 2004, he had several internships at IBM T. J. Watson Research Center, Yorktown Heights, NY, USA, where he worked towards his Ph.D. degree. His research interests are in the field of secure communications, optical communications, and coding theory. He is an author of more than 70 journal and conference papers He is a mentor of 40 M.Sc. and 6 Ph.D. candidates. Dr. Risteski was a project leader of two national research projects and also a participant in several national and international projects sponsored by European

Commission and IBM. He has also leaded and participated in a number of industry-related consultancy projects. He is a member of the National Board for Accreditation and Evaluation of Higher Education in the Republic of Macedonia. He is president of the Society for Electronics, Telecommunications, Automatics and Informatics (ETAI) of Republic of Macedonia, co-chairman of Conferences ETAI 2009, ETAI 2011, ETAI 2013, and a co-director of NATO Advanced Research Workshop. From 2005 to 2007, he was an independent member of the Board of Directors of Makedonski telekom AD Skopje. He is also a member of the IEEE.

Marjan STOILKOVSKI graduated in 2000 from the Military Academy in Skopje. From 2009 to 2011 he was working on his Mater degree on Cybercrime investigation and digital forensics with the Faculty for Information technology on the University College Dublin in Dublin, Republic of Ireland. Currently, he is working toward his PhD on Computer incidents and digital forensics with the Faculty for Information technologies on the European University in Skopje. From 2008 he was appointed as a Head of the Cybercrime Unit in Ministry of Interior and from 2013 as a Head of the Cybercrime and digital forensics department in Ministry of interior. Beside the professional experience in investigating cybercrime cases he was appointed in the working group for developing the National CERT in Republic of Macedonia and also he is leading the working group for developing a Cyber security strategy in Republic of Macedonia.

Philip SUSMANN obtained a BS from Norwich University and an MBA from Clarkson College of Technology, NY. Currently, he is the VP of Strategic Partnerships at Norwich University responsible for new business initiatives at Norwich University. Mr. Susmann has been at Norwich University for the past 27 years as a faculty member, Chief Information Officer, and recently responsible for creating a research and development activity – Norwich University Applied Research Institutes (NUARI) credited with the development of a Distributed Environment for Critical Infrastructure Exercises (DECIDE) - a platform used to deliver two large scale financial sector exercise Quantum Dawn 1 & 2. In addition, NUARI has developed, in partnership with USU Space Dynamics Lab, Cyber SMART - a cyber exercise scenario development tool.

Ashok VASEASHTA received a PhD from the Virginia Polytechnic Institute and State University, Blacksburg, VA in 1990. Before joining as the Director of Research at the Institute for Convergence of Information, Science, Technology, and Knowledge (formerly Institute for Advanced Sciences Convergence) and International Clean Water Institute, he served as a Professor of Physics and Physical Sciences and Director of Research at the Nanomaterials Processing and Characterization Laboratories, Graduate Program in Physical Sciences at Marshall University. Concurrently, he holds a visiting professorship at the 3 Nano-SAE Research Centre, University of Bucharest, Romania; and a chaired professorship at the Academy of Sciences of Moldova, Chisinau, Moldova.He served as a visiting scientist at the Helen & Martin Kimmel Center of Nanoscale Science at the Weizmann Institute of Science, Israel. In 2007-08, he was detailed as a William C. Foster fellow to the Bureau of ISN at the U.S. Department of

State working with the Office of WMDT and FCM programs. He served as a Franklin Fellow and S&T advisor to the office of VTT/AVC in the Bureau of Arms Control Verification and Compliance at the U.S. Department of State. He is a fellow of the American Physical Society, Institute of Nanotechnology, and New York Academy of Sciences. He was awarded a Gold medal by the State Engineering University of Armenia for his contribution to Nanotechnology. In addition, he has earned several other fellowships and awards for his meritorious service including the Marshall University 2004/2005 Distinguished Artist and Scholar award. His research interests include counter-terrorism; advanced and nano materials for development of chemical-bio sensors/detectors; water safety and security; environmental pollution monitoring, detecting and remediation; and green nanotechnology. He authored over 230 research publications, edited/authored five books on nanotechnology, presented many keynote and invited lectures worldwide, served as the NATO Project Director of five NATO ASI/ARW, multi-year SPS program, and co-chair of an ISNEPP conferences. He led the U.S. position on Nanotechnology in High Technology Coordination Group to joint U.S. and India delegation. In addition, he served as a member of the U.S. Department of Commerce, NIST, and ANSI delegation to the U.K. representing the U.S. position on Standards in Nanotechnologies at the inaugural meeting of the ISO/TAG to TC-229. He is a member of NATO-SET-040, an exploratory team panel investigating security and surveillance applications of nanotechnology. He serves as an expert counsel to the UNESCO, ObservatoryNANO, and COSENT – south-east consortium on Nanotechnologies on NANO-Science and Technologies. He is an active member of several national and international professional organizations.

NATO – Advanced Research Workshop Best Practices and Innovative Approaches to Develop Cyber Security and Resiliency Policy Framework June 10-12, 2013, Ohrid, Republic of Macedonia

Selected Photographs

Questions?

INEX
HOTEL GORICA

УНИВЕРЗИТЕТ
ЗА ИНФОРМАТИЧКИ НАУКИ И ТЕХНОЛОГИИ
University
for Information Science and Technology
„St. Paul the Apostle" - Ohrid

Contents

Cyber Security and Resiliency Policy Framework
A. Vaseashta et al. (Eds.)
IOS Press, 2014

doi:10.3233/978-1-61499-446-6-1

Cyber Security – Threat Scenarios, Policy Framework and Cyber Wargames

Ashok VASEASHTA[*,**1], Philip SUSMANN[*] and Eric BRAMAN[*]
[*]*Norwich University Applied Research Institutes*
57 Old Freight Way, Northfield, VT 05663 USA
[**]*IASC/ICWI, Norwich University Applied Research Institutes*
13873 Park Center Rd., Herndon, VA 05663 USA

Abstract. Securing digital assets is an extremely difficult and strategic challenge worldwide that requires technology, cooperation between the public and private sector, military and civilian education and training, and a legal and policy framework. Unfortunately, cyber-crime and cyber–terrorism are on the rise and the perpetrators operate from shadows without boundaries. The technology that is developed to enhance our capabilities has the capacity to inflict harm by way of misusing information, pilfering financial assets, jeopardizing safety, security and integrity of our critical infra-structure. The nature of the technology and our growing reliance on its reliability and security opens vulnerability on a personal to national scale. A cyber-attack by small groups or individuals capable of large consequence is now a reality. Nation states and significant sub national actors are developing skills to promote political motives into the cyberspace with cyber crime as the noise that obfuscates the methods and tactics of cyberwar. Cyber-wars are always ongoing, however events such as a "Cyber-9/11" or the "Cyber Pearl Harbor", though possible cannot be predicted. Cyber-war has escalated in a pervasive manner with advanced persistent threats infiltrating our national security and defense industrial base systems. Urgency exists worldwide to define a national cyber policy to enhance resiliency in the cyber domain. This requires examining consequence and probability while exploring methods for escalation of response to be considered. Defining what indicators and warnings will engage a national response to the cyber event is a representation of the national capability and priorities. At what point do nations collaborate with national partners to respond as a region. Each national policy will mirror the will of the society and government adopting those tenets but some basic parameters help to lead the development of the policy. The policy must be tested and processes developed and exercised to ensure resiliency. A critical element of national policy and regional collaboration must be the development of national and regional cyber exercises and war-games that hone response and refine capability. Finally, cooperation across multiple nations requires the development of trust initially to create the legal framework for sharing information and resources.

Keywords: *cyber-security, policy, cyber-exercises, war-games, legal, critical Infra-structure*

---

[1] Corresponding author email: prof.vaseashta@ieee.org

Introduction

Securing digital assets is an extremely difficult and strategic challenge worldwide that requires technology, cooperation between the public and private sector, military and civilian education and training, and legal and policy framework. Unfortunately, cyber-crime and cyber–terrorism are on the rise and the perpetrators operate from shadows without boundaries. This is compounded by the fact that the world today relies on computer and interconnectivity and cyber-criminals exploit everyone's basic necessity for their own personal gain – may it be financial, seeking revenge, or gaining personal notoriety or thrills. The New York Times reported that a speech delivered by United States Secretary of Defense Leon E. Panetta warned that "*the United States was facing the possibility of a "cyber-Pearl Harbor" and was increasingly vulnerable to foreign computer hackers who could dismantle the nation's power grid, transportation system, financial networks and government*". In another speech at the Intrepid Sea, Air and Space Museum in New York, "*An aggressor nation or extremist group could use these kinds of cyber tools to gain control of critical switches,*" Mr. Panetta said. "*They could derail passenger trains, or even more dangerous, derail passenger trains loaded with lethal chemicals. They could contaminate the water supply in major cities, or shut down the power grid across large parts of the country*"[2]. Mr. Panetta painted a dire picture of how such an attack on the United States might unfold, while reacting to increasing aggression and technological advances by the nation's top adversaries, which officials identified as China, Russia, Iran and militant groups out of middle-east. This opens a possibility of Cyber 9/11!

From a philosophical standpoint, the internet protocol is derived from ARPAnet, which was used by some scientists in a spirit of intellectual curiosity and scientific cooperation. Further evolution contributed to exceptional progress in the field with great applications in banking, social, technical, and enhanced situational awareness. A "*weaponized internet*" was not a remote intention and hence no countermeasures were contemplated. It is for this reason that the scientific society finds themselves in a situation wherein the unanticipated ill-intentions of cyber-criminals and terrorists are to use the Internet as a "*weapon*". In hindsight, the intersection of evermore and greater reliance on technology to manage our daily routines, and those of business, government and the workings of critical infrastructure with the growing enhanced sophistication and funding of cyber-war capabilities worldwide is a blueprint for significant opportunity for catastrophe.

Ubiquitous interconnectedness is a major vulnerability notwithstanding being a great capability and asset. While the administration is focused on the primary control systems or Supervisory Control and Data Acquisition (SCADA) systems, it is critical to fully understand the characteristics, principles, and challenges that underlie the development of secure information systems. Software weaknesses, user's behavior, inadequate cyber-security professional training, and under-funded projects to institute and activate countermeasures contribute to the vulnerability. Furthermore, a multidisciplinary approach along with international cooperation and a comprehensive set of complementary tools, methods, policy, and laws is likely to significantly reduce the consequences of malicious attacks.

It is with this international cooperation that the NATO Advanced Research Workshop (ARW) titled "Best Practices and Innovative Approaches to Develop Cyber

[2] www.nytimes.com/2012/10/12/world/panetta-warns-of-dire-threat-of-cyberattack.html

Security and Resiliency Policy Framework" was conducted to gather specialists who are well versed with the technical problems, case studies, legal and policy development issues related to securing critical cyber infrastructures and enhancing resilience. All aspects of research involving hardening systems, attack prevention, response and recovery, and maximizing resources was included in the ARW. A short synopsis of each chapter is described later in this chapter.

1. Cyber Security Perspectives

Cyber security is defined by the International Standards Organization (ISO) 27032 as the preservation of confidentiality, integrity, and availability information in cyberspace. In this context, it is crucial to debate and define risk, threat and vulnerability. Risk is a probability associating the impact of loss or compromise to the expectation it will occur. This association informs the asset owner of the threshold for implementing mitigation strategies. Organizations and individuals must recognize the risk and implement mitigation factors that are economically reasonable. Threat is defined as an action that can compromise the confidentiality, integrity, or availability of an asset through vulnerability. We look at threats in terms of actors and motivations. Vulnerability is the existence of a weakness in a system, either known or unknown, that renders a system vulnerable to compromise. A vulnerability can affect the confidentiality, integrity, or availability of the system. The impact of the vulnerability is related the value of the compromised system. Unknown or widely unknown defects are sometimes referred to as zero-day exploits, because no remediation or warning may exist for the exploit. Vulnerabilities may be related to any part of the system from user interactions to the operating system or network protocol. All systems have vulnerabilities by the nature of use and interaction with humans. Awareness and training of users, structured systems development, and rigorous testing can reduce vulnerabilities.

The following terms are commonly used in literature to identify, define, and/or describe unusual activities over the network:

- Cyber Attacks: computer-to-computer attack that undermines the confidentiality, integrity, or availability of a computer or information resident on it.
- Cyber Terror: The deliberate destruction, disruption or distortion of digital data or information flows with widespread effect for political, religious or ideological reasons.
- Cyber Utilization: The use of on-line networks or data by terrorist organizations for supportive purposes.
- Cyber Crime: The deliberate misuse of digital data or information flows.

As per Wikipedia[3], Cyber warfare is defined as "politically motivated hacking to conduct sabotage and espionage". Cyber warfare involves the actions by a nation-state, international organizations, or individual hackers (even thrill seekers) who have malicious intent to attack and attempt to damage another nation's computers or information networks through, for example, computer viruses or denial-of-service attacks. Such attempts are meant to severely disrupt commerce, infra-structure, flow of

[3] http://en.wikipedia.org/wiki/Cyber-attack

information, create mass confusion and panic, steal or blackmail items of interest and include terms defined above such as cyber-attack, terror, utilization, and crime. Cyber warfare is not a low intensity conflict (LIC); conversely, it is best described as asymmetric warfare with undefined borders and no rules of engagement (ROE). At present, the best line of defense is multiple layers of protection and with opposing state players, cyber warfare is increasingly characterized by engagements approximating an all-out offensive.

1.1 Cyber Security Threat and Scenarios

Numerous nuisance attack events take place in the form of unwanted email spam, phishing messages with malware in the form of viruses or Trojans, and probes of network perimeter devices. On an individual basis these types of events are classified as mere inconveniences but may also be the preambles to more significant criminal activity. Cyber attacks, as defined above, are not bound by geographic region in the same way a physical event would be defined and motivation can range from simple thrill seeking (low consequence) to critical infrastructure attacks (high consequence). The Internet was not designed with an effective foundation for threat defense, and constantly evolving Internet technologies defy relative security and confidence. Moreover, because of the constantly evolving nature of Internet technologies, there is a lack of horizon scanning – attempts to anticipate unconventional cyber threats to stay ahead of the curve. Multiple sector attacks require sophisticated technologies and coordination of action. The ability to execute these types of multiple sector attacks point to a capability of a nation-state or significant sub-national actor, such as a pan-national terrorist organization.

The National Institute of Standards and Technology (NIST) is asking government agencies to implement a cyber security framework[4] - published in February 2014. There are four levels at which the framework could be implemented to "provide context on how an organization views cyber security risk and the processes in place to manage that risk." The highest level, Tier 4, is labeled "Adaptive". An organization that "actively adapts to a changing cyber security landscape and responds to evolving and sophisticated threats in a timely manner" and has "continuous awareness of activities on their systems and networks" meets Tier 4 requirements. Though NIST admits that the tiers don't necessarily represent actual maturity of cyber security defenses; agencies should be "encouraged" to move to higher levels, as needed.

One method of describing the cyber security threat is by mapping the intent of actions with respect to the probability of the attack against the consequences of the attack. On the consequence scale, individual events are minor and although the probability of being attacked is very high; the impact is negligible. Further up on the consequence scale are attacks that are more coordinated and sophisticated with the intent to pilfer financial assets and/or damage systems. Consequences grow if the attacks are directed at cyber-physical systems; impacting the physical world through manipulation of control systems. Somewhere in the middle of the curve, the intentions may point to political motivations. We define increasing consequence when attacking critical infrastructures as shown in fig. 1. Critical infrastructure such as water, energy,

[4] http://www.nist.gov/itl/csd/launch-cybersecurity-framework-021214.cfm

transportation, financial, and health care are examples of assets essential for a functioning society. Disruption of these critical infrastructures can have significant impacts on the ability of the government to provide essential services. Impact or consequence grows as the effects are focused on multiple critical infrastructures. Nevertheless, for organizations to successfully thwart any cyber incident in the future, effectiveness will not be based on how many attackers they can keep out of their networks and systems, but how fast and how effectively they can detect and respond to attacks that are already present/taken place/in-progress.

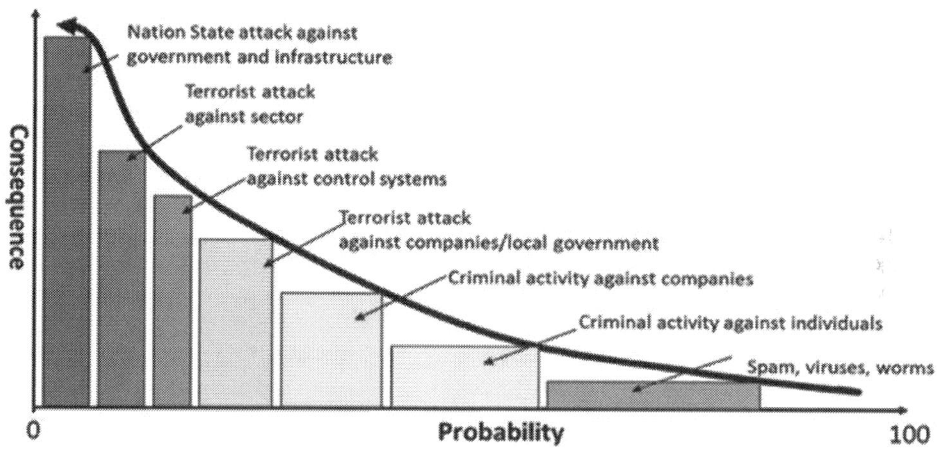

Figure 1. Consequence vs. Probability of Cyber Attacks

At the far left of the chart are low probability events due to significant sophistication of the attacks as well as organized coordination. Execution of the malware attack is a high probability event due to the low cost and effort to assemble the tools and networks. The other important factor is attribution of the event which complicates response options and legal proceedings, thus requiring a legal and policy framework.

1.2 Critical Infrastructure

An important concept when assessing cyber security is the critical infrastructure. The United States Department of Homeland Security (DHS), defines critical infrastructure as the backbone of the nation's economy, security, and health. It is the assets, systems, and network necessary for survival of an organization or nation. DHS identifies the following as critical infrastructures: Agriculture and Food, Water, Public Health, Emergency Services, Defense Industrial Base, telecommunications, Energy, Transportation, Banking and Finance, and Chemicals and Hazardous Materials. Each of these sectors represents a critical facet of society required for national prosperity and security. These critical infrastructures are often owned and operated by private sector organizations. The telecommunications sector provides the basis for telephony and network traffic and operates as the link between individuals and organizations. It is the vector by which we communicate and also the means to propagate a network based cyber-attack. The telecommunications sector is operated by private businesses that are organized and poised for making profit. A profitable business model must generate an excess of revenue beyond expenses that rewards the owners for their investment – the model of a capitalistic society. Though telecommunications companies are highly regulated and are dictated to meet secure standards, they must still generate a return on investment (ROI) large enough to attract capital to build the network and systems. It is this relationship, the cost of loss of the critical infrastructure versus the cost of implementing the physical systems that defines the assumption of societal risk. The loss of critical infrastructure in terms of costs to individuals and society can far outweigh the investment to develop and deploy the infrastructure. Constant pressure and competition forces organizations to carefully assess deployment of security against overall operating margins. National organizations aggregate across multiple sectors to identify trends and threats as well as to share best practice information as the threat environment evolves.

2. Policy Framework

Two extremes define the basis for a national cyber policy as shown in Figure 2, viz. what is the definition of due care that we expect to connect to the national and global network. It is at the far right of the graph that defines acceptable behavior as well as the threshold for criminal activity. At the far left of the graph is the development of a national capability to respond and recover. The internet does not observe national boundaries and requires nations to develop relationships and international treaties to share information and resources in the event of a catastrophic cyber event.

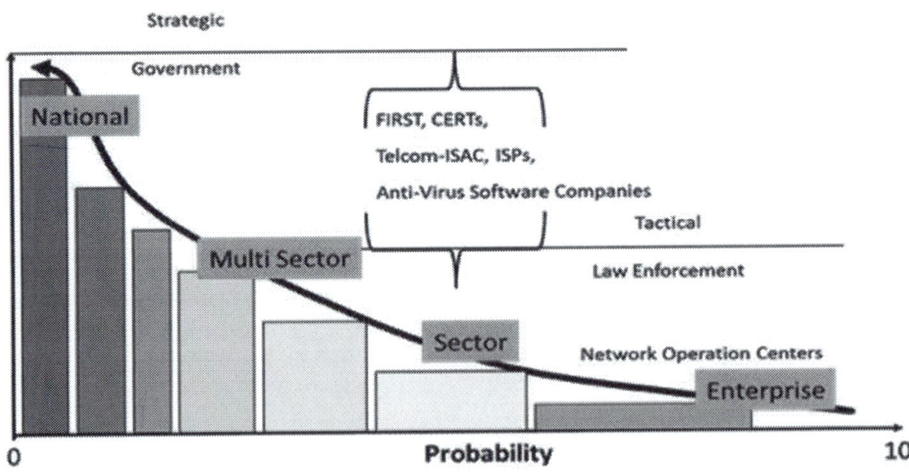

Figure 2: Strategic vs. Tactical limits

It is at these two ends that we can look at the will of the society and the tradeoffs between privacy, individual rights and security. If all data-traffic is inspected and analyzed then the opportunity to identify infected or compromised systems can be correlated and much like a strict organizational network, greater security can be ensured. The mandatory implementation for controls and limits on web sites on individual systems may mitigate some risks at the cost of loss of privacy or the right to view any website. It is this balance and the tolerance/expectations of the society that will dictate how intrusive the security policy will and should become. The same is true for the development of a national cyber security capability and architecture. A trusted enclave is created wherein resources and information can be shared. The perimeter of the enclave is constructed to limit actions and information through hardened systems that enforce cyber security policies. The perimeter should be monitored most certainly for traffic entering the enclave but also for traffic exiting the enclave. Rules are developed that will either alert and/or limit access when the policy is violated and the perimeter compromised.

As events grow in consequence from an attack on an individual or a single enterprise to a sector and then further to a multi-sector, responses must increase in sophistication. There must be an awareness of the threshold where the enterprise must reach out for assistance from law enforcement and where law enforcement must escalate the incident handling to regional or national entities. Law enforcement needs legal jurisdiction to respond, analyze, investigate, and a framework to prosecute and punish across traditional geographical investigative and prosecutorial boundaries. As an event grows in sophistication across multiple entities, the ability to share information becomes important. Operational specifics for a sector or critical infrastructure through aligned business models or systems have created information sharing and analysis centers that are both national and global in nature. These centers take in incident information from multiple critical infrastructure operators and correlate the events looking for common tactics, exploits, and vulnerabilities. These centers then share the threat information with members of the sector. National organizations aggregate across multiple sectors to identify trends and threats as well as share best practice information as the threat environment evolves. The point at which the event invokes a national response and engages the national security apparatus will vary greatly on the coordination that exists between organizations, sector, and between multiple sectors.

3. Cyber Wargames

Cyber war games are designed to examine how (a): an organization responds to realistic simulated cyber crises; (b): an organization enacts & adapts business continuity plans, (c): an organization has appropriate contingency plans, and (d): under which conditions an organization is most likely to fail. Such simulations provide insights to a prolonged and persistent Red Team attack in several multifaceted phases; specifically to mobilize an organization's full Blue Team capability through an escalating attack, and challenges the various responses, methods, teams, and decision-makers to cope with complex scenarios. In recent times, discussions relating to cyber war capabilities and associated terrorist organizations have been reported in the popular press. This revelation signals an increase in the breadth and depth of sophisticated techniques by which threat actors have attacked critical infrastructure. Companies, such as Symantec, CISCO, IBM, etc. employ cyber war games to prepare for hackers. Cyber war games employ fictitious firms and execute events that simulate actual attacks. These "cyber-readiness challenges" help understand the hackers, their *modus-operandi*, and tactics so as to better recognize and respond to their corporations' vulnerabilities. With this is a common objective, this ARW organized several cyber exercises with the following objectives:

- Who has the responsibility of protecting against cyber-attacks targeting the critical infrastructure?
- How does current legislation and regulation address the consequences of Cyber-attack?
- What are the roles of government, NATO, Industry Organizations, and critical infrastructure providers in the development of coherent Cyber Security Policy?

The outcomes of these exercises respectively were:

- Parameters for identifying - "Who's in Charge?" and identification of event classification: private, information sharing, law enforcement, nation response, international response. What are the dimensions to allow for a national response to a private infrastructure event? This helps to define the legal construct required for governmental intervention or support of critical infrastructures operated by the private sector.
- The evolution of the technology outpaces the ability of the judicial branch to create legislation that balances the private sector operators of critical infrastructures with the societal responsibilities of essential services, continuity of government, and a safe and secure cyber infrastructure. The elements of this gap between legislation and technology begin to be identified and considerations for the legislative approach emerge.
- Understanding of the stakeholders required in the development of a cyber security policy and their inherent conflicts. How the interests of the stakeholders create natural tensions in policy setting and how we can describe these tensions. Using a model for understanding the nature of the problem across the spectrum of severity describe what is the expectations of the stakeholders from actions of each other.

4. Synopsis of Chapters

The report from Milan Maric described how the Ministry of Information society of Government Montenegro initiated an ambitious e-Government project based on a Multipurpose E-Government Web Portal with an e-Service generator, payment gateway and delivery service included, serving as "a one stop government" for all end-users (citizen, business, and government agencies). The article describes how to improve the security of e-Government services and override the problem of potential malicious or improper usage by identifying who is responsible, what needs to be done and when to do it.

The report of Risteski et al. deals with complex security issues dealing with the telecommunications infra-structure and interconnectedness. In addition to the interplay of different technologies, the overall dynamics involves passive monitoring to active countering of destructive attacks disabling the normal operation of ICT (information and communication technology) infrastructure. Therefore, security issues for the telecommunication infrastructure must be thoroughly addressed by all relevant stakeholders. Since each technology includes certain security mechanisms, it is necessary to create a well-designed security concept for the infrastructure as a whole, taking into consideration not only the technical issues, but also the policy framework and legal aspects. The case of Republic of Macedonia is elucidated.

Cveto Andreeksi from the University of St. Kilemnt-Ohridski discusses security issues related to mobile devices. Since such devices hold sensitive information and are used with different type of wireless and mobile communication lines, such communication increases the risk of unintended data transfer. Their characteristics (dimensions, processing power, networking etc.), working environment, stored information and their value, makes them suitable for theft and abuse. This article addresses the problem of countermeasures needed to make smart phones and tablets more secure.

Gevorg Margarov, the Head of the Information Security and Software Development Department at the State Engineering University of Armenia makes the case of endpoint security and importance of education and training.

Metodi Hadji-Janev, COL. and Dean of the Military Academy "General Mihailo Apostolski, in Skopje discusses future cyber security and strategy path-forward for Macedonia and the region of South East Europe (SEE), in general. The article discusses several aspects including a comprehensive approach addressing cyber-crime; cyber defense; intelligence and counterintelligence, critical information infrastructure protection and crisis management; and cyber diplomacy and cyber governance. Given that most of the SEE countries share the same history and political, social and security dynamics with small adjustments, the findings and recommendation could apply to the rest of the SEE countries.

Sabina Barakovic et al. provides an overview of the complex security management organization for the territory of Bosnia and Herzegovina and how technological innovations lag in comparison to advanced European countries. The Ministry of Security of Bosnia and Herzegovina has initiated an establishment of the Computer Emergency Response Team in Bosnia and Herzegovina – BIH CERT. This article aims to provide an overview of the activities of the Ministry of Security of Bosnia and Herzegovina in the area of cyber security focusing on establishment of the BIH CERT body. The BIH CERT has been envisioned as a preventive body which gives recommendation for the application and improvement of the security measures for protection of the information systems of Bosnia and Herzegovina's governmental institutions. In addition, this body will represent the Bosnia and Herzegovina's central point for cooperation with the international CERTs and thereby contribute to the security of the overall cyber space.

Nazife Baykal argues a need to develop national and international cyber security strategies for holistic, integrated, comprehensive approach supported by strong leadership, enhanced governmental coordination, reinforced public-private co-operation, and improved international co-operation. The report presents national strategy that resulted in National Cyber Security Strategy document and 2013-2014 Action Plan. The strategy document lists cyber security risks and measures, 7 major topics, 29 key actions and 30 governmental organizations responsible of these actions. In the 2013-2014 Action Plan, 29 actions in the scope of the major topics, sub-actions and organizations responsible of these actions are reported. An evaluation of cyber security studies in Turkey is also reported.

Galit Ben-Israel describes an app developed by Israeli civilians living in Tel Aviv during the Operation Pillar of Defense in November 2012. At the time when the IDF (Israel Defense Forces) was engaged in a military attack on Gaza, code-named "Pillar of Defense", the armed Palestinian militant groups Hamas and Palestinian Islamic Jihad were firing Grad and Kassam rockets at civilians in the State of Israel's home front. The new applications were designated to mark and map the locations of public shelters during emergencies in Israeli cities and towns for the benefit of civilians regularly using smartphones and applications. This illustrates a case of a citizen driven defense–oriented smartphone app in an interconnected world that materialized out of necessity more quickly than it could have been done from within the bureaucracies of government.

Predrag Pale from University of Zagreb makes a case for an accelerated, mandatory and prompt education and increased awareness of cyber security for all age groups. Cyber security educations should be a major component of everyone's continuous, lifelong education. He suggests that to support this strategy, national centers for increased awareness and broad education should be established, strongly linking academia both because of academia's deep insight in cyber security development and its involvement in the development of educational methods and tools.

Luben Boyanov and Zlatogar Minchev address cyber security issues related to smart homes. With the introduction of smart devices and systems in our homes, the risks and threats linked to them and correspondingly to the smart home inhabitants will grow. The digital world as we know it has gradually developed standards, protocols, interfaces, operating systems, programming models and architectures, making both computing and networking a type of plug-and-play environment. The smart house and its services, as we know them, form a highly heterogeneous environment, which presents a significant challenge for future users and manufacturers. Healthcare services contain unknown dangers to human life, and present real vulnerabilities in interconnected medical devices.

Konstantine Papatheodorou from the Institute of Serres, Greece reports an application concerning case studies for the identification and delineation of ground water (GW) recharge areas using remote sensing. The methodologies proposed in this report have been tested in various areas of Northern Greece providing reliable results at minimal costs. Their combined application can provide the tools to constantly monitor GW quality, to detect GW pollution at a very early stage, to select and apply remediation measures and to continuously rate them, to detect pollution sources, to support decision making regarding land uses, to help raise public awareness and overall, and to ensure GW protection and sustainability.

Our debt of gratitude to NATO, the key speakers, and many discussions with participants who contributed enormously to the contents. Many sectors of the society – such as University, Government agencies, Military, Legal professionals, Financial institutions, Computer scientists, and lawmakers were represented leading to many new and innovative ideas to counter a silent threat that we all face.

Cyber Security and Resiliency Policy Framework
A. Vaseashta et al. (Eds.)
IOS Press, 2014

doi:10.3233/978-1-61499-446-6-11

E-Government 3 Web Security Issues: Who, What, When?

Milan MARIC[1]
S&T Crna Gora d.o.o
Bulevar Revolucije 5
81000 Podgorica, MONTENEGRO

Abstract. The millennium project was created with an intensive development of ICT systems development in support of E-Government applications which enables administrative authorities in several countries and municipalities that have considered E-Government as a helpful tool for better informing public and changing quality of their core business services to citizens and to improve constituent satisfaction. Usually E-Government was initiated by different authorities and refers to government use of technology, particularly web-based Internet applications to enhance the access to and delivery of government information and service to citizens, business partners, employees, other agencies and government entities. We noticed that in several stages of development of E-Government, there were security vulnerabilities in government services as sensitive information remained accessible to different subjects, citizens, and institutions of government. In this article, we will highlight how to improve security of E-Government services and override the problem of potential malicious or improper usage. The Ministry of Information society of Government Montenegro initiated an ambitious e-Government project based on Multipurpose E-Government Web Portal with an e-Service generator, payment gateway and delivery service included, serving as "a one stop government" for all end-users (citizen, business, and government agencies).

Keywords. E-Government, government services, decision-making, transparency

Introduction

"*In the beginning was Information*" [1]. Authorities around the world promote usage of E-Government services to provide more useful information to the public, improve efficiency, effectiveness, and transparency of government service delivery, and on the other hand improve active participation of citizens in public decision-making processes – therefore developing democracy. But, information technology is sometimes used to reinforce existing administrative and political arrangements [2]. This may be perceived by a wide audience as E-Government an as extended Government tool for controlling. Thus could also lead to a malicious user, negatively oriented towards government authorities, and other authorities in general, such as characteristically younger population, to try to disable and block E-Government services. Unstable E-Government services could be their small victory against authorities, symbolically showing their power against Government. Cyber-attacks could be directed to support different

[1] E-mail : milan.maric@snt.me

political subjects against government, or simply to block normal Information and Communication Technology (ICT) on national level and produce panic or psychological unstable impression of current situation in a country. It is not possible to develop modern, open E-Government system and at the same time prevent access. But we could apply a "need to know" restriction system, implemented through Enterprise System Bus, dealing with main security issues. We recognized three web security issues about access and use of information: **What - Who - When**?

1. Web-security issues

1.1 First: Information publishing (What)

From a technical perspective, an e-government model utilizes technology to accomplish reform by fostering transparency, eliminating distance and other divides, and empowering people to participate in the political processes that affect their lives [3]. In the initial stage of e-government development, Government is the main initiator, where information about activities of the government is available online. The government published information to citizen through website and all other important information is posted on the website and citizens access governmental Web sites more often to obtain information than to transact [4]. However, it is not enough to establish advanced technical infrastructure for E-Government, moreover, governments must develop a user-centric model that involves key stakeholders outside of government – such as businesses, commerce, artist, scientists, NGOs, etc., without which e-Government projects are unlikely to succeed, because end-users will not use a system that does not fits to their needs [3]. The first stages of e-government had been mainly focused on IT introduction in order to improve the quality and quantity of data, Figure 1b, and to foster horizontal and vertical integration of back office and front-office systems, following generally the ′stages of growth′ model of Layne and Lee [5,6].

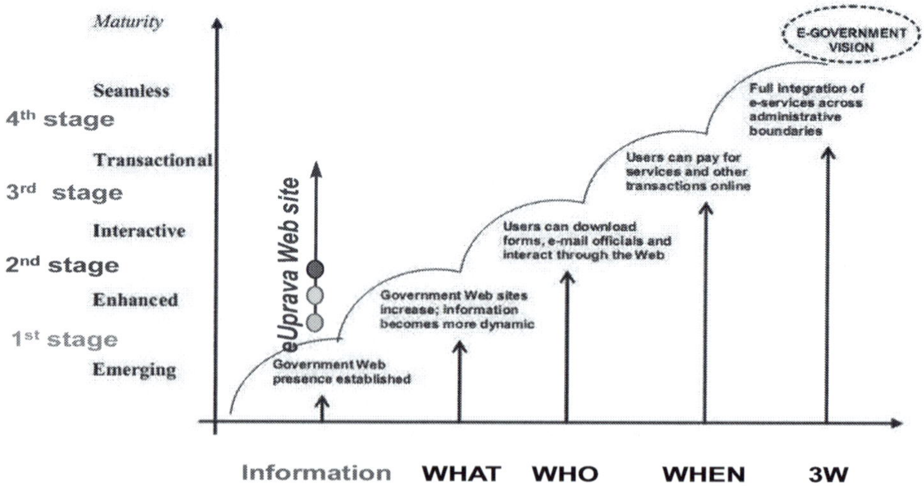

Figure 1. E-Government phases

This approach within the information publishing phase enabled self-service, but most often in the form of PDF files that can be downloaded, completed, and then returned either as an attachment to e-mail or by mailing the completed form to government. The organizations in this group are not likely to focus on digital services, and will rarely have work processed and displayed through the net.

1.2 Second: Interactivity & Users (Who)

The Public Sector Process Rebuilding (PPR) model [7-9] uses an activity and customer centric approach rather than that of technological capability. The interactivity phase is the extension stage with extensive use of intranet and adoption of personalized Web user interface for customer processes. The Web user interface is targeted towards the registered end-users rather than other unknown public authorities or the agencies themselves. At this stage there are still many manual routines, and while the user might be likely to find many forms and information, each agency is equally interested in re-directing the users to information at other agencies.

1.3 Third: Transactional ON line (When)

The transaction ON line phase is characterized by data mobility across organizations as business subjects, application mobility across vendors, and ownership to data transferred to customers. In this phase, the employees' actions can be traced through the Internet and there is information available online about progress in, for example, case handling. This is possible through intra and extra organizational mobility of data and services. The Internet is not seen exclusively as a means to create increased mobility within the government.

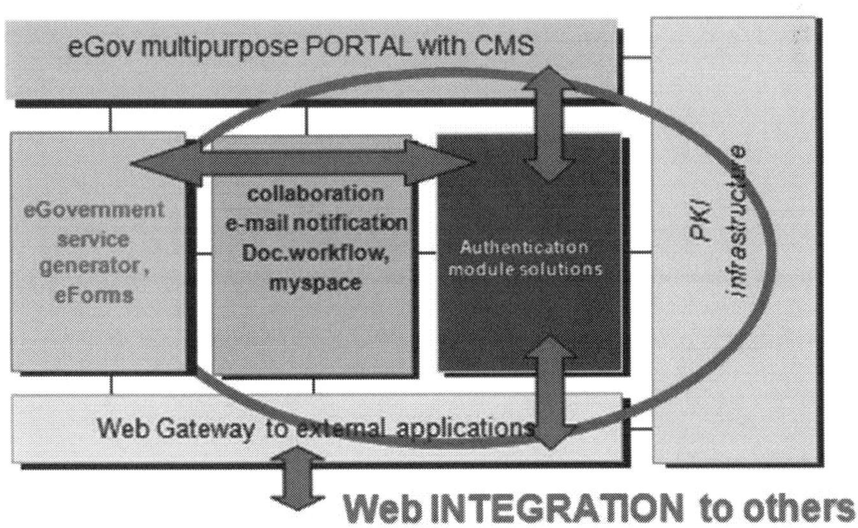

Figure 2: IT e-Government architecture

Business is the initiator of on-line transactions, as this is most efficient way to finish administrative processes initiated from end users and also businesses can be an active part of it. In this phase, saving time is a critical factor for adoption and businesses tried to decrease time spent on administrative processes.

1.4 Seamless Integration (Who-What-When)

Seamless integration is a never ending phase where the basic goal is to integrate all the BackOffice applications, directly attached to one front-end Web office, which we might call "One stop Government". To achieve this aim, technically speaking, interoperability framework is needed as a basic act for re-engineering existing processes by reducing bottlenecks and intermediaries, enabling special applications of Web Interfaces to connect back offices. This is seamless and an ideal vision in which processes initiate sophisticated, unified, and personalized services to every user, according to their own needs and preferences. The last phase is a long-term goal for e-government development, where Government is offering tools such as online voting, polling and surveys, which is an attempt to improve political participation, citizen involvement, and political transparencies. At the same time, e-Government gradually changes the way in which people make political decisions.

2. E-Government project in Montenegro

2.1 Information to citizen (What)

In 2006, the initiator of E-Government project in Montenegro was Ministry of Information Society of Government Montenegro, and it adopted three methodologies, for measurement, development and maintenance of E-Government systems [10,11]. This was an emerging stage where an official government online presence was established. At this stage government sets up websites (static) for providing information to citizen /users, communication is one-way, and information is limited, basic and static on Web site. At the end of this stage, in 2009 Government Web sites increase to Web portal, and information becomes more dynamic (www.gov.me). Content and information is updated with greater regularity. The government publishes all information to citizens over the Web portal, with a Content Managed System (CMS) administrated and created from Government Administrators. Citizens, business users, and Government Institutions were still informed in a static manner.

2.2 Authentication & Interactivity (Who)

The government established a Government Certificate of Authority (CA) for issuing public key infrastructure (PKI) certificates for internal employees and Public CA (Post Montenegro) which issued certificates for public subjects. Hence, users are authenticated and enabled to start interactive personal communication with the E-Government system. Authentication and physical identification of subjects enabled two way transactions, when information are transacted and exchanged between citizen as users and government/agencies as service providers. Registered users can download forms, e-mail officials, interact through the web and make appointments and requests.

Government Certification Authority (GOV-CA) issued credentials to Super Administrators and Administrators in several Institutions, authorizing them with PKI strong authentication to administrate and issue their own content and forms for end-users. Government Institutions, as authorized and independent subjects were enabled to generate new services on a daily basis, using a Service Generator module on e-Government Portal. On the other hand, end-users were authorized by Public CA, again with strong PKI, and therefore were enabled to register their own profile with on-line request form repository and facilities to follow up status of their service requests. In this phase all subjects in the e-Government system, if they request so, where identified, with personal data, registered in the GOV-CA or Public CA, became trusted partners in all, possibly sensitive process, giving them individual data protection .

As the user requests more information, government sites increase and information becomes more dynamic. The Montenegro government uses a single service portal (www.euprava.me) as a single point of entry to effectively provide services to its departments, agencies and citizenry; which provides citizen/users with the opportunity to customize the portal based on their desired features, where end-users manage their own profile on multipurpose e-Government portal. They will be informed automaticaly, on-line about the status and changes of all their requests and open issues via personel email or sms.

There are different services, some of them are for anonymus users, some of them for simple registration, but some of them need user PKI identification, especially if the chosen service involves payment process.

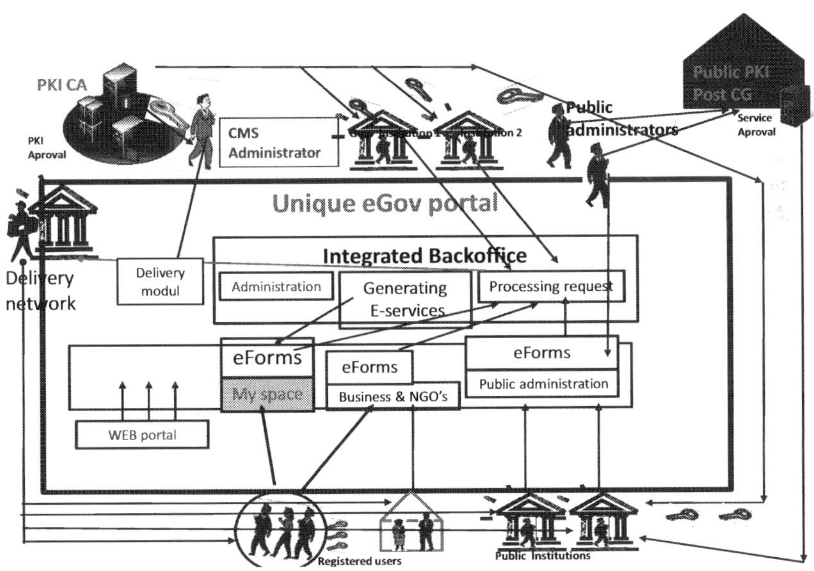

Figure 3. One stop shop E-Gov portal with PKI

2.3 On line transactions (When)

This is the transactional stage where users can actually pay for services and other transactions online, and this was initiated mostly by the banking sector, as they wanted to be active business partners of E-Government projects. Due to needs to provide end users one stop for solving their service request, in this phase different operational processes in different Institutions will be connected, enabling an authorized request to travel between Back-Office applications and collect data needed to solve each issued request and complete documentation on same folder where it is open. When requested service needs payment, the user is offered to appoint his bank account from which it is possible to transfer money to Institution which is serving his request. Different payment methods were enabled: cash, bank card, or electronic bank account. All transactions are done in secure mode, certified by issuer and replier, logged and audited on both side of the transaction, in payment process on three or four sides.

2.4 Integration (What-Who-When)

It is noticeable, during the development of E-Government project that each process itself will initiate integration with another one, as some requests coming from end users couldn't be finished inside isolated processes. As the number of processes grow, due to increasing number of government services becoming on-line, system becomes seamless with maximum mobility, with an ultimate goal for full integration of e-services across administrative boundaries. Citizens could finish all requests from one service point, including home delivery. Government changes its structure and provides full sophisticated, integrated and personalized services to citizens. Government of Montenegro, with third party partners, will enable delivery of such requested service, directly to home of request issuer, upon issuer's request. From the experience on Montenegro project it is clear that E-Government involves multiple stages or phases of development and is not a one-step process. The process of E-government implementation occurs in different phases, these phases are not dependent on each other, nor do they need one phase to be completed before another can begin.

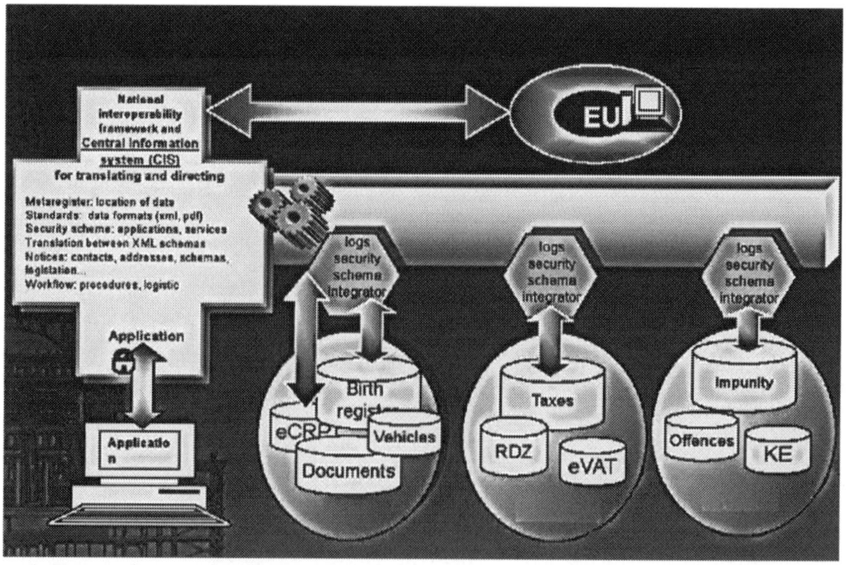

Figure 4. Enterprise service bus

The Montenegro Government must start working on the National Interoperability Framework (NIF) and Enterprise Service Bus (ESB), which will assure smoothly and continual efficient connectivity between different applications, registers and back office administration in Government institutions. **ESB** will enable, through defined secure data scheme and interfaces, secure interchange of data between different users and institutions requiring. We couldn't block access to the sensitive information, at least to some subjects, but an ESB log audit scheme will always provide answers on three important questions: **What** is accessed? By **Whom** and **When**?

3. Conclusion

Definitely, an E-Government system requires much planning and preparation, and does not happen just because a government buys more computers and publishes a Web portal. It is clear that E-Government involves multiple stages or phases of development and is not a one-step process. The process of E-government implementation into different phases, these phases are not dependent on each other, nor need one phase to be completed before another can begin. We have to monitor at least 3 web security issues: Access (What – to publish) Interaction with authentication (Who – access the information), Transaction (When – access or activity happen) and Integration (What – Who-When). To solve above issues efficiently we need to finish NIF, ESB and Central Information System (CIS), as shown in Figure 4. The E-Government portal should be connected with CIS which is responsible for central supervision and log auditing, authentication, authorization, translating and redirecting inquiring addressed to National registers and databases. It is important to integrate existing Public and Government PKI systems into the future ESB, which will enable reliable authentication and authorization of users attempting to access sensitive data, mostly in national registers and databases.

References

[1]. Werner Gitt, *Am Anfang war die Information* 1994 by Hänssler.

[2]. The World Bank, *A definition of e-government*. Washington, DC (2003).

[3]. S. Bretschneider Information technology, e-government, and institutional change. Public Administration Review, (2003).

[4]. J. N. Danziger_& K. V. Andersen. Impacts of IT on politics and the public sector: Methodological, epistemological, and evidence from the Golden Age of transformation. *International Journal of Public Administration*, (2002).

[5]. K. L. Kraemer & J. L. King._Information technology and administrative reform: Will the time after e-government be different? Irvine, CA7 *CRITO,* University of California. (2003).

[6]. K. Layne &, J.W. Lee Developing fully functional e-government: A four stage model. Government Information Quarterly, (2001).

[7]. S&T Montenegro, IPMIT, Methodology for development e-Government, Methodology for ICT measurement (2006)

[8]. UN, "Benchmarking E-government: A Global Perspective", Assessing the Progress of the UN Member States. (20010.

[9]. J. C. Thomas & G. Streib, The new face of government: Citizen-initiated contacts in the era of e-government. *Journal of Public Administration Research and Theory* (2003).

[10]. UNPAN, Benchmarking e-government. A global perspective. New York 7 *United Nations Online Network in Public Administration and Finance.* (2002).

[11]. Center for Democracy and Technology (2002). *E-Government Handbook.* Retrieved October 10, 2008, from Gartner Research. (2003).

[12]. K. V. Andersen & H. Z. Henriksen. "E-government maturity models: Extension of the Layne and Lee model", *Government Information Quarterly,* vol. 23, (2006)

Cyber Security and Resiliency Policy Framework
A. Vaseashta et al. (Eds.)
IOS Press, 2014

doi:10.3233/978-1-61499-446-6-18

Cyber Security Issues of Telecommunication Infrastructure

Aleksandar RISTESKI[a], Mitko BOGDANOSKI[b], Marjan STOILKOVSKI[c], Miroslav JOVANOVIC[d]

[a] *Faculty of Electrical Engineering and IT*
University "Ss. Cyril and Methodius" in Skopje, MACEDONIA
[b] *Military Academy "General Mihajlo Apostolski"*
An associated member of "Goce Delcev" University, MACEDONIA
[c] *Ministry of Interior, Cyber Crime Unit, MACEDONIA*
[d] *Makedonski Telecom AD Skopje, MACEDONIA*

Abstract. We live in a well-connected and technology dependent world. People, institutions, companies have increasing need for communication in everyday life. Global and seamless connectivity today is enabled by complex telecommunications infrastructure consisting of a large variety of different technologies which are in a continuous process of development and innovations. But, the global connectivity and easy access to modern technology also enables malicious users and their activities. These activities might be of a different nature: starting from passive monitoring to destructive attacks disabling the normal operation of ICT (information and communication technology) infrastructure. Therefore, security issues of the telecommunication infrastructure must be thoroughly addressed by all relevant stakeholders. Although each technology includes certain security mechanisms, it is necessary to create a well-designed security concept for the infrastructure as a whole, taking into consideration not only the technical issues, but also policy framework and legal aspects. The concept must be a subject of constant revision in order to be up to date to current threats. Therefore, the network infrastructure must be always monitored and analyzed, in order to create efficient measures against the security threats. The telecommunication infrastructure in the Republic of Macedonia is owned and operated by state institutions, telecom operators and providers, other companies and universities etc. All of them are faced with a number of malicious activities and attacks exploiting vulnerabilities of the systems, which are well monitored and statistically analyzed. Also, all of them have defined a more or less effective security concept including proactive and reactive measures. However, a common practice of cooperation and exchange of information and experience among the subjects is missing. A national strategy and policy framework are also missing that will benefit all stakeholders resulting in more effective and less expensive solutions as a response to cyber-attacks.

Keywords. Cyber security, telecommunication infrastructure, attacks, LEA, incident handling

Introduction

Modern society is characterized by a populace compelled to follow the latest technological achievements. The dependence of individuals and society on computer systems, communications, robotics, drones and other advance technology, becomes greater each day. To take full advantage of the capabilities of modern technology it is necessary to be connected with the outside world through a global network, because otherwise investments in the rapid technological development would be unacceptable for the simple reason that one of the basic needs of all (whether they are individuals, groups, industrialists, government officials, etc.) is to be always and everywhere connected and up to date. People, machines, businesses, organizations and even things have an ever increasing need for communication in everyday life.

Global and seamless connectivity today is enabled by complex telecommunication infrastructure consisting of a large variety of different technologies which are in continuous process of development and innovation. Cheap and easy access to the globally connected world (provided by new devices, applications, services and so on) are the reason for increased number of users which operates on everyday Internet usage. In the last few years there has been a huge expansion in the telecommunications infrastructure usage. Moreover, the ICT is one of the key drivers for general growth.

In order to make this possible, researchers are working on improving existing technologies for increased Internet speed, increased mobility, increased security and so on. However, besides the positive effects, global connectivity and easy access to modern technologies also enables the activities of malicious users. They can access systems and networks without authorization, and moreover the global network offers them an opportunity to bind together across the globe, thus increasing their capacities and capabilities. Recently, there are many examples of cyber-attacks where the effects turns from passive into destructive, which includes disabling the normal operation of the ICT infrastructure or even destroying data and systems, attacks on critical infrastructure, entire nations, even the global society.

Due to the increased number of cyber-attacks enabled over non secured computer systems and networks resulting in blockades of the nation's critical information infrastructure, the protection of information and communication system has become a major global security concern. For these reasons, this chapter focuses on the description of the current threats to the security of telecommunication infrastructures as a part of the overall critical infrastructure and measures taken to respond on these threats.

The rest of the chapter is organized as follows. Section 2 gives an overview of the treatment of cyber-attacks by the world's superpowers, as well as large security related organizations. This section also covers the most modern and most destructive cyber-attacks which can disrupt the global security, including the most resent concepts of cyber warfare. Section 3 gives explanation about the telecommunication infrastructure in Macedonia and its exposure to attacks with special attention to the defense infrastructure of one of the main telecommunication operators in Macedonia, Makedonski Telekom. The current situation with identified cyber-attacks in Republic of Macedonia is described in Section 4. Section 5 explains the typical incident handling process of cyber-attacks in Macedonia. Finally, Section 6 concludes our work.

1. Cyber-Attacks and the Global Security

In the last several years, malwares, Trojans, vulnerabilities of computer systems, network vulnerabilities, intrusions, data theft, identity theft, botnets and critical infrastructure protection are becoming common major issues related to the security threats. Many public discussions are focused on threats and methods to develop better defense mechanisms. On the other hand, the governments do not want to talk about the methods of cyber-attacks and operations as a matter of policy related to countermeasures to conduct cyber operations. The reason for this concealment is perhaps the fear that people may not approve these operations.

Due to the increased usage of cyberspace to attack not just a computer system or a critical infrastructure, but the entire nation's functionality, the world's superpowers and large organizations take appropriate and timely measures and strive to follow the progress of a growing army of malicious users. Thinking in this direction resulted mostly after the cyber-attacks against Estonia in 2007 followed by similar attacks in several other countries, where "army" of attacker's and zombie's machines completely blocked functionality of several critical institutions in this country.

One of the main counter-measures taken by the USA in 2010 against the increased number and power of the malicious users was the establishment of a new Cyber Command (also known as USCYBERCOM) whose main objectives are to coordinate cyber defense of military networks and conduct full spectrum military cyberspace operations in order to enable actions in all domains.

Similar commands/institutions are established or under establishment by the other superpowers and organizations. The investments in this field are more than acceptable if one considers the frequency by which cyber-attacks occur among global security threats [1-6] and financial losses caused by these attacks [7,8]. A review of literature regarding organizational security concerns as well as national strategies and policies [9-12] shows that cyber-attacks rank among the highest security threats.

In June 2011, then the USA CIA (Central Intelligence Agency) Director Leon Panetta stated that "*The next Pearl Harbor we confront could very well be a cyber-attack that cripples our government, security and financial systems*" [13]. Later, he also gave an interview for CBC News [14], but now as a Secretary of Defense, where he showed concerns from these attacks and the possible consequences. U.S. Department of Defense Secretary Paneta said that "*cyber warfare can threaten the grid system, the financial system, and even it could paralyze whole nation*".[13]. On the other hand, since 2009, the FBI (Federal Bureau of Investigation) has ranked cyber-attacks as the third most dangerous threats behind nuclear war and weapons of mass destruction [15].

Table 1 shows the most known cyber-attacks targeting important state's public and private institutions. Most cyber-attacks are largely limited to denial of service (DoS), espionage and sabotage [16].

Among the attacks shown in Table 1, we emphasize the attack on U.S. military network in 2008. The Pentagon had never openly discussed the incident. According to the statement given in 2009 by the Deputy Secretary of Defence, William Lynn, this attack is treated as the most serious attack on classified U.S. military networks. It began when an infected flash drive was inserted into a U.S. military laptop at a base in the Middle East. The flash drive's malicious computer code, placed there by a foreign intelligence agency, uploaded itself onto a network run by the U.S. Central Command. That code spread undetected on both classified and unclassified systems, establishing what amounted to a digital breach, from which data could be transferred to servers under foreign control. It was a network administrator's worst fear: a rogue program operating silently, poised to deliver operational plans into the hands of an unknown adversary [17].

Stuxnet and especially Duqu, targeting the Iranian uranium enrichment centrifuges, are operating in a very similar way to this malicious code, especially considering how each spreads among the networks and systems and sends the stolen information back to the attacker [18].

Table 1. Most known cyber-attacks on national/global security and critical infrastructure

Year	Attacker	Target	Consequences
1982	USA-CIA	Logic bomb targeting USSR Siberian gas pipeline	Destruction
1999 and 2000	Russia	Pentagon, NASA, National Labs	Stealing information, espionage
2004	China	Sandia National Laboratory, Lockheed Martin and NASA	Espionage
2007	China	U.S. Computer Network (750,000 computers)	Denial of service
2007	Русија	Estonia's government websites and other important institutions/banks	Denial of service
2008	Unknown	U.S. Military Network	Malicious code and zombie machines
2008	China and/or Russia	U.S. Presidential Election	Intrusion into email systems
2008	Russia	Georgia's government websites and other important institutions/banks	Denial of service
2010, 2011	Unknown (unofficial Israel/USA)	Iranian uranium enrichment centrifuges	Sabotage
2010-2013	Anonymous "Operation Avenge Assange"	Multiple western targets (public and private)	Denial of service
April 2011	2 anonymous groups/ supported by unknown state	RSA Secure ID	Phishing, Espionage
August 2012	Unknown (unofficial Iran) Cutting Sword of Justice	Saudi Aramco oil company	Destruction, Espionage
2013	USA - NSA	United Nation's video conferencing system European Union building on New York International Atomic Energy Agency	Surveillance

The telecommunication providers and infrastructure are not resistant to these attacks. There are many examples for malicious activities against telecommunications infrastructure. Very recently, there was an advanced massive cyber-attack on Telenor, the telecommunication giant of Norway [20]. It's perceived that cyber-criminals may have filched a significant volume of information stored on computers that the executives of the major organization used. To be able to enter in the provider's infrastructure the attackers initially dispatched crafty emails that hit the inboxes of high-profile officials, while seemed as arriving from trustworthy sources as internal employees and organization. The email attachments carried advanced malicious software undetectable by security software. Even more, in December 2012, during the World Conference on International Telecommunications (WCIT) held in Dubai, hackers disabled the ITU's (International Telecommunication Agency) main meeting and several websites [19].

2. The most recent concepts of the cyber attacks

Although cyber security came into use in the ICT sector since the first computer systems, it was only in 2007, when large-scale cyber-attacks affected entire nations that the topic was catapulted to the center of international attention. This was a warning to all the world's superpowers that telecommunications infrastructure attacks have become one of the greatest threats to the global security [21]. For better understanding of this global security threat, first, this section will describe the most common attacks that fall into this group of threats. In the list that follows, the attacks are listed according to their impact, from the simplest to the most destructive [18].

- **Cyber espionage**
  Cyber espionage is the act or practice of obtaining secrets (sensitive, private or classified information) from individuals, competitors, rivals, enemies and governments for military, political or economic advantage using illegal methods for exploitation of internet, networks, software and / or computers.
- **WEB vandalism**
  Web vandalism are attacks that deface or deny service to websites.
- **Propaganda**
  Propaganda attacks distribute political messages to anyone who has access to the Internet.
- **Information gathering**
  Information gathering attacks seek to intercept or modify information, enabling espionage from any part of the world.
- **Distributed denial of service attack**
  A DDoS attack uses multiple compromised system, which are usually infected with a Trojan to target a single system causing a Denial of Service (DoS) attack. Victims of a DDoS (Distributed DoS) attack consist of both the end targeted system and all systems maliciously used and controlled by the hacker in the distributed attack.
- **Equipment disruption**
  Equipment disruption attacks target military operations that are used to coordinate computers and satellites. Using this attack, malicious users can intercept or modify orders and communications, putting soldiers at risk.
- **Attacking critical infrastructure**
  Critical infrastructure attacks attempt to control systems supporting electricity, water, fuel, communications, transportation and similar key infrastructure elements.
- **Compromised counterfeit hardware**
  Counterfeit hardware attacks have malware hidden inside software, firmware or even in microprocessors within computer hardware in order to enable attacks to the larger network infrastructure.

At year end, the experts and organizations concerned with computer security predict possible threats for next year. Many of the threats that occur or increase in an upcoming year have been identified in the current year's security assessment.

According to [22-24], the top cyber threats predictions for 2013 are:

- Criminals will benefit from unintended consequences of espionage,
- Attackers will increasingly use apps, movies and music to install malware,

Drive-by attacks and cross-site scripting attacks will be attacker favorites,

- Software updating gets easier and exploiting vulnerabilities gets harder,
- An increase in large-scale attacks, designed to destroy infrastructure rather than based on purely financial gain, will firmly take hold in 2013,
- Hacking "as a service" is expected to rise,
- Rootkits will evolve in 2013,
- Cyber-attacks will be directed to cloud servers and mobile devices,
- The decline of Anonymous, but a rise in extreme hacktivism.

The analysis of these five predictions associated with cyber threats gives a bleak picture about cyber-attacks in 2013. Threats seem extremely challenging, if not a bit overwhelming and reveal that this is a modernized form of armed conflict in its infancy where questions exceed answers. The most recent analysis for cyber-attacks made by Hackmageddon for August 2013, shows that US, India and UK collected together 54% of the attacks reported in the timelines (Figure 1) [25].

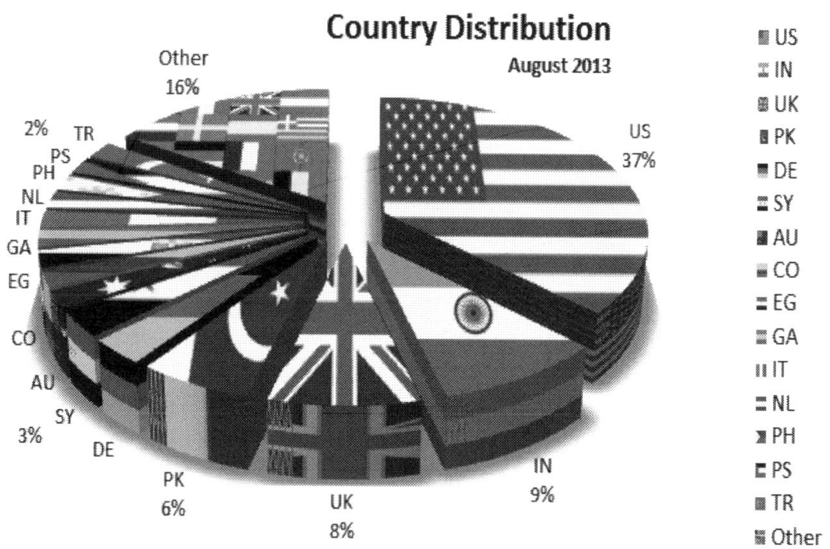

Figure 1. Cyber-attack country distribution for August 2013

The same source gives a statistic showing that cyber crime is a leading motivation behind cyber-attack with 57% followed by hactivism. Historically, SQLi (Structured Query Language Injection) and DDoS are among the first three most frequent types of cyber-attacks [26], although in the last period Defacements lead the Distribution of Attack Techniques Chart (Figure 2). Finally, account Hijackings are becoming very popular.

Apparently it is increasingly difficult to track actual techniques used to carry out the attacks. According to the statistics, the reasons and mechanisms used for almost one of four attacks are unknown. However, DDoS, as usual, leads the Distribution of Attack Techniques chart for the known cases (Figure 2). The Syrian Electronic Army is one offender, and instances of Account Hijacking becoming more evident every month. SQLi (Structured Query Language Injection) attacks are decreasing but it is difficult to estimate how many "unknowns" were effectively related to SQLi.

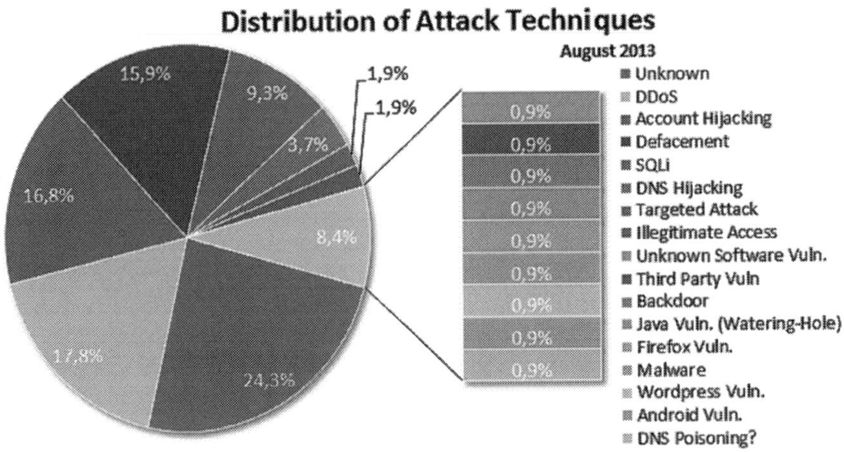

Figure 2. Distribution of attack techniques for August 2013

Governmental and Industry targets lead the Distribution of Target chart with 26% and 17% respectively (Figure 3) but are constantly vying for first and second place. It is interesting to note that attacks on individuals rank third as a result of account hijackings.

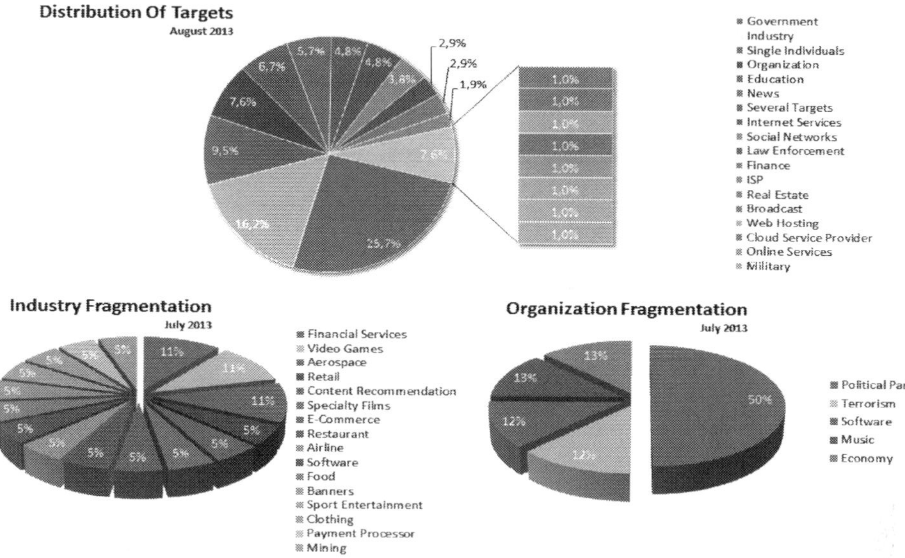

Figure 3. Distribution of targets for August 2013

Over the past few years, there has been a rapid increase in the proliferation of new cyber weapons that are being used as part of coordinated cyber-attacks on computer networks around the world. In some cases, these cyber-attacks are part of sustained, multi-year operations that target governments, corporations and research institutions. The most dangerous cyber weapons of 2013 with the greatest potential to change how we think about the relationship between national security and cyber security are briefly described in the following sub-sections.

2.1. Red October

At the very beginning of 2013, Kaspersky Lab published a comprehensive report that included the results of a study of the global cyber espionage operation known as “Red October”. The earliest evidence indicates that the “Red October” cyber espionage campaign was active since 2007. The attackers have been focused on diplomatic and governmental agencies of various countries across the world. The information harvested from infected networks was reused in later attacks [27].

Figure 4 shows a distribution of nations affected by the sinkhole, where it can be seen that Macedonia, as well as other countries from the region (Greece, Bulgaria, Croatia and Serbia) are represented in very large percentages. Namely, nearly one-third of the espionage attacks occurs on countries from this region.

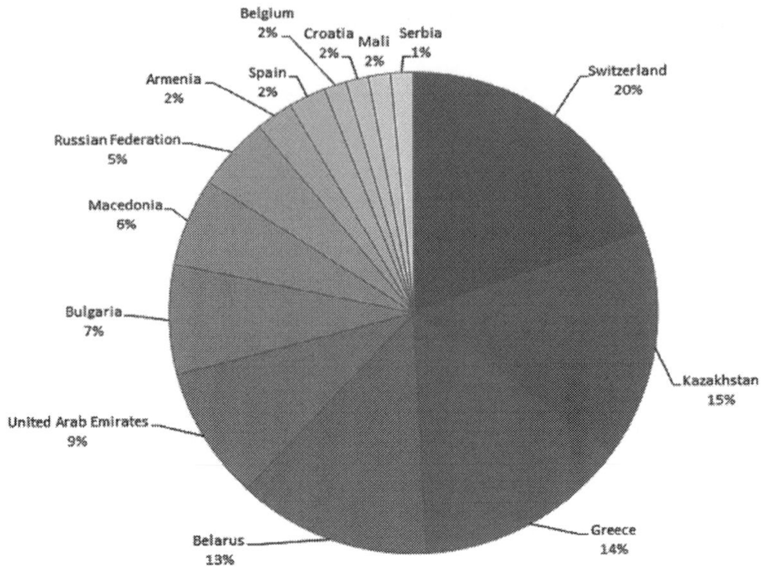

Figure 4. Red October operation - country distribution of connections to the sinkhole

2.2. MiniDuke

In February 2013, Kaspersky Labs identifies 'MiniDuke', a new malicious program designed for spying on multiple government entities and institutions across the world. Cyber criminals have targeted government officials in more than 20 countries, including Ireland and Romania, in a complex online assault seen rarely since the turn of the millennium. The attack was conducted using an Adobe PDF bug [28].

2.3. APT1 (Advanced Persistent Threat)

In February 2013, the U.S. information security company Mandiant published a comprehensive report on attacks by a group of Chinese hackers known as APT1. At the beginning of the report, Mandiant states that APT1 is believed to be a unit of the Chinese Army. Mandiant even cites the possible postal address of this unit and builds an estimate of its numbers and the infrastructure it uses. Mandiant suspects that the APT1 group has been operating since 2006 and that over the past six years has managed to steal terabytes of data from at least 141 organizations. Most of the targeted companies are in English-speaking countries.[29]

2.4. TeamSpy

In March 2013 the Laboratory of Cryptography and System Security (Crysys) at Budapest University of Technology and Economics, released their research around a targeted attack they have identified, named TeamSpy. This cyber surveillance operation targets high level political and human rights activists through CIS and Eastern Europe nations. Victims also include government agencies as well as private companies. The attacks have been ongoing for almost a decade and were previously mentioned by Belorussian activists in 2012 [30].

2.5. Stuxnet

In March 2013 Researchers at Symantec traced the origins and design of Stuxnet, the first cyber weapon designed to shut down industrial facilities. It was found that Stuxnet 0.5, the older version of the virus widely considered to be a joint effort between Israel and the U.S., was actually first deployed in 2007, several years before it was detected in 2010. Moreover, its virus codes trace back to 2005. The discovery of Stuxnet was followed by other dangerous cyber weapons. After Stuxnet was discovered, engineers found similar viruses with the names Duqu, Gauss, and Flame. The basis of Stuxnet malware code was similar to its followers [31].

3. Cyber Security Threats & Defense Challenges of Telecommunication Service Providers in Republic Of Macedonia

As previously mentioned, the telecommunication infrastructure is vulnerable to cyber-attacks. Frequently, telecommunications organizations report cyber-attacks against their systems and infrastructure, but many attacks go unreported as well. Cyber security threats and defense challenges of the telecommunication service providers in Republic of Macedonia will be considered through the case of the biggest telecommunication service provider Makedonski Telekom (MKT). MKT infrastructure has 3 key segments exposed to the Internet (Figure 5):

- IP Backbone: Backbone interconnection between the corporate network, the T-Home ISP network, business clients, residential clients, mobile broadband users and the Internet.
- T-Home ISP Services: Main services provided by MKT are E-mail hosting, web hosting, cloud services, authoritative DNS for the hosted domains, customer business solutions.
- Corporate Services: Corporate network infrastructure with Internet facing services (VPN, DNS, customer self-care, public web content, email, partner interconnection).

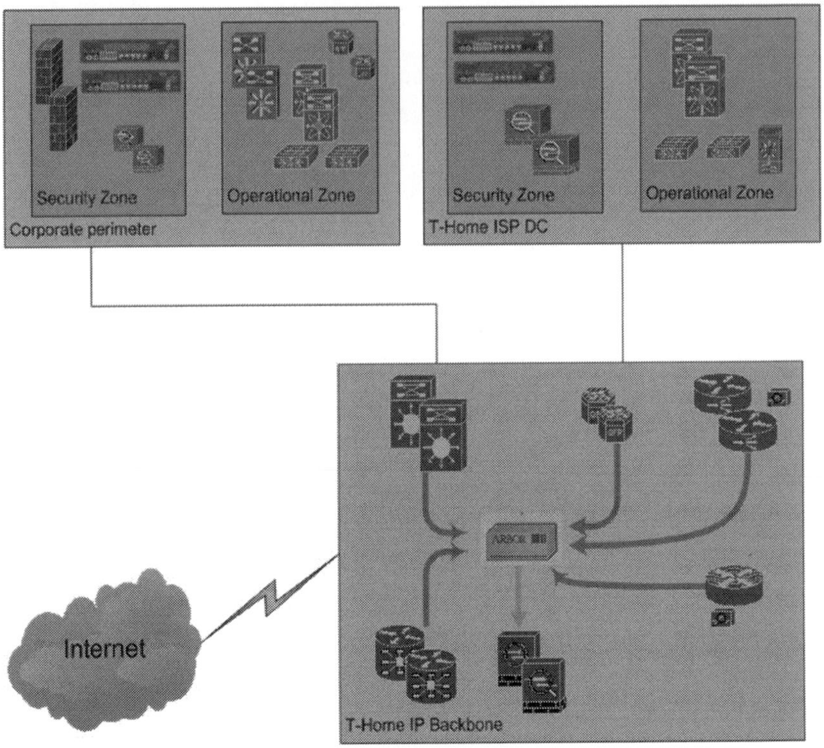

Figure 5. MKT Infrastructure

According to the company's traffic statistics, the defense infrastructure of the MKT handles in average 8 Gbps of traffic, with monthly volume of more than 14TB. More than 50% of the processed traffic is HTTP, while Browser related services (HTTP, SSL and Flash) are responsible for two thirds of the total internet traffic (Figure 5). However, not all traffic is legitimate. Namely, 20% of the traffic is filtered out as malicious.

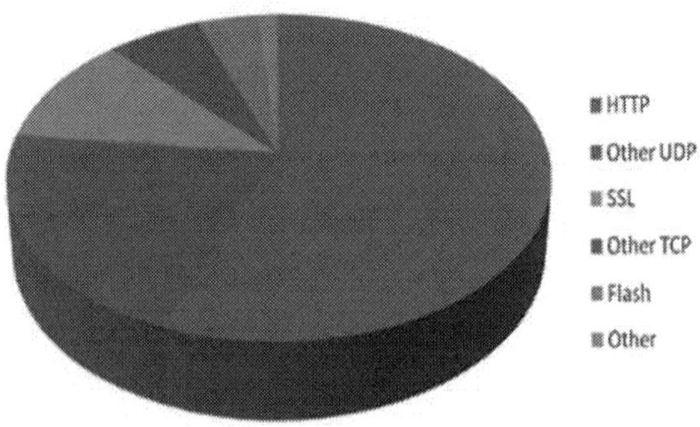

Figure 6. MKT infrastructure traffic statistic

The most frequent target within the T-Home (MKT) ISP (Internet Service Provider) segment are: web hosting, authoritative DNS, customer business solutions and cloud services. Successful attack is almost impossible if the malicious user is not well informed about the vulnerability of the potential victim. For this reason the attacker must conduct network and system reconnaissance attacks in order to gather information that can be further used in more sophisticated attacks. The most frequently used information gathering methods against MKT systems are port scanning, DNS zone analysis and web server traversal.

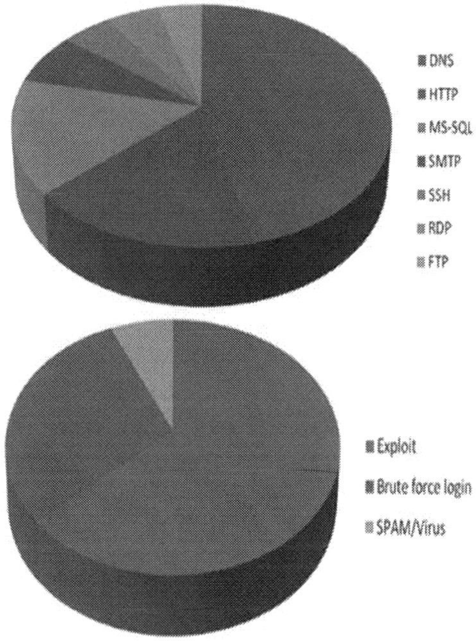

Figure 7. MKT infrastructure traffic statistic. a) Attack distribution by protocol; b) Attack distribution by type

When the attacker conducts successful reconnaissance operation, he is on his way to the victim's vulnerable systems and sensitive information. The most frequent techniques and exploits used against MKT systems and information are: (D)DoS, website defacement, brute force password attacks, exploiting know web server/CMS vulnerabilities and SPAM/virus propagation (Figure 7).

Makedonski Telekom, as the biggest telecommunication service providers takes all necessary measures against malicious activities. MKT created a defense infrastructure which can effectively counter attacks from malicious users. The defense infrastructure is customized and set around the critical infrastructure, with knowledge of traffic and profiled to respond to typical attacks (Figure 8). MKT has enabled so called defense-in-depth mechanisms which significantly improve cyber security. The MKT implemented new advanced firewalls (smart gateway devices) capable for full event analysis and application level detection. MKT also uses modern IPSs (Intrusion Prevention

Systems). Unlike IDSs (Intrusion Detection Systems) IPSs devices are in-line installed and they are able to actively prevent/block intrusions that are detected.

As we already explained, MKT is very often exposed on (D)DoS attacks. For this reason, MKT makes efforts to prevent (D)DoS attacks. MKT installed special anomaly detection systems which are shown as very effective mechanism against these attacks. Also, in order to monitor and detect the possible attacks in their early phases, MKT incorporates known measures that involve commercial and open source based monitoring.

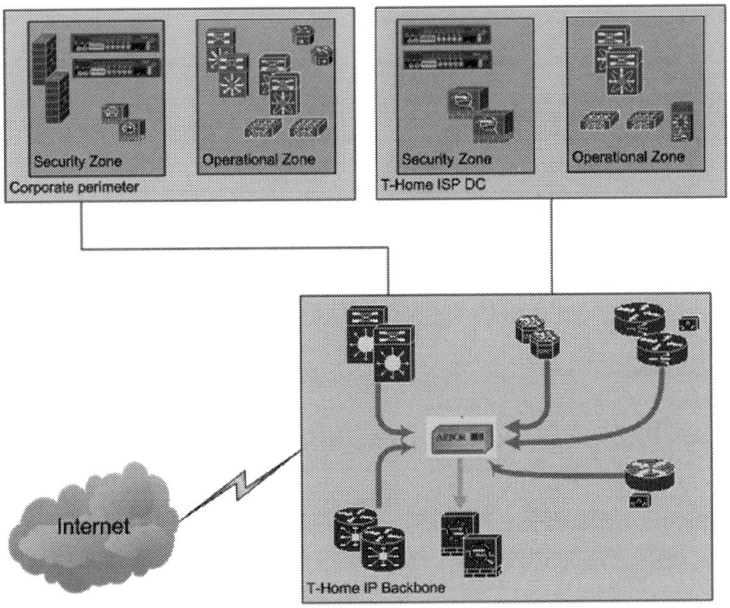

Figure 8. MKT Defence Infrastructure

Makedonski Telekom implemented all security-related principles, standards, regulations. MKT is an ISO 27001 ISMS (Information Security Management System) Certified Company. MKT has implemented the Payment Card Industry Data Security Standard (PCI DSS). MKT has paid special attention to systems and applications processing payment card data - E-commerce (webshop) and e-Top-Up. MKT also implemented the policies related to personal data protection. One of the main security objectives for the MKT is vulnerability and advisory management. MKT implemented effective software and hardware tools for vulnerability assessment of the entire infrastructure. The implemented QualysGuard security and compliance suite systems enables MKT to execute vulnerability scans of the public network. Finally, MKT has significantly improved their capabilities of tracking security advisories and following up on remediation.

4. The current situation with identified cyber-attacks in Republic of Macedonia

The status of cyber-attacks in Republic of Macedonia is not different from the other countries from the region and Western Europe. This was shown through the case study of MKT, which does not differ at all from the status of other telecommunication service providers and other providers in Macedonia. Many cyber-attacks on information systems of private and public institutions are identified on daily basis. Many attacks are not reported to the law enforcement agencies (LEAs) responsible for investigating cyber-crimes. In many cases, cyber incidents are handled by the IT security teams from the institutions, but it exacerbates national cyber security readiness when they fail to report the illegal activities on their systems to the LEA. By reporting cyber security incidents to the LEA, the national cyber security posture is strengthened because it increases awareness of cyber security incidents, and enables improved incidents handling mechanisms throughout the country.

The most common identified cyber incidents in Republic of Macedonia are:

- *DDoS (Distributed Denial of services) attacks.* DDos attacks are directed to the private institution (financial sector) or public sector and governmental institutions. In most cases, the end goal is online extortion or attempts to make public services unavailable. In some cases, more serious attempts to exploit the complete system is the attacker's goal and it bears mentioning that all DDoS attacks are illegal according to the National penal code.
- *Web page defacement.* Using different approaches of attacking and exploiting web pages, the aim of web page defacement attacks are to send messages or express "power" on Internet. Quite frequently, young people (working alone or as a part of some "hacker" groups) conduct such attacks in order to learn more and exploit the vulnerable web pages, not understanding that with those activities they are committing criminal acts. On the other hand, more sinister groups have defaced web pages with goals of seriously damaging the reputation and thereby causing the organization to incur great costs in reparations.
- *Scanning or probing IT systems for illegal intrusions in the systems and data alteration.* The administrators of the IT system in corporations and public sectors in Macedonia have indentified many scans with system metadata collection. Those scans are coming from different IP addresses and locations. While it is possible that these scans are the results of reconnaissance missions with no criminal intent, organizations must treat all scans as if the perpetrators intend harm to the system.. In-house IT experts usually monitor and respond to these types of attacks as a routine part of their responsibilities.
- *Phishing.* Phishing is a more advanced technique for acquiring sensitive data such as usernames, passwords, and financial information from users. The targets of phishing attacks are often banks, financial, and commercial institutions. Phishing attacks that result in the acquisition of usernames, passwords, financial, and personally identifiable information can also enable identity theft operations.

Besides the aforementioned attacks in the Republic of Macedonia, there are several other identified types of cyber incidents, committed by individuals with different purposes. Those cyber incidents are not always committed by advanced "hackers". According to the available statistics from the incidents handling institutions in

Macedonia, about 92% of the attacks are conducted by the so called "script kids", who are using online freely available tutorials and software for performing the attacks, 7% of the attacks are conducted by the computer specialists that understand the topologies of the computer programs and are able to use exploits and malwares for gaining access into the systems and only 1% are conducted by advanced computer experts who understand and know how the malware and exploits work, and they are able to produce new exploits and malware for concrete systems and purpose.

5. Handling cyber incidents in Republic of Macedonia

Handling computer/cyber incidents is a complex process and cannot be generalized, because the incidents differ by their nature and goal. Furthermore, as a consequence of the fast development of new technologies and IT solutions, the way by which attacks are conducted is changing, so we are constantly facing new, more advanced and more dangerous cyber-attacks and incidents.

In Macedonia, a two phase process defines the response to cyber security incidents, In the first phase, upon recognition of cyber-attacks, responses are handled by the IT teams responsible for systems' development, administration and security. These teams are responsible for ensuring functional and secure systems by performing daily activities that identify unexpected processes or states of operation, and consequently are the first responders to incidents. They must respond to the incident while preserving all the information necessary for incident reporting and investigation in later phases by the LEAs. The second phase in responding to cyber incidents involves LEAs and requires handing over the case from the Cybercrime Unit responsible for collection and analysis of all available information to the Investigators in order to identify the relevant digital evidence for the person or group that committed the illegal act. The Cybercrime Unit is responsible for investigating the cyber incidents using all necessary measures for identification and collection of the digital evidence on the scene. Digital evidence that are not available on the national level are obtained using the international legal instruments of MLA (Mutual Legal Assistances). One of the main steps during incident handling is the phase of involving a Public prosecutor in the investigation process. The prosecutor plays an important role in specifying the methods of obtaining digital evidence, and it is his obligation to present the evidence in court.

Practically speaking, in almost all cases of cyber incidents reported by the public/private sector, including the telecommunication service providers, investigation goes beyond the national borders, which means that the digital evidence must be obtained from international or multinational service providers. On November 23, 2001, the Republic of Macedonia signed the Budapest Convention for Cybercrime of Council of Europe [32], and in doing so, adopted all the procedures recommended by this Convention to be fully and properly implemented in the national law. Fulfillment of the Convention's requirement allows the possibility to obtain digital evidence from multinational service providers.

According to the LEAs in Macedonia that deal with cyber incidents, investigation of the most incidents on the national level is seldom possible. Almost always, during the cyber incidents handling process, the national LEAs need assistance from the regional and international LEAs. This experience of Macedonian LEAs does not differ from the experience of the LEAs of the other countries which is one of the main reasons for signing the above mentioned Convention. Considering the fact that the cyber incidents in almost all cases are caused by attacks which are based on the usage of global telecommunication network (Internet), it is more than obvious that the cybercrime cannot be considered as a national issues but as an international issue and should be treated on that level.

6. Conclusion

Cyber attacks in the last few years are moving from disruptive to destructive in nature. They have become the leading threat to the state and multinational organizations security. The public and private agencies / institutions have incurred large financial losses and leaks of sensible data that are caused by the malicious usage of the ICT infrastructure by the attackers.

This chapter gave a detailed description of the treatment of the cyber threats among other threats to national and global security. Furthermore, the chapter gave a detailed overview of the most important cyber threats throughout history, followed by a description of the latest concepts of cyber warfare and the most dangerous cyber weapons in 2013. Afterwards, the chapter gave a review of the problems encountered by telecommunication operators in Macedonia (with special emphasis on the largest telecommunications service provider - Makedonski Telekom) and the security measures taken to prevent against potential cyber threats.

LEAs are the authorities that should take appropriate measures for reports of cyber incidents by the public / business sector. One of the major problems encountered by the national LEA in Macedonia is that the institutions which should report registered incidents are very much closed and in many cases they do not cooperate with the national cyber authorities. In fact, those responsible for cyber security and management of the organizations very rarely decide to report such incidents, mainly assuming that this might lead to loss of their own reputation or the reputation of their organization/institution. Furthermore, it should be emphasized the importance of regional and international cooperation during the cyber incidents handling. The reason for this is that in most of the registered cyber incidents in Macedonia, the attacks are conducted by the attackers, or machines that operate outside the Macedonian border, which means that national LEAs cannot respond to these threats without regional or international cooperation.

References

[1] M. Bogdanoski, D. Petreski, Cyber Terrorism–Global Security Threat, *Contemporary Macedonian Defense-International Scientific Defense, Security and Peace Journal*, 13(24), 59-73.

[2] "GCHQ chief reports 'disturbing' cyber-attacks on UK", BBC news UK, 31.10.2011, http://www.bbc.co.uk/news/uk-15516959, Last accessed 29.09.2013

[3] E. Kain, "Cyber-attacks take down two Israeli websites - is cyber warfare the next front in the middle east conflict?", FORBES, 16.01.2012, http://www.forbes.com/sites/erikkain/2012/01/16/cyber-attacks-take-down-two-israeli-websites-is-cyber-warfare-the-next-front-in-the-middle-east-conflict/, Last accessed 29.09.2013

[4] B. Acohido, Cyber-attacks likely to escalate this year, US Today, 10.01.2012, http://usatoday30.usatoday.com/tech/news/story/2012-01-08/hacktivism-lulzsec-anonymous/52489606/1, Last accessed 29.09.2013

[5] Cyber-attacks now the most feared EU energy threat, Euractive, 25.01.2011, http://www.euractiv.com/energy/cyber-attacks-feared-eu-energy-threat-news-501547, Last accessed 29.09.2013

[6] J. P Mello Jr, Cyber-attacks the greatest threat to nations, say global execsm , CSO, 13.06.2013, http://www.csoonline.com/article/735485/cyberattacks-the-greatest-threat-to-nations-say-global-execs, Last accessed 29.09.2013

[7] 2012 Cost of Cyber Crime Study: United States 2012, Ponemon Institute, October 2012, http://www.ponemon.org/local/upload/file/2012_US_Cost_of_Cyber_Crime_Study_FINAL6%20.pdf, Last accessed 29.09.2013

[8] J. Kirk, Deep cyber-attacks cause millions in losses for U.S. banks, Computerworld, 22.09.2013, http://www.computerworld.com/s/article/9241852/Deep_cyberattacks_cause_millions_in_losses_for_U.S._banks, Last accessed 29.09.2013

[9] "Strategic Concept For the Defense and Security of The Members of the North Atlantic Treaty Organisation", Adopted by Heads of State and Government in Lisbon, November 2010, http://www.nato.int/lisbon2010/strategic-concept-2010-eng.pdf, Last accessed 29.09.2013

[10] "A Strong Britain in an Age of Uncertainty: The National Security Strategy, United Kingdom", October 2010,http://www.direct.gov.uk/prod_consum_dg/groups/dg_digitalassets/@dg/@en/documents/digitalasset/dg_191639.pdf, Last accessed 29.09.2013

[11] "National Security Strategy, Unite States of America", May 2010, http://www.whitehouse.gov/sites/default/files/rss_viewer/national_security_strategy.pdf Last accessed 29.09.2013

[12] "International Strategy For Cyberpace, Prosperity, Security, and Openness in a Networked World", President of the United States, May 2011, http://info.publicintelligence.net/WH-InternationalCyberspace.pdf, Last accessed 29.09.2013

[13] H. Mirza, "Cyber-Attacks Are the Biggest National Security Threat", Policymic, August 2011, http://www.policymic.com/articles/1518/cyber-attacks-are-the-biggest-national-security-threat, Last accessed 29.09.2013

[14] S. Pelley, Panetta: Cyber warfare could paralyze U.S., CBS News, 05.01.2012, http://www.cbsnews.com/8301-18563_162-57353420/panetta-cyber-warfare-could-paralyze-u.s/, Last accessed 29.09.2013

[15] R.C. Hodgin, "FBI ranks cyber-attacks third most dangerous behind nuclear war and WMDs", TD Daily, 7 January 2009, http://www.tgdaily.com/security-features/40861-fbi-ranks-cyber-attacks-third-most-dangerous-behind-nuclear-war-and-wmds, Last accessed 29.09.2013

[16] "Investigating Cyber Security Threats: Exploring National Security and Law Enforcement Perspectives", Frederic Lemieux, GW-CSPRI-2011-2. http://www.cspri.seas.gwu.edu/uploads/2/1/3/2/21324690/2011-2_investigating_cyber_security_threats_lemieux.pdf 07 Apr 2011. Last accessed 29.09.2013

[17] Worst Cyber Attack on U.S. Military Came Via Flash Drive: U.S., Defence News, 25.09.2010, http://www.defensenews.com/article/20100825/DEFSECT04/8250303/Worst-Cyber-Attack-U-S-Military-Came-Via-Flash-Drive-U-S-, Last accessed 29.09.2013

[18] M. Bogdanoski, A. Risteski, M. Bogdanoski, Industrial Cyber Attacks – Global Security Threat, March 2012; In proceeding of: International conference "The Faces of the Crisis"

[19] Cyberattack against Telenor, The Norway Post, 26.05.2013, http://www.norwaypost.no/index.php/business/general-business/28565-cyberattack-against-telenor-, Last accessed 29.09.2013

[20] Hacking Attack Hits ITU Website During Ongoing Meet In Dubai, CBR, 07.12.2012, http://www.cbronline.com/news/security/hacking-attack-hits-itu-website-during-ongoing-meet-in-dubai-071212, Last accessed 29.09.2013

[21] H. T. Klaar, "Cyber Security Threats and Responses at Global, Nation-State, Industry and Individual Levels", 2011, http://www.sciencespo.fr/ceri/sites/sciencespo.fr.ceri/files/art_htk.pdf, Last accessed 29.09.2013

[22] T. Rains, Using the Past to Predict the Future: Top 5 Threat Predictions for 2013, Microsoft Security Blog, 13.12.2012, http://blogs.technet.com/b/security/archive/2012/12/13/using-the-past-to-predict-the-future-top-5-threat-predictions-for-2013.aspx, Last accessed 29.09.2013

[23] 2013 Threats Predictions, McAfee Labs, 2012, http://www.mcafee.com/us/resources/reports/rp-threat-predictions-2013.pdf, Last accessed 29.09.2013

[24] D. Banning, J. Hainaut, Top Cyber Threats: Making Sense of All the 2013 Predictions, Experis Manpower Group, March 2013, http://www.experis.us/Website-File-Pile/Webinar-Recordings/Experis/Presentation-Materials/Cyber-Threats-Presentation-Material, Last accessed 29.09.2013

[25] P. Passeri, July 2013 Cyber Attacks Statistics, Hackmageddon, August 2013, http://hackmageddon.com/2013/09/07/august-2013-cyber-attacks-statistics/, Last accessed 15.09.2013
[26] M. Bogdanoski, T. Shuminoski, A. Risteski, Analysis of the SYN Flood DoS Attack, *International Journal of Computer Network and Information Security (IJCNIS)*, 5(8), 1., 2013
[27] Kaspersky Lab Identifies Operation "Red October," an Advanced Cyber-Espionage Campaign Targeting Diplomatic and Government Institutions Worldwide, Kasperky Lab, January 2013, http://www.kaspersky.com/about/news/virus/2013/Kaspersky_Lab_Identifies_Operation_Red_October_an_Advanced_Cyber_Espionage_Campaign_Targeting_Diplomatic_and_Government_Institutions_Worldwide, Last accessed 29.09.2013
[28] Kaspersky Lab Identifies 'MiniDuke', a New Malicious Program Designed for Spying on Multiple Government Entities and Institutions Across the World, Kastersky Lab, February 2013, http://www.kaspersky.com/about/news/virus/2013/Kaspersky_Lab_Identifies_MiniDuke_a_New_Malicious_Program_Designed_for_Spying_on_Multiple_Government_Entities_and_Institutions_Across_the_World, Last accessed 29.09.2013
[29] APT1: Exposing One of China's Cyber Espionage Units, Mandiant, February 2013, http://intelreport.mandiant.com/Mandiant_APT1_Report.pdf, Last accessed 29.09.2013
[30] TeamSpy – Obshie manevri. Ispolzovat' tolko s razreshenija S-a. v1, Laboratory of Cryptography and System Security (CrySyS Lab), Technical Report, March 2013, http://www.crysys.hu/teamspy/teamspy.pdf, Last accessed 29.09.2013
[31] G. McDonald, L. O Murchu, S. Doherty, R. Chien, Stuxnet 0.5: The Missing Link, Symantec, February 2013, http://www2.gwu.edu/~nsarchiv/NSAEBB/NSAEBB424/docs/Cyber-088.pdf, Last accessed 29.09.2013
[32] Cybercrime Convention Committee (T-CY), Council of Europe, Convention on Cybercrime, Budapest 23.11.2001, http://conventions.coe.int/Treaty/en/Treaties/Html/185.htm, , Last accessed 29.09.2013

Cyber Security and Resiliency Policy Framework
A. Vaseashta et al. (Eds.)
IOS Press, 2014

doi:10.3233/978-1-61499-446-6-36

Security Issues for Mobile Devices

Cvetko ANDREESKI[a,1]
[a]*University St. Kliment Ohridsk, FTU – Bitola*
Ohrid, M. Tito 95, 6000 Ohrid, REPUBLIC OF MACEDONIA

Abstract. The history of smart phones and tablet computers is relatively short from a historical point of view, yet these devices are widely used for personal and business tasks daily. We present the advances of these devices in comparison to laptop and other computers with an awareness of their abilities to safeguard data. They are used as devices that hold sensitive information; and they are intended for use with different type of wireless and mobile communication lines. This kind of communication increases the risk of data transfer. Their characteristics (dimensions, processing power, networking etc.), working environment, stored information and their value, makes them suitable for theft and abuse. This paper addresses the problem of countermeasures needed to make smart phones and tablets more secure. Besides the fact that the first commercially available tablet computer was presented only three years ago, sales increase significantly each year. According to the analysis of the web site statista.com, in the last quarter of 2012 76% more tablet computers were purchased in comparison with the same quarter in 2011. According to the research expectations, this trend should continue in the next few years, and in 2016 we can expect around 283 million tablet computers to be purchased which will exceed purchases of laptop computers.

Keywords. Mobile devices, security, communication. Protection

Introduction

Mobile personal devices are powerful computer like machines and even in standard configurations are equipped with GPS, high definition cameras, capabilities of different kind of wireless communication (Wi-Fi, mobile communication – 3G, 4G, LTE, NFC, Bluetooth), memory cards with 32 or more gigabytes (GB) storage, high screen resolution, and multi core processors. These devices operate many hours without any need for battery charging rendering them portable and flexible. With all these capabilities, they are ideal tools for remote and mobile working and communicating with corporate servers and networks. Outside of the corporate network, they should be reliable and secure in acquiring data, processing, storing and communicating with the corporate infrastructure. The ubiquitous usage of mobile computing devices occurred only six years after introduction of the first iPhone, and less than 5 years from the introduction of the first version of the Android OS in September 2009.

In the last few years we have witnessed an increasing number of mobile devices for individual and professional work. Mobile networks have evolved from 2G to 3G to the common 4G standard which offers a maximum speed of an impressive 1Gb/s.

[1]E-mail: cvetko.andreeski@uklo.edu.mk

According to the Cisco Virtual Network Index, in 2012, the number of mobile-connected tablets increased to 36 million and by 2016, more than 280 million tablets will be purchased which will exceed laptops and desktops purchases in that year. Figure 1 presents forecasted traffic through mobile networks.

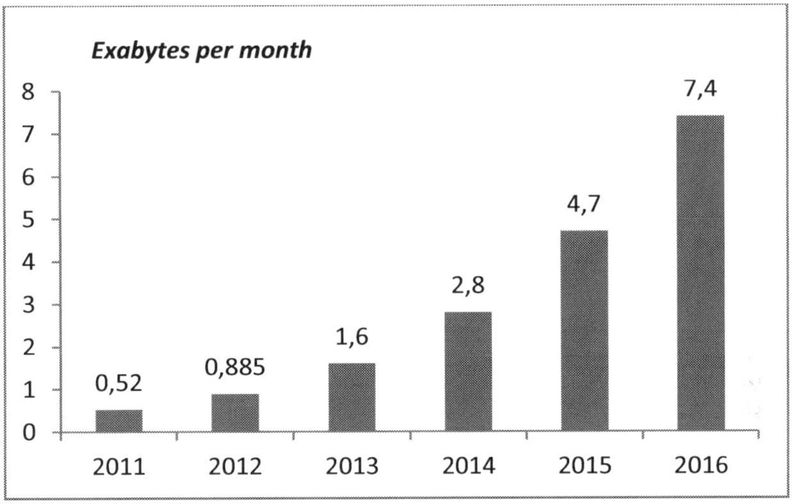

Figure 1: Realized and expected traffic created on mobile networks,
Source: Cisco VNI Mobile forecast 2013

There are many papers that deal with security of mobile devices on many aspects like: secure communications, security of platforms for mobile devices, working and maintaining secure applications, preserving and protecting data on mobile devices and protecting the device from being stolen or damaged. In an analysis by Ernst&Young – "Mobile device security" [17], we can find many aspects of mobile device security, starting from application security, device security, encryption mechanisms and vulnerability audit and identification. In the paper of J. Crowcroft, D. Cottingham, G. Mapp, and F. Shaikh, "Y-comm: A global Architecture for Heterogeneous Networking" [25], the Y-comm framework is presented with a review of the security model of the Y-comm architecture.

Some aspects of encrypted communication and data stream via BlackBerry devices are presented in the paper of K. Sangani, "Secrets of the data stream" [30]. A comparison between different mobile platforms is presented by Gandhewar and Sheikh in "Android: An Emerging Software Platform for Mobile Devices" [7] with accent on Android platform its architecture and features. In this paper we are analyzing many different aspects of mobile device threats and security followed by proposals on these aspects towards increasing mobile device safety.

The following sections of this paper are organized as follows: Section 1 presents characteristics of mobile and wireless networks which are essential for communication and transfer of files and data over mobile devices. Section 2 analyzes different mobile platforms: Apple IOS, Android and Windows. Section 3 discusses aspects of application security and application markets. Finally, Section 4 discusses issues about mobile data security. Section 5 concludes the paper and provides some advice for improving security on different aspect for mobile devices.

1. Mobile networks and communication

Mobile devices are designed to communicate via different types of standards and protocols for wireless and mobile networks. Recent devices capable of using different standards of 802.11 based networks, and all GSM based mobile networks (3G, 4G). They can also send information though other kinds of wireless communication like Bluetooth and NFC. Mobile devices are mainly used outside corporate networks, so they cannot count on corporate protection on secure connections and secure communication. These realities expose mobile devices to several information security risks.

As a first line of defense, users should use only certified vendor access points for communication to avoid risk of third party intrusion into communications channels. As late as 2012, most users used the 3G standard for sending data over mobile networks. Only 0.9% of the connections were established via 4G standard comprising 14% of the mobile traffic.

Basic mobile network security authentication assumes connection to wireless networks and is enabled via authenticated key agreement (AKA) protocol conducted between the mobile device and mobile base station. The authentication process requires use of a 128 bit secret key that is sent between the mobile infrastructure and mobile devices with the appropriate protocol of communication. The core of the communication protocol is an algorithm based on the Kasumi block cipher, a cryptography technique based on blocks of data transformed by symmetric key. Besides the improvement in the cryptography techniques used in 3G standards (ECB – electronic codebook or CBC – cipher block chaining), there are several attacks that can occur within the secure communication over this standard. Meyer and Wetzel presented the possibility of a man in the middle attack on UMTS based networks under some circumstances [31]. However, if all of the recommendations for safety are obeyed, CBC provides very secure communication. If the network is a combination of 3G and WLAN, it is easier to attack the communication by a man in the middle attack [27].

The newest standard of mobile communication, the 4G standard is based on a layered structure similar to the OSI model. Security issues are implemented in the design of the framework. As the design is structured in layers, the security is also implemented in many layers of the architecture. According to the research by Crowcroft, Cottingham, Mapp and Shaikh there are three levels of security Network Architecture Security - NAS, Network Transport Security - NTS and Service and Application Security – SAS [25]. The Y-Comm framework has two branches, one for the core network and one for the peripheral network. The NAS I connects to the network management of the core network and policy management of the peripheral network. This layer makes decisions about redirection of communication for the process of vertical handover. NTS is a security measure connected with the core transport layer for the core network and end system transport for the peripheral network. This security layer has the role of a firewall, intrusion detection system, and implements secure transport for the core network. The SAS is the top level of security and it's connected with service platform on the core network and application environment on the peripheral network. This level is concerned with authentication algorithms, access to some resources on the net and possible communications with other networks.

For wireless networks, there are plenty of software tools for monitoring and hacking wireless networks. Some of them are already in use for mobile devices like Sharkfor Root and Fing for Android, and SubNetInsight for IOS. These applications are suitable for network analysis and hacking. By using these application, hackers can create a virtual wireless router, using their own devices and give them an SSID of some known wireless provider. By using specialized applications they can get access to login passwords of the users, as well as other information and password for corporate networks and applications. These applications also offer tools for hacking devices like port scanning and network analysis. If the mobile device isn't protected well, it can be infected by malware and the intruder can gain full access to the mobile device. He can redirect the communication to its SD card, and the content of that communication can be subject of further analysis. Taken information may influence the work of some corporate services. Many tools for network analysis and tutorials can be found on the web site of Stanford University by the year of publication (http://www.slac.stanford.edu/xorg/nmtf/nmtf-tools.html).

Virtual private networks are a good solution for distributed work between entities that are geographically dispersed. By tunneling data through public networks and by use of secure protocols like IPSec and SSL, VPNs offer a high level of security. Recent offers from several communication providers offers possibilities to mobile users to use VPN security with mobile device as well as other computer devices. Providers of mobile and wireless internet are offering connections on VPN networks on different locations with guaranteed security and privacy.

Another approach toward establishing safe communication over mobile and remote networks is following data transfer via validation of MAC addresses of the users. In the case of lost or stolen devices, employees should report the device as stolen in order to block the access of that device to the corporate resources.

2. Mobile platforms security

Only six years ago there were two major platforms for mobile devices: Symbian and Windows Mobile. In these six years, many things in this field have changed. In 2002, the Blackberry OS was released. In 2007, the Apple IOS emerged closely followed by the Google Android platform. Symbian was most popular platform till 2007, but today Symbian is not even listed in a market share analysis of mobile platforms. Symbian was replaced by the Windows Mobile platform, and Android is emerging as most popular mobile platform (Fig. 2). Many of these platforms are taking their roots from known previous platforms, proved in the past like: Apple IOS, MS Windows, and Linux – Android. Blackberry is a new platform, created by RIM Company, specially constructed for mobile devices.

Mobile platforms are analyzed by several aspects of security. All of these aspects are presented in Table 1 for the dominant mobile platforms: Android, IOS, Blackberry and Windows. Figure 2 presents a breakdown of 99.2% of all mobile platforms in use as of May 2013.

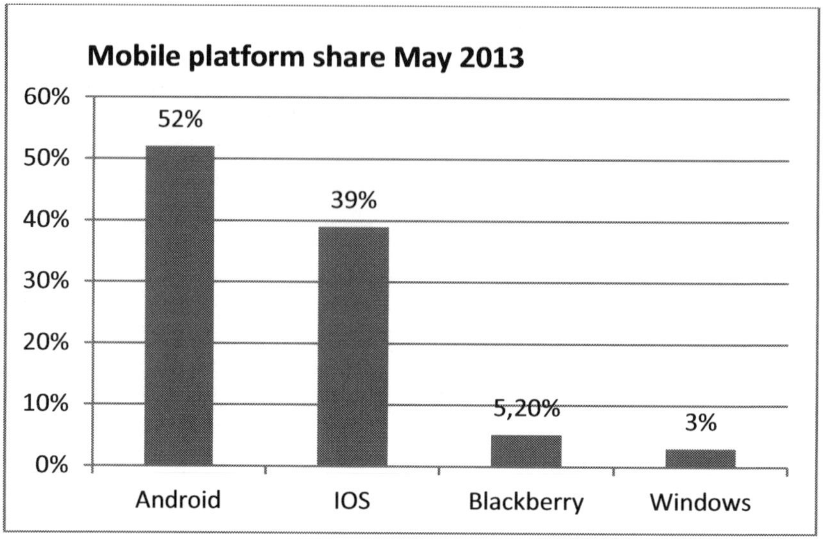

Figure 2. Market share of mobile platforms. Source: comScore, May 2013

In Table 1, a comparison of the security features of different mobile platforms are presented according to specifications of the companies that produce the operating systems, as well as some papers dedicated to mobile platform security ([17], [11], [13]). All of the analyzed mobile platforms have the ability to remotely wipe data. If the device is stolen, the owner can send a request to wipe the data from the device. This feature is not enough to protect data from experienced users. It is more secure to encrypt the data with strong passwords and keys.

Table 1: Security features of mobile platforms

Feature	Blackberry	iPhone	Android	Windows
Remote wipe capability	✓	✓	✓	✓
Encrypted backup files	✓	✓	✓	✓
Mandatory code signing	✓	✓	•	•
Type safe programming	✓	•	✓	✓
Application sandbox	✓	•	•	•
Manageability and policy enforcement	✓	•	•	✓
Full disk and memory encryption	✓	•	☒	•
End-to-end data encryption	✓	•	☒	✓
	✓	•	☒	
	Implemented	Partially implemented	Not implemented	

All of the mobile platforms support data encryption and backup of files. But there are some differences between the platforms. Blackberry offers several levels of data encryption. The user can choose which data should be encrypted and which should be in plain text format. Even the main memory can be encrypted, so the data on the device will stay secure. There isn't any other platform that offers this kind of flexible encryption. There are some third party tools that provide some of these features for different platforms.

All platforms represented in Table 1 ask for mandatory code signing. For the Android mobile platform, signing is not required by a certificate authority. The developers can use self-signed certificates. Some of the mobile platforms use third party products for security code signing. Windows Mobile uses signing certificates from Symantec Corporation. All of the analyzed mobile platforms offer software development kit –SDK and tutorials for software development. An Android application can be tested on simulator without a need for a certificate issued by a trusted source.

Application sandboxing is fully covered by RIM for the Blackberry mobile platform. Apple IOS and Google Android also declares that every application runs in sandbox and are separated in a different virtual space. There are also many different tools for different mobile platforms that can be used for sandboxing. Sandboxing is a mechanism for limitation of available resources on the device, in order to inspect the behavior of the software and protection of the devices' software. Sandboxing is based on emulation via virtual machine and the virtual machine acts like a separate mobile device by itself. If the application performs illegal activities, they are reported and it can be shut down without after-effects.

Only RIM and Microsoft ensures full end-to-end communication for the users. Besides the mobile platform and applications for them, RIM offers the BlackBerry Enterprise Server for safe data, communication, possibilities for data wiping and processing. Microsoft has a variety of applications for managing corporate policies like ActiveSync and Exchange. There is also a Microsoft System Center Mobile Device Manager which provides end-to-end user security via mobile VPN and software distribution. It's intended for corporate use. With the Microsoft Mobile Device Manager, users have opportunity to take advantage of the Microsoft Active Directory features.

3. Mobile application security

As opposed to personal computers, mobile platforms support application markets for the users. From this type of market, users can purchase and download different kind of software tools, utilities, games, communication software and so on By installing new applications on the mobile device, users agree that some of the device resources should be available to software, and the companies that produces software for mobile devices can receive information from installed applications for their own analysis. Sometimes, these data gathered is statistical in nature in order to make more thorough analysis for future software development.

Figure 3 shows an installation agreement for the Tango application. This application requires the user to allow access to device resources including storage, messages, current location, microphone, and camera among others. The communication established with this application is sent via servers of the application vendor. This communication together with other information about the device location can be recorded on the server site.

The application requires access to user accounts, and can add or remove previously created accounts. In addition, the application asks for access to personal information like your name and contacts as seen (fig. 4.). This information allows the application to connect users via the application and its servers with information about relations of the users.

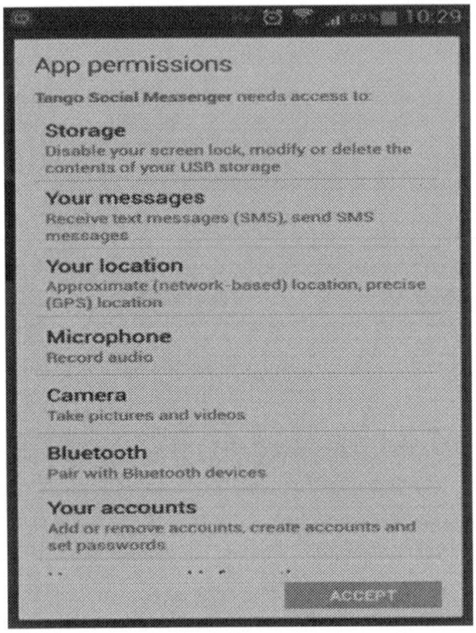

Figure 3. Application installation agreement

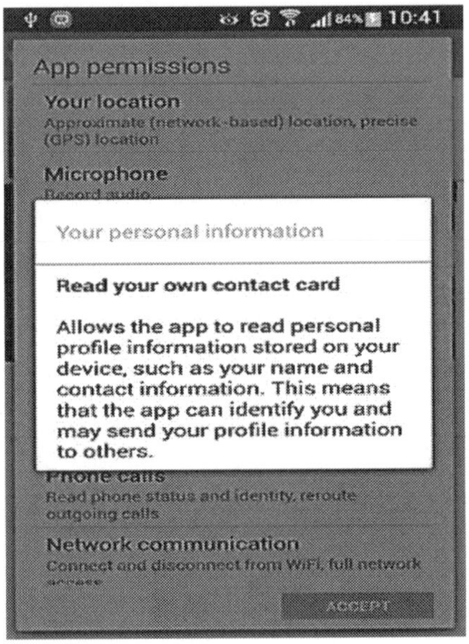

Figure 4. Explanation about personal information

Different platform vendors have different approaches towards developing new applications. While the Apple SKD is based on Objective C, the base for development on the Android platform is Java. All mobile applications are web based applications. For the Android market, produced software should be signed by the producers. There isn't any additional control for application security. This approach increases the risks for the end users to install malicious code on the mobile device. Furthermore, certificates and keys for the applications can be taken from one location of the mobile device: /etc/security/cacerts.bks.

On the market, there are many reverse engineering tools for the Android platform. In theory, they are not intended for breaking the code of the application, but for customizing parts of the applications. Tools like apktool or Dex2Jar are popular tools for Android reverse engineering. Adb shell is a base for analyzing data and application on android based devices. Command logcat is basically intended for viewing log files, can be used for opening log files and buffers of any application, even for the application used for financial transactions. Even some information sent via SSL protocols are stored in the log files of the device.

IOS have many security issues implemented, like sandboxing of every application and mandatory code signing. All these measures are meaningless if the device is jailbreaked. There are several tools for jailbreak, even specialized web services (www.jailbreaknation.com) that take only a few minutes to execute.

Microsoft Windows 8 has a variety of languages, libraries and tools for developing mobile applications. The successor of older versions of Windows have many advances and ready to use tools, but also many drawbacks and threats. Standard .NET framework offers different languages like C#, Visual Basic, Java etc., as development environment for mobile and desktop applications and there are lots of libraries for different aspects like .dll, directx etc. In the Windows SDK, the Windows App Certification Kit (ACK) is included. This kit is intended for testing applications for the Windows 8 Certification program. Also, there are many software tools and tutorials for reverse engineering of windows applications. As compared to previous versions of the Windows platform, Windows 8 has an invisible folder for Program Applications, but the users can gain access to this folder via the security tab. Tutorials about accessing this folder can be found on many sites on the web. Applications downloaded from the Windows store are installed in this folder. Reverse engineering is straight forward for languages like javascript, html and css that are not compiled in executable files. The source code can be changed in any text editor and changes can be visible immediately.

Executable files written in C# are joined with xaml files that are text files. Many software updates include these types of files. There are also many tools for reverse engineering of executable files such as JetBRains dotPeek[2]. Most of the web services that are used by applications are given in plain text in the code. These links can be changed and forwarded to another web site which can intercept the mobile communication. Signing of the application can prevent some aspect of reverse engineering, but text files cannot be protected from reverse engineering. Some secure protocols like SSL, can prevent reverse engineering for html and other plain text files. They can be encrypted and signed as executable files.

4. Mobile data security

Data stored on mobile devices often contain important and confidential data which can bring loses of confidentiality, finances, and reputations of individuals and companies. As discussed previously, mobile devices are vulnerable in many ways and subject to attacks aimed at acquiring data on the device or through its communication channels.

Data stored on mobile devices can be accessed from the device itself where it can be transferred to another computer, or data can be retrieved from removable storage devices like memory cards, SSD disks. Access to data can be acquired over device's network connection by malware, phishing and social engineering, interception of data communications and spoofing.

There a lot of new malware created especially for mobile devices (AccuTrack, Acnetdoor, Adsms, BeanBot etc.). Even current anti-malware software cannot detect the emerging forms of malware. Some malware tracks users and their actions, some are intended for intrusion and opening a backdoor to the device, but some of them are intended for obtaining files and other information stored on mobile devices (contacts, sms, and other personal data). Malware can be found for every different type of mobile

[2] http://www.jetbrains.com/decompiler

device and every different platform (J. Friedman, D. V. Hoffman – [26]). Malware on mobile devices can be used also for other purposes like DoS attacks and attacks on corporate networks.

The most challenging attacks are phishing and social engineering attacks. They are managed by cyber criminals (individuals and groups) in order to gain access to confidential information stored on devices and servers. They usually mislead users to some web service where they should register, and by this procedure they are expecting to collect information about usernames and passwords (spoofing). In most cases, they send e-mail messages with information that they should register themselves to some service to verify their login information, or to update the software they use for protection of the device. If the user "updates" the software they get malicious software and gives access to the device. Some web pages are intended for infecting computers when they visit these sites. Most mobile devices use WEbKit based browsers to surf the internet. Vulnerabilities of WEbKit are listed on the web site http://www.cvedetails.com/, - the ultimate security vulnerability datasource. Tools like Metasploit offer tools for cyber criminals who aren't knowledgeable programmers to easily infect many devices upon visiting certain websites. Mobile devices have many advantages one of which is the ability to use them as removable storage. Many companies have corporate policies forbidding employee use of USB devices while allowing mobile devices for internal and remote work for the company. These mobile devices are also USB storage devices, with even greater storage capacity.

If the device is lost or stolen, all the information stored on the device is available to potential criminals. Besides the fact that users have some tools allowing remote connections to the mobile device (GPS tracking, taking camera pictures, wiping data), stored data on the mobile device can be revealed even when data is erased, or the memory is formatted. Figure 5 presents one utility for undeleting files for the Android OS.

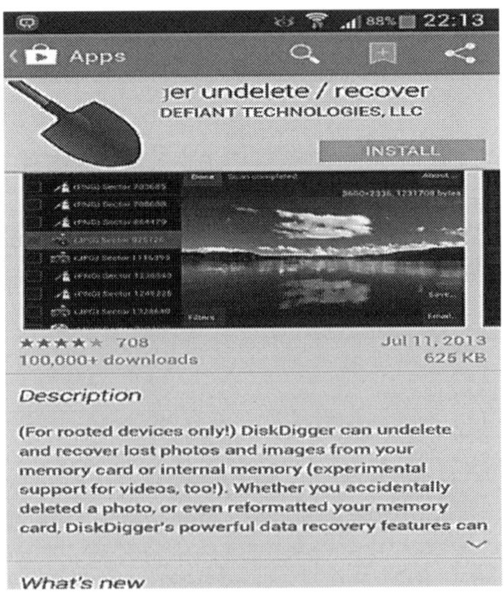

Figure 5. Undelete utility from Android play market

Researchers Glisson, Storer, Mayall, Moug, & Grispos purchased 49 mobile devices from secondary market, such that the devices were produced by different vendors. They have used mobile forensic toolkits for extraction of data (C-UFED, XRY Forensic Examination Kit and Radio Tactics Aces - RTA) and they gained access to 11, 135 artifacts stored on purchased devices (call information, calendars, e-mails, files, images, messages, notes, and videos) [8]. There are also some utility tools on mobile markets for undeleting previously deleted files. They can be used for restoring data and can store the files on other device or computer for further analysis.

5. Steps to increase security of mobile devices

In order to minimize the risks of data and device loss, users should follow several steps:

- Know the risks and assets associated with mobile devices and communication
- Follow security policies for mobile devices
- Test the platform and applications
- Avoid or limit the transfer of sensitive data over the network
- Use secure protocols for logging and sending sensitive data
- Employ sandboxing for untrusted (or all) applications
- Test the end to end communication and services

When acquiring new devices, they should be aware of possible risks and assets they have on the mobile device. In that manner, companies should give information and training for the employees about all possible aspects of mobile device security. Most of the security issues should be controlled by software, and for all different user actions on potential decrease of security, software should give warning of reduced safety (disable of firewall, disable of anti-malicious code for faster work etc.).

Most of the problems that occur on mobile security issues are connected with noncompliance with corporate policy for mobile device security. Every company has internal policies and procedures for maintaining computer, software and network safety. Quite frequently, regulations related to cyber safety policy is violated by employees (J. Friedman, D. V. Hoffman – [26]). Companies should control the implementation of cyber safety, but for mobile devices in most cases employees are outside the corporate facilities – “mobile blind spot”. Corporate safety policy for mobile devices often includes many aspects of safety like:

- Require safe authorization and authentication (strong password policy, use of safe certificates, secure protocols and networks for communication and transfer of files and data)
- Require both the device and login procedure to be protected with passwords and authentication
- Employ policies regarding screen lock and duration of idle sessions
- Require all of the confidential documents to be encrypted, on the device and during transfer
- Consider that a mobile device is and has removable storage; and extend existing policies forbidding use of some kind of removable storage (flash memory, external disks etc.) to mobile devices

- Perform regular updates for safety software and safety measures (driver by triggers or time stamps)
- Forbid downloading and installing software that is not intended for corporate purpose
- Forbid sharing of corporate software and documents and data
- Use certified network providers (with preference for authentication of the provider and network for wireless networks)
- Define procedures for lost or stolen mobile device (declaration of stolen device as soon as possible)

If the users don't follow the corporate policy for mobile safety, they increase the possibilities of intrusion or data loss. Education, training and control of employees and devices are one approach towards increasing safety measures for mobile devices.

Safety measures expire as technologies advance and consequently measures should be upgraded and improved constantly. Malicious software (viruses, Trojans, worms, malware) are changing and improving their capabilities. Anti-malware software is always one step behind new threats. Mobile devices, operating system and applications should be occasionally tested for vulnerabilities or possible infections. Most of the software protection tools often track suspicious behavior of different applications and they can prevent data loss, changes of important system and application settings, and accessing protected areas and files.

Characteristics of mobile platforms should be analyzed before authorizing the types of mobile device and platform to be used for corporate purposes. Section 3 of this paper compares many security features of mobile platforms. Companies can choose one of the platforms with ready solutions for safety, or they can choose an open platform and create their own solutions regarding safe working practices and communication. Changing the mobile platform on the corporate level can be expensive and time consuming plan. Development of new solutions is often much more expensive than implementation of the shelf solutions, but custom created solutions can address unique security needs for the company.

One measure to increase the security of data is to avoid or limit the transfer of sensitive data over the network. Transferred files via network should be encrypted and sent via secure protocols. If a confidential file is no longer needed on the mobile device, it should be deleted, but bear in mind that even deleted files can be recovered by undelete utilities. Formatting memory will not protect the memory from an undelete utility. If we really want to remove some file for good, we should fill that part of memory by some other file or data. Files on corporate sites are often better protected than on the mobile device.

Connecting and using bandwidth of mobile and wireless networks is another potential risk for mobile users. Corporate policy should dictate which provider of mobile and wireless internet should be used for corporate purposes. Hackers can easily set wireless network access points on public places with same SSID as known internet providers. Besides the authorization and authentication measures, safe encryption and communications protocols should be mandatory for transfer of sensitive information over internet, in order to countermeasure hacking techniques as man-in-the-middle and spoofing attacks whereby hackers can gain access to the username and password of a connected user. Username and password credentials are often used to further attacks on corporate sites. In [27], an example of man-in-the-middle attack is described where the attacker gained access to the mobile device and changed the contents of the ROM on the device.

If the user is connected via mobile network, he should know the risk of transferring data over mobile network. Whenever possible, they should use faster and safe mobile networks for corporate purposes. The Y-comm framework includes security in the model and it's proposed as a best approach towards safe communication over mobile networks.

Sandboxing is another measure for safe work on mobile devices. All applications that are driven on mobile devices that are not signed by trusted vendors should be sandboxed, or even better, they should not be used on corporate mobile devices. Sandboxing can prevent potential harmful activities of application on the platform of the device. Virtually surrounding the application is a work frame where the application is allowed to work. Apple IOS, and Android platform are running every application in sandbox mode. Each application is separated from others. Any suspicious behavior of the application will be detected and possible harm to the system will be prevented. Each application declares the resources needed for their work, and the user should accept the permissions for each application (fig. 3). Some applications want to share data with other applications on the platform (contacts, calendar, etc.). These types of applications should be avoided for corporate use, or trusted applications should be listed or preinstalled on mobile devices.

Finally, security analysis for mobile devices should examine the end to end communication channel and services. Clients and servers should communicate over a secure net, with secure protocols and the transfer of data and files should be validated by a server site. Some actions after safe communication can be driven by a server site (wiping data, sending triggers for activities on the user site).

References

[1]. Benjamin Speckmann, (2008) " The Android mobile platform", A Review Paper Submitted to Eastern Michigan University

[2]. Carnegie Mellon Software Engineering Institute, with the US Secret Service and CERT Coordination Center. (2005), *Insider Threat Study: Computer System Sabotage in Critical Infrastructure Sectors*

[3]. Ray-Guang Cheng, and Shiao-Li Tsao. (2004) 3G-based access control for 3GPP-WLAN interworking. 2004 IEEE 59th Vehicular Technology Conference, 2004. VTC 2004-Spring. Volume 5, Page(s): 2967-2971 Vol.5.

[4]. Chou-Chen Yang, Kuan-Hao Chu, and Ya-Wen Yang. (2006) 3G and WLAN Interworking Security: Current Status and Key Issues. *International Journal of Network Security* , Vol.2, No.1, PP.

[5]. Damianos Gavalas and Daphne Economou, "Development Platforms for Mobile Applications: Status and Trends", A Review Paper Submitted to the University of the Aegean Mytilene, Lesvos, Greece

[6]. P. Dempsey (2013). Mobile Apps are Gathering Data on our children. *Engineering & Technology* (17509637), 7(12), 13.

[7]. N. Gandhewar & R. Sheikh. (2011). Google Android: An Emerging Software Platform For Mobile Devices. *International Journal On Computer Science & Engineering,* 12-17.

[8]. W. Glisson, T. Storer, G. Mayall, I. Moug, & G. Grispos. (2011). Electronic retention: what does your mobile phone reveal about you? *International Journal Of Information Security*, 10(6), 337-349. doi:10.1007/s10207-011-0144-3

[9]. S. S. Gold (2012). Hacking on the hoof. *Engineering & Technology* (17509637), 7(3), 80-83. doi:10.1049/et.2012.0313

[10]. V. Gratzer, D. Naccache, D. Znaty (2006) Law enforcement, forensics and mobile communications. *In: Proceedings of the 4th Annual IEEE International Conference on Pervasive Computing and Communications Workshops*, p. 256. IEEE Computer Society
[11]. http://developer.android.com
[12]. http://developer.windowsphone.com
[13]. http://us.blackberry.com
[14]. http://www.cisco.com
[15]. http://www.comscore.com
[16]. http://www.cvedetails.com/vulnerability-list/vendor_id-49/product_id-10007/cvssscoremin-5/cvssscoremax-5.99/Apple-Webkit.html
[17]. http://www.ey.com
[18]. http://www.jailbreaknation.com
[19]. http://www.jetbrains.com
[20]. http://www.jgoldassociates.com
[21]. http://www.slac.stanford.edu/xorg/nmtf/nmtf-tools.html
[22]. http://www.symantec.com
[23]. E. M. Huang, K. N. Truong. (2008) Breaking the disposable technology paradigm: opportunities for sustainable interaction design for mobile phones. *In: Proceeding of the Twenty-Sixth Annual SIGCHI Conference on Human Factors in Computing Systems*. ACM, Florence, Italy
[24]. Ian Goldberg, David Wagner, Randi Thomas, and Eric Brewer (1996). "A Secure Environment for Untrusted Helper Applications (Confining the Wily Hacker)". *Proceedings of the Sixth Usenix Unix Security Symposium*
[25]. J. Crowcroft, D. Cottingham, G. Mapp, and F. Shaikh, (2007) "Y-comm: A global Architecture for Heterogeneous Networking"
[26]. J. Friedman, D. V. Hoffman (2008) Protecting data on mobile devices, A taxonomy of security threats, *Information Knowledge Systems Management* 7, 159-180
[27]. L. Zhang, W. Jia, S. Wen, D. Yao (2010) A man in the middle attack on 3G-WLAN Interworking, *International Conference on Communication and Mobile Computing*, 121-125, doi: 10.1109/CMC.2010.34
[28]. D. H. Nguyen, A. Kobsa, G.R. Hayes. (2008) An empirical investigation of concerns of everyday tracking and recording technologies. *In: Proceedings of the 10th International Conference on Ubiquitous Computing,* pp. 182–191. ACM, Seoul, Korea
[29]. B. Preneel (2007). Mobile and Wireless Communications Security, Katholieke Universiteit Leuven, Dept. Electrical Engeneering – ESAT
[30]. K. K. Sangani. (2010). Secrets of the data stream [security system]. *Engineering & Technology* (17509637), 5(15), 28-29. doi:10.1049/et.2010.1501
[31]. U. Meyer, S. Wetzel (2004) A man in the middle attack on UMTS, *Wireless Security Connference*, 90-97, doi:10.1145/1023646.1023662

Cyber Security and Resiliency Policy Framework
A. Vaseashta et al. (Eds.)
IOS Press, 2014

doi:10.3233/978-1-61499-446-6-49

Strengthening Cyber Security Policy by Means of End-Users Dedicated Training

Gevorg MARGAROV [a,1]
[a] *State Engineering University of Armenia (Polytechnic)*
Information Security and Software Development Department
105 Teryan str., Yerevan, ARMENIA

Abstract. This article is devoted to problems of end-users dedicated training based on the latest methods and practice of endpoint security. Aims and objectives of endpoint security training are revealed. The basic ideas of security and privacy when using social networking services in the training are considered. It is concluded that endpoint security will continue to hold the attention of almost all enterprises, but most important in this list will be the education sector.

Keywords. End-point security, end-users privacy, security training, security awareness, security threats and risks

Introduction

Modern organizations and enterprises are increasingly using information technology to support the regular activities of the staff, while the security landscape can become a harsh environment. Hackers and cyber criminals are using more sophisticated attack methods to penetrate networks and steal sensitive data. Gaining overall popularity, social networks are being compromised and used to distribute malware and instigate phishing attacks. At the same time proliferation of mobile and cloud technologies are opening new vulnerabilities ripe for exploitation. Precisely these vulnerabilities are equally dangerous for government bodies and large enterprises, as well as small and medium enterprises and even individuals. End-users often wrap themselves in a false sense of security believing that they are not as interesting or valuable to hackers and cyber criminals [1]. That belief is completely wrong and too risky for not only specific users but the global security infrastructure at all. What most end-users fail to realize is that they are dealing with the same vulnerable security environment as those most famous enterprise players and must be mindful to the threats posed by social networks, mobile devices and conventional attacks.

The common indicators in any security breach are insecure and unmanaged endpoints. The problem is only getting more complicated for enterprises as they operate under broad consumer oriented environment and "bring your own device" (**BYOD**) trends [2]. Mobile devices, tablets, smartphones and next-generation ultralight notebooks will open up new vulnerabilities. Enterprises have to overcome bigger challenges in managing an increasingly complex mix of hardware diversity and applications with limited resources and expertise, and end-users that are unaware of the threats. One of the most effective solutions associated with large-scale end-users

[1] Corresponding Author E-mail: gmargarov@gmail.com

dedicated training based on the latest methods and practice of endpoint security particularly during implementation of extracurricular research projects [3].

1. Aims and Objectives of Endpoint Security Training

The global aim of training is to develop and maintain the necessary level of qualification, taking into account constantly changing requirements in the field of information security, as well as features and techniques for using of modern hardware and software [4]. Thus the policy objectives in the field of information security training can include:

- Development and compliance with rules on data protection;
- Development and implementation of training environment, including the identification of training needs, planning of activities, organization of training and monitoring of its effectiveness;
- Construction of a study program in accordance with the specific future career of trainees;
- Formation of relevant training standards, including well-founded learning outcomes;
- Enabling best practices, modern knowledge and efficient management methods in the process of endpoint security training;
- Motivating end-users to improve security and ensure reliability of operation;
- Regular assessment of knowledge, skills and competences in endpoint security and their application in practice.

2. End-Users Information Security Awareness Improvement Program

Awareness program refers to introduction of a process of regular knowledge, skills and competences improvement in endpoint security [5]. Basic requirements that all considered solutions must satisfy may include:

- Providing the possibility for regular training of end-users, regardless of their territorial location and without interruption of regular workflow;
- Presentation of the materials to end-users in a simple and understandable manner;
- The value of all implemented solutions should be adequate, and should not be in direct proportion to the number of trainees.

Based on the requirements listed above, it is clear that that this task must fit different system of classroom and distance learning solutions based on wide use of modern information technology, including cloud, tools and solutions. In particular, widely used social networking services can be used to support both classroom and distance learning.

3. Security and Privacy When Using Social networking services in the Training

Trainers and trainees can use social networking services to communicate with each other, information exchange and teamwork. However, some public services, such as **Facebook** and **Twitter**, have a fairly wide range of users, while others may limit the number of participants, becoming essentially private services [6]. When users share information on the Internet, they should understand the potential risks and, accordingly, be careful when choosing what to share and with whom. Security and privacy risks may be associated not only with the purposeful actions of cyber criminals, but also with inadvertent disclosure of information by the user.

Malefactors can use social networking services to spread malicious software, compromise (hack) users' computers or gain access to information about a user's identity, his location, contact information, as well as personal or professional relationships [7]. At the same time, the user could inadvertently disclose such information to unauthorized persons, improperly placing it in a social network or carelessly performing certain actions.

3.1. Potential Threats in Social networking services

The main potential threats for the user in social networking services may include:

- **Viruses**. The popularity of social networking services makes them ideal targets for attackers who naturally seek the greatest effect at the lowest effort. By creating a virus, and inserting it into a website or third-party applications, the attacker can infect millions of computers mainly due to the spread of malicious links to user's contacts.
- **Special Tools.** Attackers can use specially designed tools (software) that will enable them to take control of a user account in a social service. Further, an attacker can gain access to a user's personal data and by his contacts to the data of other users who share information with him. Furthermore an attacker who gains access to a user account may distribute any information, in particular malicious content on his behalf.
- **Social Engineering Attacks**. Attackers can send email or leave a comment that will appear as coming from a trusted social service or user. Thus this message may contain a link to a malicious Website or request for personal information. If the user follows the instructions, the user may disclose confidential information or compromise the security of his system.
- **Identity Theft**. Attackers can gather enough personal information from social networks to disclose the identity of the user or one of his contacts. Even a few identifying factors of personal data can provide attackers with enough information to guess the answers to questions asked by systems for secure recovery of e-mail, credit card or bank account password (PIN code).
- **Third-Party Applications**. Some social networking services may allow users to extend the functionality by adding third-party applications (software), such as additional tools, games, etc. One must be very careful when using these applications because, even if the application does not contain malicious code, it can gain access to information in a user's profile without his permission. Then this information can be used for various purposes, such as sending spam e-mail,

an adaptation of advertisements, marketing research or access to the user's contacts.

3.2. Professional and Personal Risks

A list of professional and personal risks [8] that may arise as a result of placement of certain types of information in social networking services may include:

- **Overhead Information**. Placement in social networking services of sensitive information intended for use only within the enterprise can have serious consequences. Disclosure of information on intellectual property, human resources, structural changes, or other activities of the enterprise may lead to untimely or inappropriate publicity, loss of demands and other undesirable consequences.
- **Professional Reputation**. Inappropriate photos or content posted on the social network can threaten educational and career prospects of users. Universities and training centers can conduct online searches for information about the students in the learning process or entrants in the process of reviewing applications. In addition, many companies-employers may also conduct online searches for information about the candidates applying for employment during the interview process. Information which indicates that the applicant may be unreliable, untrusted or unprofessional may threaten a career of candidate. In other words, placing some information may affect the credibility and professional reputation of the user.
- **Personal Relationships**. Given the fact that users have the ability to post comments on social networking services from any computer or even a smartphone with access to the Internet, they can impulsively place comments, which will be regretted later. Even if comments and photos will be deleted by the user, it may be too late to avoid the consequences. Essentially, once the information gets to the social service, there is no practical way to gain control over who sees the information, where it is redistributed, or whether it is stored in the service archive or not. Such information can naturally affect the user's relationship with the other persons.
- **Personal Safety**. The user may endanger his/her personal safety, placing certain information in social networks. For example, placing travel plans (absence from home) at a certain time, especially if the home address is placed in the user's profile, increasing the risk that his apartment will be robbed.

An important point to remember about social networking services is that the user can post information about other people as well. Without even realizing it, the user can compromise someone else placing a comment or photo that could jeopardize the privacy or safety of that person. Sometimes, information or comments with negative content about someone else are not casual. Social networking services can provide services to deal with complaints about cyber bullying or compromising information, which is a growing problem that can lead to significant psychological damage.

3.3. Self-Defense in Social networking services

Social networking services are undoubtedly useful and pleasant tools for education and other forms of activity, but it is important that the user is taking active steps to protect his computer and personal information. Defending himself, the user also helps to protect people who are connected jointly with him to services.

Applications of the following general safety measures may allow significantly reduce professional and personal risks:

- Use of reliable (strong) passwords, and use of different passwords for each service;
- Maintenance of up to date anti-virus software;
- Timely installation of the system and application software updates, especially updates that affect web browsers.

3.4. Reasonable Practice of Work with Passwords

Passwords are the most common form of authentication and are often the only barrier between the user's personal information and other people. There are many available software tools which attackers can use for finding or "hacking" passwords. Nevertheless, choosing complex passwords and ensuring their confidentiality can make the task of unauthorized access to user's personal information rather difficult to solve. However, choosing a good password is quite a challenge based on a compromise between convenience and security. On the one hand, a complex password that is difficult for a hacker to decipher is also difficult for a user to remember. On the other hand a simple password is easy to remember, but it is also easy to decipher.

The following tactics may assist a user in choosing a cryptographically strong password:

- Do not use passwords that are based on personal information (name, date of birth, etc.), which may be easily available or found;
- Do not use words that can be found in any dictionary of any language;
- Choose within the constraints long enough (at least 8 characters) passwords;
- Develop mnemonic rules for creating and remembering complex passwords;
- Use combinations of uppercase and lowercase letters, numbers, punctuation marks and special characters;
- If necessary, take care to safely and securely store passwords;
- Use different passwords for different services.

3.5. Practical Recommendations for Reducing Security Risks

In addition, security risks can be reduced with careful adherence to the following guidelines:

- **Use Robust Privacy and Security Settings**. Use the security configuration options provided by social networking services. Choose the most secure option over convenience. Social networking services periodically change their options to improve security and privacy, so review configuration settings periodically.
- **Avoid Suspicious Third-Party Applications**. When selecting third-party applications, choose applications developed by trusted manufacturers and avoid

applications that seem suspicious. In addition, restrict access by third-party applications to sensitive information.

- **Assume that Everything May be Available to the Public**. Limit the amount of information placed on social networking services. This recommendation applies not only to the information in the user profile, but also to any comments or photos, which identifies the user.
- **Share Information Only with Acquaintances**. While many users try to establish as many contacts as possible in social networking services, it is best to limit interaction with unfamiliar persons. If the user decides to expand their contacts outside people known to him, then contacts must be grouped and assigned different levels of access to groups. Malicious users can masquerade as different people in a bid to be added to user contacts, so he should try a roundabout way to authenticate any contact that he/she considers.

Even the most restrictive security settings cannot provide complete privacy. An attacker or malicious software can use vulnerabilities in the system and application software, or someone else can redirect the user information to an untrusted entity. Therefore, use social networking services responsibly and always consider the possible risks. Despite best efforts at securing information, assume that any information placed on social networking services can become public and therefore available to everyone. In this regard, consider cryptographic and steganographic means for securing information that requires high levels of confidentiality [9, 10].

4. Protecting Sensitive Information from Malicious Software

One of the most important components of an information security policy is to protect the end-user, or more precisely his workplace (endpoint) against malicious software. The two techniques employed to protect the workplace (endpoint) from malicious software are to detect known bad software, referred to as blacklisting, or approve known good software, referred to as whitelisting.

With blacklisting, users can download and run any application that isn't banned. Blacklisting is generally considered more efficient than whitelisting, because the number of good known applications exceeds bad known applications. But recently attackers have overwhelmed the ability of security companies to develop full blacklists by regularly creating variants of their malware or providing transformability of malicious software. Nevertheless, there are some ways to further improve blacklisting technologies, first to focus on the initial download of or attached files and the reputation of their source. As an example, within its intrusion prevention software, Kaspersky labs uses a combination of techniques, such as source reputation and the blocking of exploits for known vulnerabilities to stop malicious software from getting to the hard drive. These systems ensure security in several consistent steps: use of an intrusion prevention system to block downloads, use of antivirus signature and heuristic technologies to scan downloaded files, and use of behavioral detection tools to block malicious behavior.

Security companies also link endpoints together to create something like a network of end-users as exemplified in the Kaspersky Security Network (KSN) [11] that creates a private cloud, using information gathered from across the customer base. When one endpoint detects a malicious file through behavioral analysis, information on the malware is passed to the network (cloud), turned into a signature and is available for download by the entire customer base through antivirus updates. By continuously updating information on suspicious files in this way, companies can more quickly react to malware.

Whitelisting, which allows the download and installation of only approved applications, are becoming increasingly popular since attackers have gotten better at hiding the malicious files and applications. Like blacklisting, whitelisting is no longer just about comparing an executable file to a list of signatures. Instead of just approving application binaries, whitelisting has become a set of sophisticated policies. Increasingly, whitelisting is about evaluating behavior and reputation and giving applications a score that places them on a list of a comparative evaluation, and they take into account who's asking to run an application.

5. Conclusion

The difficulty of ensuring information security can be summed up by a famous quote by Albert Einstein "Problems cannot be solved with the same level of awareness that created them". The problem of end-user mistakes cannot be solved by adding more technology; it has to be solved by radically increasing awareness of information security, most particularly at the level of endpoint security. The benefit of a properly educated information security user base is economically valuable. Rather than mediating security breaches caused by an uninformed user base, information security personnel can discover and plug hidden threats that are beyond technological means. Without the help of the end-users, an information security staff can feel as a certain extent helpless against growing security threats. The three fundamental countermeasures for defending infrastructure and data are technology, operations and awareness, training and education. [12]. Endpoint security will continue to hold the attention of almost all enterprises, but the ability to educate the user base about best practices in information security is the most important and significant step towards reducing costs of information security assurance.

References

[1] T. DeZabala, R. Baich, *Cyber crime: a clear and present danger. Combating the fastest growing cyber security threat*, Deloitte Development, 2010

[2] B. Morrow, *BYOD security challenges: control and protect your most sensitive*, Network Security, Volume 2012, Issue 12, December 2012, 5–8

[3] G. Margarov, *Information Security Studying by Means of Extracurricular Research Projects,* NATO Security through Science Series, E: Human and Societal Dynamics, Volume 16, ISO Press, 2007, 286–293

[4] M. Whitman, H. Mattord, *Management of Information Security*, Stamford: Cengage Learning, 2013

[5] T. Loveček, V. T. Míka, J. Ristvc, *Advanced Tools for Acquirement of Competencies by Crisis and Security Managers,* In 11th WSEAS International Conference on Education Technology "Latest Advances in Educational Technologies" (Singapur, May 11-13) 2012, 65–70

[6] P. A. Tess, *The role of social media in higher education classes (real and virtual) – A literature review*, Computers in Human Behavior, Volume 29, Issue 12, September 2013, A60–A68

[7] I. Kotenko, A. Chechulin, *Computer attack modeling and security evaluation based on attack graphs,*
IEEE 7th International Conference on Intelligent Data Acquisition and Advanced Computing Systems (Berlin, September 12-14) 2013, 614–619

[8] Z.Xuan, N. Wuwong, L. Hao, Z. Xuejie, *Information Security Risk Management Framework for the Cloud Computing Environments,* IEEE 10th International Conference on Computer and Information Technology (Bradford, June 29- July 1) 2010, 1328–1334

[9] G. Margarov, S. Chopuryan, *Public Key Cryptosystem Based on Finite Automata for Multilateral Antiterrorist Activity Support,*NATO Security through Science Series, E: Human and Societal Dynamics, Volume 67, ISO Press, 2010, 183–198

[10] G. Margarov, *Investigation of Web Based Hidden Data,* NATO Security through Science Series, D: Information and Communication Security, Volume 27, ISO Press, 2010, 93–107

[11] D. Maslennikov, *IT Threat Evolution: Q1 2013*, Kaspersky Lab (http://www.realphantom.com/sites/default/files/images/computers_internet/142043837-Malware-Report-Q1-2013-Kaspersky-Lab.pdf)

[12] C. D.Schou, K. J. Trimmer, *Information assurance and security,* Journal of Organizational and End User Computing, Volume 16, Issue 3, September 2004, i – vii

Cyber Security and Resiliency Policy Framework
A. Vaseashta et al. (Eds.)
IOS Press, 2014

doi:10.3233/978-1-61499-446-6-57

Toward Effective National Cyber Security Strategy: The Path Forward For Macedonia

Metodi HADJI-JANEV[1]
Military Academy "General Mihailo Apostolski – Skopje"
University "Goce Delcev" – Stip, Skopje, REPUBLIC OF MACEDONIA

Abstract Cyberspace has become the dominant place for social, economic and political activities in the region of South East Europe (SEE). However like in the rest of the World the growing dependence of the cyberspace in the SEE in general and in Macedonia in specific has not been matched by a parallel focus on security. This article explains why Macedonian government needs to consider concrete strategic guidance for cyber security. The main argument of the article is that future cyber security strategy must have a comprehensive approach addressing cyber crime; cyber defense; intelligence and counterintelligence, critical information infrastructure protection and crisis management; and cyber diplomacy and cyber governance. Given that most of the SEE countries share the same history and political, social and security dynamics with small adjustments the findings and recommendation could be applicable to the rest of the SEE countries.

Keywords: national cyber security strategy, cyber crime, cyber defense

Introduction

Globalization and technological development have affected security in a unique way. On one hand they have brought progress and success. On the other hand these processes have brought serious challenges to national security. Today most of the social, political and economic activities are taking place in the so-called "cyber world". Although virtual this world in many forms influences one state's progress and economic development. At the same time, cyberspace has become an opportunity for negative forces whose activities directly or indirectly affect our security and the way of living.

As the rest of the World the region of SEE depends on cyberspace. However the security risks to cyberspace have not been addressed with strategic guidance. Thus effective cyber security strategy is a must for the region itself. Since the Republic of Macedonia shares a common history, tradition, culture, ambitions and challenges with most of the SEE countries, this article goes to in-depth analyses of existing legislation and security concepts to propose the path that the political elite needs to consider in order to protect cyberspace. The main hypothesis is that while building the future cyber security strategy Macedonian Government needs a comprehensive approach that will

[1]E-mail: metodi.hadzi-janev@ugd.edu.mk

establish an appropriate balance between security on one hand and social, political and economic needs on the other hand.

To prove this, this article first defines the problem by addressing global security trends and explain how these trends affect cyberspace in the region of SEE in general and Macedonia more specifically. Then by analyzing current political and security dynamics, the article will address the need for a national cyber security strategy within Macedonia. Then, the article will offer some recommendations for the future cyber security strategies. These recommendations are based on the analyses of existing legislation, security concepts, and the role that appropriate stakeholders should play in protecting cyberspace. The article will also address some issues that may offer guidance that although well intended may also create counterproductive measures and outcomes.

1. Global security trends and Macedonia

The intensified processes of globalization and technological development after the Cold War have dramatically changed the concept of security. The dissolution of the opposing communist block in the international arena had flattened the world and opened the door for new relations and exchange.[2] At the same time, technological development has lowered the costs of communication and prompted communications among corporate, groups and individuals. Eventually hierarchical corporations that were once predominantly controlled by government and wedged among geographical, political and cultural boundaries have almost disappeared. Today many of the global systems and services that they provide are run by private non-state actors. These systems and services are interlinked, interconnected and go beyond national borders. Global processes run through such systems and services and bring a fundamental shift in the spatial scale in human social organizations that links distant communities and expand the reach of power.[3]

Even though many see these processes as a success, it is evident that global flows of technology, goods, information, ideologies, and people can have destructive as well as productive effects. Today many argue that globalization introduced many side effects by scrambling everything and thus affecting the previously designed international order.[4] Unlike the Cold War, modern security threats are hybrid. Relying on modern technology (especially information technology) and by (ab)using modern technologies, both state and non-state actors pose asymmetric and unconventional threats which are far more unpredictable. Governments around the globe have lost their monopolies of power. At the same time, modern non-state adversaries are (what is considered under contemporary regulations) a mix of terrorists, criminals, insurgents and religious extremists.

As for the rest of the World, information and communication technology (ICT) and the use of a cyberspace plays a crucial role in the region of South Eastern Europe (SEE). The pursuit of modernization, the Euro-Atlantic integration and the necessity for foreign investments among others, urged SEE countries to invest in the

---

2 Friedman. L. Thomas, *The World is Flat,* Farrar, Straus & Giroux, 2005

3 Mcgrew, Anthony, "The Globalization of World Politics", in ed. J Baylis; S Smith and Patricia Owens, "An Introduction to International Relations", 5th. ed. Oxford, 2010, p. 14-31.

4 Brian Forst, *Terrorism, Crime and Public Policy*, Cambridge University Press, 2009, p. 86

development of ICT and cyberspace. Thus although virtual, cyberspace has become the dominant place for social, economic and political activities in the region of SEE. These activities have brought both positive and negative effects.

Its geographical position and Euro-Atlantic aspirations of its populace and political elites urge the Republic of Macedonia to seriously consider current political and security dynamics. The Government of the Republic of Macedonia among others has pledged to improve the Macedonian people's welfare.[5] It clearly understood that to achieve this, it must follow current trends in cyber domain and have seriously invested in the development of the so called informatics society.[6] Nevertheless although there is a significant technological improvement and there is an evident increase in cyber technology usage[7], Macedonia does not have a comprehensive cyber security strategy.

2. Does Macedonia Need a Cyber Security Strategy?

In step with global trends, the growing dependence on cyberspace in the SEE has not been matched by a parallel focus on security. Cyberspace, for all its practical utility, has arguably become a space that negatively affects the social order security, everyday life, and introduces new forms of crime and security threats. At the same time, recent practices show that the cyber - world has become both a battle-space for modern terrorists' ideological and information warfare and a medium for global radicalization. Hence economic, political and security reasons urge the Macedonian Government to consider a national cyber security strategy.

Building an effective cyber security strategy also complements political and security requirements due to the Macedonian Euro-Atlantic aspirations. Both the revised NATO Policy on Cyber Defense of 8 June 2011[8] and the Chicago Summit Declaration of May 2012[9] stressed the importance of cooperation with partner nations in order to achieve greater cyber security. Although a "storm cloud still emerges from European Union's cyber security strategy"[10] regarding its lack of clarity to protect cloud computing this document clearly confirms the importance of addressing cyber security too.

---

[5] Government of the Republic of Macedonia - Ministry of Finance, "The Ctrategy for development of Public Internatl Finansial Control in the Republic of Macedonia", Jully 2013, (Original: Стратегија за развој на јавната внатрешна финансиска контрола во Република Македонија од 2013 до 2016")

[6] Government of the Republic of Macedonia - Ministry of Informatic Society,"National Strategy for e-Government 2010-2012", January 2010, Original: „Национална стратегија за е Влада, 2010-2012")

[7] Compare for example The official UN findings between 2008 and 2012, UN E-Government Survey 2008: From E-Government to Connected Governance, New York, 2008 (E-Government Readiness Data 2008), retrieved from: UN E-Government Survey 2012: E-Government for the People, The UN New York, 2012 (E-Government Readiness Data 2008), retrieved May 13, 2013.
from: http://unpan1.un.org/intradoc/groups/public/documents/un/unpan048065.pdf

[8] NATO Public Diplomacy Division, "Defending the Netwroks, The NATO Policy on Cyber Defence", June 8, 2011

[9] NATO Homepage, Chicago Summit Declaration, Issued by the Heads of State and Government participating in the meeting of the North Atlantic Council in Chicago on 20 May 2012, retrived (May 3, 2013 from: http://www.nato.int/cps/en/natolive/official_texts_87593.htm)

[10] European Union, "The cybersecurity strategy – "An Open, Safe and Secure Cyberspace"", The European Commission and High Representative of the Union for Foreign Affairs and Security Policy, February 7, 2013 retrieved May 5 2013.
from: http://www.eda.europa.eu/info-hub/news/2013/02/08/european-union-strategy-for-cyber-security

Cyber security challenges pose serious security threats that can directly and indirectly undermine peoples' trust in the system when the former is incapable to provide effective protection. Many argue that the cyberspace was not designed with legal and security considerations. In short, as Gary Chapman asserts *"...while the Internet and the concept of "national security" share common roots in history, they developed along separate and divergent paths. This makes it all the more interesting that these paths are now converging again, but in a way that makes the Internet problematic and even threatening to national security..."* [11]

Today technical issues of cyberspace also represent a serious challenge to national securities in many states and in Macedonia too.[12] Thus the "paradox of modernity"[13] in the context of cyber security also affects Macedonia. The more we depend on modern technology the more vulnerable we are.

It seems that common wisdom dictates that if the Macedonian Government is about to ensure economic development, it needs to invest in a safe and secure environment. Achieving such an environment requires measures, instruments and mechanisms that will convince clients, investors, consumers and citizens in cyber security too.

3. Towards An Effective National Cyber Security Strategy

Addressing a nation's cyber security issues is not an easy task. The development of a Macedonian national cyber security strategy must be understood as a tool that will help the society to reach a desired state of affairs. It is not an end in itself. Therefore the Macedonian leadership needs to recognize the emerging problem and set forth goals and adequate strategic framework to address it.

Current cyber security threats straddle the boundaries between different public sectors. These include (but are not limited to) law-enforcement, national defense, crisis management, economic efficiency and public diplomacy and governance. Furthermore, current practice shows that cyber security threats could be interconnected and interlinked affecting different social sectors at the time. Thus, while considering cyber security threats, Macedonian leadership must balance the economic, legal and social importance of the free flow of information to the security needs of government, industry, and citizens. Hence the national cyber security strategy should span over five cornerstone areas. These cornerstone areas are: countering cyber crime; cyber defense addressed by the military cyber stakeholders; intelligence and counterintelligence; critical infrastructure protection and crisis management; and cyber diplomacy and cyber governance.

Effective response to cyber security treats thus must be comprehensive and highly coordinated among all stakeholders. Consequently this will require responses from different stakeholders (public including private sectors too). So far all of these areas have been addressed by the specific documents in the broader national security context, separate from cyber threats. Therefore nesting the cyber challenges under current

[11] Gary Chapman, *National Security and the Internet*, The 21st Century Project, LBJ School of Public Affairs, July 1998, p.5

[12] See in depth discussion in: Weber H. Rolf, "Internet of Things New security and Privacy challenges", Computer Law & Security review 26, 2010, 23-30

[13] For more general discussion on this topic see:

Macedonian security strategic documents requires careful analyses of existing legislature regarding the leading national authorities in different areas.

3.1. Finding the Right Balance Under the Appropriate Security Concept For Future Cyber Security Strategy in Macedonia

Existing strategic security documents in the Republic of Macedonia prioritize different national authority. This usually depends on the nature of the threat and the situation. The closest model for strategic guidance that could be useful for comparative analyses in Macedonia (which is relevant for the rest of the South-East European Countries if not wider) in the context of cyber security strategy is the current Crisis management system. The analogy comes from the nature that a crisis management system addresses (i.e. comprehensive approach and multi-institutional approach-the one that cyber security requires).

However, when comparing the recent developments in the Macedonian crisis management system while building cyber security strategy, one can expect to meet different and competing considerations among the all stakeholders.[14] The former could be a serious challenge to the existing matrix of Macedonian national security strategic documents. This however should not be discouraging since many nations still face similar challenges.

Macedonian legislation that builds the framework for a crisis management system in Macedonia gravitates over the, Ministry of Interior,[15] Ministry of Defense,[16] Protection and Rescue Directorate,[17] Crisis Management Center,[18] Ministry of Transport and Communication,[19] Directorate for Protection of Classified Information[20]and Ministry of Environment and Spatial Planning.[21] Logically when comes to cyber security along with the former, one should definitely consider the Ministry for Informatic Society's related and other relevant legislative considering the ITC.[22]

---

[14] Hadji-Janev Metodi, "Threats to the Critical Infrastructure in South-East Europe posed by Al Qaeda and its Associated Movements", In: Caleta, D., and Shemella, P., (Eds), *Counterterrorism challenges regarding the Critical Infrastructure protection*, (2011), Center for Civil - Military Relation, Monterey, USA, S-4,2, pp. 187-201, ISBN: 9-789619-286029, available at: http://www.ics-institut.com/research/books/2

[15] The Official Gazette of R.M no.92/09

[16] The Official Gazette of R.M no.5/03, 06 and 08

[17] Official Gazette of RM", No. 36/04,49/04,86/08,18/11

[18] The Official Gazette of RM" No. 29/05

[19] The Official Gazette of RM, No. 40/07

[20] The Official Gazette of RM, No.9/04

[21] The Official Gazette of R.M No. 48/10, 124/10 and 51/11

[22] The list of these document is conists of: Law for electronic data and electronic signature, 2001 "The Official Gazette of RM", No. 34/01 from 03.05.2001, National Strategy for development of Information Society with action plan (2005) available at: http://www.mio.gov.mk/files/pdf/dokumenti/Strategija_i_Akcionen_Plan.pdf.; Law for electronic communication (2005) ("The Official Gazette of RM", No. 13/05 from 25.02.2005 13/05,14/2007,55/2007,98/2008 and 83/2010)"; Law for personal data protection (2005)(, "The Official Gazette of RM", No. 7/05 from 01.02.2005"); Two bylaws for issuing digital certificates in accordance with the law available at: //e-demokratija.mk/documents/10157/46173/; Law on free access to public communications (2006), ("The Official Gazette of RM", No. 13/06 from 24.08.2006); Law on interception of communications (2006-2013) ("The Official Gazette of RM", No. 116/12 од 27.09.2012); Law on electronic commerce (2007) ("The Official Gazette of RM", No. 133/07 from 02.11.2007); National strategy for development of electronic communications with information technologies (2007) ("The Official Gazette of RM", No. 136/07 од 12.11.2007) and Government of the Republic of Macedonia - Ministry of Informatic

Considering the nature of complex cyber security threats and the numbers of documents without strategic guidelines, this could easily create confusion. Thus although well designed and organized when put together, the overall response by national stakeholders could turn into disaster. This is not to say that the current crisis management system, or existing documents are not well designed or do not recall appropriate institutions to address specific threats. This means that absence of strategic guidance is unacceptable in the age of cyber threats.

The complexity of comprehensive approach further requires one to consider the model of shaping the strategic guidance i.e. strategic concept. A brief overview of the existing security documents will emphasize serious security challenges that might have fatal consequences in the context of security concepts designed to address cyber security threats. To avoid such scenarios, future strategists must consider existing security concepts which address cyber security challenges. These concepts should be in compliance with the political elites' efforts, i.e. the Euro- Atlantic integrations. Nevertheless future strategists must avoid establishing defaults or just copies of the concepts that are suitable for different societies that share different history, tradition and culture.

Although well intended, Euro-Atlantic integration processes might cause complex confusion especially when security responses need to be implemented in practice on operational or tactical level. More precisely, confusion may occur if a nation fails to develop an appropriate security concept that will be followed by all responsible stakeholders. Moreover this concept should be vertically (top-down and bottom-up from strategic through the operational too tactical level) and horizontally (between different institutions) harmonized.

For example, the European Union and NATO cyber security documents produce guidance that is designed to enhance national cyber security responses in different sectors. Usually defense sectors follow NATO guidance and standardizations and law enforcements follow EU guidance and standardizations. At first glance, there is nothing wrong with these, even some will argue that there are many areas where NATO and EU guidance complement each other. However it should be also considered that not all NATO members are EU members and some of these members (arguably among the strongest and most influential, the US and Turkey) have serious influence in the security sector of SEE. Turkey and the U.S. for example are among the biggest donors to the Macedonian security sector (considering the equipment and the training).[23]

Hence, if the security concepts' guidance are not careful and under coordinated mode transferred into practice they can create "separate worlds" on operational and tactical responsive level. Eventually such mistakes will result in the development of different standardization processes (including but not limited to risk assessment, resilience building, the overall consequence management, etc.). Such discrepancies will

Society,"National Strategy for e-Government 2010-2012", January 2010, Original: „Национална стратегија за е Влада, 2010-2012")

[23] See for example Macedonian Ministry of defence's statement about this in: "Military cooperation With Turkey is at the high level", Kurir, April 22, 2013, (Original: "Воената соработка со Турција е на високо ниво"), retirieved in May17, 2013.
from: http://kurir.mk/makedonija/vesti/113068-Voenata-sorabotka-megu-Makedonija-i-Turcija-na-visoko-nivo
or see Mijanovic Vladimir, "We are Partners with US and Turkey but we need Germany, Russia and China", Nova Makedonia, September 9, 2012 (original: "Партнери сме со САД и Турција, но ни требаат Германија, Русија и Кина"), retrieved May 17, 2013.
from: http://www.novamakedonija.com.mk/NewsDetal.asp?vest=914121719479&id=9&setIzdanie=22680

be evident not just in defense or law enforcement but also in other cornerstone areas i.e. crisis management and critical infrastructure protection, intelligence and countering intelligence, cyber governance and cyber diplomacy.

3.2. Additional Guidance That Future Cyber Security Strategists Must Consider

From the previous analyses it becomes clear that countering cyber crime; cyber defense; intelligence and counterintelligence; critical infrastructure protection and crisis management; and cyber diplomacy and cyber governance are areas that strategists must cover in order to design effective strategic guidance for cyber security. Nevertheless to avoid legal collisions that could undermine faith in the government and challenge liberal and democratic values, each of these cornerstone areas must be matched by five "bipolar variables". These variables stem from practice and attempts to regulate cyber domain. All of the bipolar variables represent a specific balance which is situation-dependent. Different surrounding dynamics influence a shift in the balance which ultimately affects specific cornerstone areas. These variables are: economic development vs. improved national security; modernization of infrastructure vs. critical infrastructure protection; private sector vs. public sector; data protection vs. information sharing; and individual freedoms vs. public safety.

Finally, given the complexity which a future cyber security strategy must address, the overall approach (i.e. developing a national cyber security strategy) must rely on centralized planning and decentralized execution. Thus the strategy will avoid one of the biggest challenges that each cyber security strategy faces i.e. the lack of coordination.

4. Conclusion

Globalization and technological development have urged many countries and organizations to consider cyber security as a top security priority. Marching towards modernity and following their own ambitions for Euro-Atlantic integrations, among others, like in the rest of the SEE countries, the Macedonian Government has pledged serious efforts to improve their own information and communication technologies. So far; however, the growing dependence on cyberspace in the SEE in general and in Macedonia in specific, has not been matched by a parallel focus on security.

Economic, political and security reasons urge Macedonian and the rest of the SEE governments to consider a national cyber security strategy. While considering cyber security threats, the Macedonian and SEE countries' leadership must balance the economic, legal and social importance of the free flow of information to the security needs of government, industry, and citizens. Hence, a future national cyber security strategy should span over countering cyber crime; cyber defense; intelligence and counterintelligence; critical infrastructure protection and crisis management; and cyber diplomacy and cyber governance. To avoid legal collisions that could undermine faith in the government and challenge liberal and democratic values, each of these cornerstone areas must be matched by the following variables: economic development vs. improved national security; modernization of infrastructure vs. critical infrastructure protection; private sector vs. public sector; data protection vs. information sharing; and individual freedoms vs. public safety. Nevertheless to avoid a potential mis-communication, future strategists must consider centralized planning and decentralized execution.

References

[1]. Chapman Gary, *National Security and the Internet*, The 21st Century Project, LBJ School of Public Affairs, July 1998,

[2]. European Union, "The cybersecurity strategy – "An Open, Safe and Secure Cyberspace"", The European Commission and High Representative of the Union for Foreign Affairs and Security Policy, February 7, 2013

[3]. Forst Brian, *Terrorism, Crime and Public Policy*, Cambridge University Press, 2009,

[4]. Friedman L. Thomas, *The World is Flat,* Farrar, Straus & Giroux, 2005

[5]. Government of the Republic of Macedonia - Ministry of Informatic Society,"National Strategy for e-Government 2010-2012", January 2010, Original: „Национална стратегија за е Влада.

[6]. Government of the Republic of Macedonia - Ministry of Finance, "The Ctrategy for development of Public Internatl Finansial Control in the Republic of Macedonia", Jully 2013, (Original: Стратегија за развој на јавната внатрешна финансиска контрола во Република Македонија од 2013 до 2016")

[7]. Hadji-Janev Metodi, "Threats to the Critical Infrastructure in South-East Europe posed by Al Qaeda and its Associated Movements", In: Caleta, D., and Shemella, P., (Eds), *Counterterrorism challenges regarding the Critical Infrastructure protection*, (2011), Center for Civil - Military Relation, Monterey, USA, S-4,2, pp. 187-201, available at: http://www.ics-institut.com/research/books/2

[8]. McGrew Anthony, "The Globalization of World Politics", in ed. J Baylis; S Smith and Patricia Owens, "An Introduction to International Relations", 5th. ed. Oxford, 2010Mijanovic Vladimir, "We are Partners with US and Turkey but we need Germany, Russia and China", Nova Makedonia, September 9, 2012 (original: „Партнери сме со САД и Турција, но ни требаат Германија, Русија и Кина"), from: http://www.novamakedonija.com.mk/NewsDetal.asp?vest=914121719479&id=9&setIzdanie=22680

[9]. NATO Public Diplomacy Division, "Defending the Netwroks, The NATO Policy on Cyber Defense", June 8, 2011

[10]. NATO Homepage, Chicago Summit Declaration, Issued by the Heads of State and Government participating in the meeting of the North Atlantic Council in Chicago on 20 May 2012.

[11]. National Strategy for development of Information Society with action plan (2005) available at: http://www.mio.gov.mk/files/pdf/dokumenti/Strategija_i_Akcionen_Plan.pdf.

[12]. The UN "E-Government Survey 2008: From E-Government to Connected Governance", New York, 2008

[13]. The UN, "E-Government Survey 2012: E-Government for the People", The UN New York, 2012

[14]. The Official Gazette of R.M no.92/09

[15]. The Official Gazette of R.M no.5/03, 06 and 08

[16]. The Official Gazette of RM", No. 36/04,49/04,86/08,18/11

[17]. The Official Gazette of RM" No. 29/05

[18]. The Official Gazette of RM, No. 40/07

[19]. The Official Gazette of RM, No.9/04

[20]. The Official Gazette of R.M No. 48/10, 124/10 and 51/11

[21]. The Official Gazette of RM", No. 34/01 from 03.05.2001

[22]. The Official Gazette of RM, No. 13/05 from 25.02.2005 13/05,14/2007,55/2007,98/2008 and 83/2010

[23]. The Official Gazette of RM, No. 7/05 from 01.02.2005

[24]. The Official Gazette of RM, No. 13/06 from 24.08.2006

[25]. The Official Gazette of RM, No. 116/12 from 27.09.2012

[26]. The Official Gazette of RM", No. 133/07 from 02.11.2007

[27]. The Official Gazette of RM", No. 136/07 from 12.11.2007

[28]. Weber H. Rolf, "Internet of Things New security and Privacy challenges", Computer Law & Security review 26, 2010.

[29]. "Military cooperation With Turkey is at the high level", Kurir, April 22, 2013, (Original: „Воената соработка со Турција е на високо ниво"),: http://kurir.mk/makedonija/vesti/113068-Voenata-sorabotka-megu-Makedonija-i-Turcija-na-visoko-nivo

Cyber Security and Resiliency Policy Framework
A. Vaseashta et al. (Eds.)
IOS Press, 2014

doi:10.3233/978-1-61499-446-6-65

Overview of the Current Situation in Bosnia and Herzegovina with Focus on Cyber Security and Fighting Cyber-Crime by Establishment of BIH CERT Body

Sabina BARAKOVIĆ[1 1], Mladen MRKAJA[1], Amir HUSIĆ[1], Adnan KULOVAC[1] and Jasmina BARAKOVIĆ HUSIĆ[2]
[1] *Ministry of Security of Bosnia and Herzegovina*
Trg BiH, 71000, Sarajevo, BOSNIA & HERZGOVINA
[2] *Faculty of electrical engineering, University of Sarajevo,*
Zmaja od Bosne bb, Sarajevo, BOSNIA & HERZGOVINA

Abstract. Communication networks and information systems in Bosnia and Herzegovina have experienced phenomenal growth throughout the last decades and became fully present in everyday life, since the majority of records and processes have been computerized and automated. Due to a low cyber security awareness together with the complex security management organization on the territory of Bosnia and Herzegovina (country's specific organization and multiple police agencies) and light technological lag in comparison to advanced European countries, this country is more susceptible to risks and threats in the cyber security domain. Therefore, in order to avoid serious repercussions for individuals, business and society in the case of cyber attacks, the Ministry of Security of Bosnia and Herzegovina has initiated the establishment of the Computer Emergency Response Team in Bosnia and Herzegovina – BIH CERT. This paper aims to provide an overview of the activities of Ministry of Security of Bosnia and Herzegovina in the area of cyber security focusing on establishment of the BIH CERT body. The BIH CERT has been envisioned as a preventive body which gives recommendation for the application and improvement of the security measures for protection of the information systems of Bosnia and Herzegovina's governmental institutions. In addition, this body will represent the Bosnia and Herzegovina's central point for cooperation with the international CERTs and thereby contribute to the security of the overall cyber space, since cyber attackers know no borders. The mission of BIH CERT will be to increase reliability of the critical infrastructure through a constant dedication, work on prevention and minimization of possibilities for occurrence of security emergency together with the provision of the assistance to the administrators of the critical infrastructure in application of the proactive measures for risk reduction from security emergency, as well as provision of the assistance in prevention of consequences of security emergency. The process of the institutional formation of BIH CERT has not yet started due to opposite political stances and interests.

Keywords. Bosnia and Herzegovina, BIH CERT, cyber, establishment, security

[1] Email: Sabina.Barakovic@msb.gov.ba

Introduction

As Vice-President of the European Commission responsible for the Digital Agenda, Neelie Kroes, put it in December 2010, "*Nowadays, no one would deny that our societies' prosperity and many aspects of our day-to-day life depend upon the unimpeded functioning of Internet and other IT networks.*" [1]. Communication networks and information systems worldwide have experienced phenomenal growth throughout the last decades and became fully present in everyday life reflecting in the way people communicate, obtain and exchange information, entertain, do business, take care of their health and environment, learn, govern, do arts, etc. The Information and Communications Technology (ICT) sector and the Internet have become the backbone of the economy, since, besides their own share, they have a great impact on other sectors such as finance, health, energy and transport as well.

Each of these daily activities includes some form of information exchange. In general, the information may be defined as data with meaning and purpose. In that context, data may be a document or any other record, knowledge or treatment, as well as oral statement, etc. [2]. According to the International Organization for Standardization/International Electrotechnical Commission (ISO/IEC) 27001 standard, information is an asset as any other vulnerable asset in business that has a value for the organization and must be continuously and appropriately protected [3]. Information has a purpose only if it has quality and it is not exposed to any form of degradation, loss or attack, together with being placed at the right location and time, and assigned to corresponding person.

Since today the majority of records and processes containing information have been computerized and automated, society has become extremely vulnerable to disturbances which may affect the functioning of ICT systems and the Internet, and jeopardize the reliability and security of the information they contain. This information mismanagement literally translates to millions of losses – either direct ones or opportunity losses for the individuals or organizations. Led by this knowledge and common sense, one can conclude that assuring the information security in this interdependent, multipurpose electronic data processing environment called cyber space is a priority for each individual, organization and society in general.

Information security management (ISM) represents the maintenance of reliability, integrity and availability of data, which is accomplished by implementation of written provisions and standards together with the institutional support for organizational affairs, implementation, check and update of provisions and standards [4]. Therefore, information security covers security issues of all the information, whether written, oral, electronic, etc., i.e., refers to all aspects of protecting information [5].

However, assuring the information security in cyber space, i.e., cyber security, falls under the umbrella of information security management and refers to security of electronic data and information systems that are isolated or related to the global computer network, i.e., the Internet. The explanation of cyber security given by the European Commission [6] is as follows: "Cyber-security commonly refers to safeguards and actions that can be used to protect the cyber domain, both in the civilian and military fields, from those threats that are associated with or that may harm its interdependent networks and information infrastructure. Cyber security strives to preserve the availability and integrity of the networks and infrastructure and the confidentiality of the information contained therein." Also, cyber security may be conceived as a wide area in information security that covers cyber crime, protection of electronic information systems, hacker attacks, together with proactive activities aimed to prevent the compromise of information systems and data.

Activities aimed at compromising cyber space and threats against it are constantly increasing and are present everywhere: while working on computers or laptops at office, browsing the Internet or socializing at home or elsewhere, while using modern smartphones and other mobile devices, even when turning on the lights or pouring a glass of water. That is why they have increasingly serious consequences for individuals, business, private and public institutions, and society in general as well, since they could disrupt the supply of essential services that we take for granted such as water, electricity, mobile services, etc. Moreover, the executors of the attacks are far more professional than before and today the threats even include state actors. In some countries, governments may also misuse cyberspace for surveillance and control over their own citizens. Cyber attacks that tend to jeopardize the professional and personal data also can be used as a means of political and economic pressure, but as an instrument of influence alongside traditional means of military force as well.

All previously mentioned incidents leave no doubt that countries all over the world must significantly improve their cyber security capabilities in order to ensure effective crisis management, to establish the coordination of the operational response to cyber attacks, to develop synergies at national levels and to enhance the international cooperation in this field. Additionally, government, academia and industry must work together to enable the development and adoption of cyber security solutions to keep pace with this dynamic threat environment. After all, one of the main goals for the government of each country is to encourage the free, safe and efficient use of cyber space by its citizens, while at the same time to ensure the protection of the critical information infrastructure, i.e., the ICT sector and the Internet that are the drivers of innovation, growth, jobs and social development.

Additionally, investment in cyber security can be considered from another economic aspect, i.e., the cyber space may be seen as a possibility and a resource. A safe cyber space makes it easier for both individuals and businesses to plan their activities, which in turn boosts economic activity. In addition to these, cyber security itself is a new and strengthening business area. In addition to the increasing job opportunities and tax revenue, society accrues benefits from this strengthening business sector in many other ways [7].

Advanced European countries have raised awareness regarding previously mentioned issues, since their citizens require trust and confidence when conducting various activities online such as purchasing over the Internet, banking, or disclosing their personal information. Consequently, their governments have not only established and strengthened the specialized units for enhancing the cyber security capabilities, but also have harmonized their legislation accordingly.

On the other hand, Bosnia and Herzegovina hitherto has made quite small steps in this field. Due to the low cyber security awareness together with the complex security management organization on its territory (country's specific organization and multiple police agencies) and light technological lag in comparison to advanced European countries, this country is more susceptible to risks and threats in the cyber security domain.

Therefore, in order to avoid serious repercussions for individuals, business and society in case of cyber attacks, and additionally motivated by EU recommendations on formation of the cyber security bodies in all member countries, as well as in the potential member countries, the Ministry of Security of Bosnia and Herzegovina has initiated the establishment of Computer Emergency Response Team (CERT) in Bosnia and Herzegovina – BIH CERT.

The authors of this paper aim to give the overview of the current situation in area of cyber security in Bosnia and Herzegovina, specially focusing on the activities of the Ministry of Security of Bosnia and Herzegovina on establishment of the BIH CERT body. This paper is organized as follows: Section 1 provides the overview of the current situation in Bosnia and Herzegovina regarding many topics such as the structure and organization of its security sector, legislation in terms of cyber security, internal and international cooperation, etc. Section 2 discusses the motives of BIH CERT formation together with systematic description of activities that have been conducted towards its establishment. In addition, this section gives the brief overview of the proposed structure of the envisioned BIH CERT. Finally, Section 3 concludes this paper.

1. Overview of the Current Situation in Bosnia and Herzegovina

In order to understand the current circumstances in Bosnia and Herzegovina that determine and constrain the activities in area of cyber security in this country, this section will provide an overview of the current situation in many fields. Therefore, the description of security management organization in Bosnia and Herzegovina will be given, together with the survey of the legislation in terms of cyber security. Cooperation between public, private and academic sector in Bosnia and Herzegovina in the field of cyber security, as well as international cooperation with relevant bodies will also be addressed. Additionally, this section will provide an overview of current qualification level of the existing institutions in terms of technology and level of staff training.

1.1. Structure of Security Management Organization in Bosnia and Herzegovina

Bosnia and Herzegovina is a country organized in a complex way: two entities, Federation of Bosnia and Herzegovina, which consists of 10 cantons, and Republic of Srpska, and Brčko District (fig. 1). Consequently, the security management sector in Bosnia and Herzegovina is equally complex. Due to that fact, there exist multiple security bodies and police agencies operating on the territory of Bosnia and Herzegovina, but on different levels including state, entity, and canton level.

On the state level, Bosnia and Herzegovina have several security management bodies. Firstly, there is the Ministry of Security of Bosnia and Herzegovina. The competences of this institution are not defined in the Constitution of Bosnia and Herzegovina [8], but within the Law on ministries and other administrative bodies in Bosnia and Herzegovina [8]. According to the subject law, this Ministry is competent for the following:

- protection of international borders, internal border crossings, and regulation of traffic at the border crossings of Bosnia and Herzegovina;
- prevention and detection of perpetrators of crimes relating to terrorism, trafficking in drugs, forgery of domestic and foreign currencies, trafficking in humans, and other crimes with international or inter-entity element;
- international cooperation in all the fields of the Ministry's competence (cooperation with INTERPOL, EUROPOL, SELEC, MARRI, etc.);
- protection of persons and facilities;

- collection and use of data relevant for security of Bosnia and Herzegovina;
- organization and harmonization of activities of the Entity Ministries of Interior and the Brčko District of Bosnia and Herzegovina in performing security tasks of Bosnia and Herzegovina's interest;
- implementation of international obligations and cooperation in matters relating to civil protection, coordination of activities of entity services for civil protection in Bosnia and Herzegovina, and harmonization of their plans for cases of natural or other disasters striking Bosnia and Herzegovina territories, as well as issuance of agenda for protection and rescue;
- creation, monitoring and implementation of policy on immigration and asylum in Bosnia and Herzegovina;
- settlement of procedures and means of organization of service dealing with movement and stay of aliens in Bosnia and Herzegovina;
- provision of support to police bodies of Bosnia and Herzegovina;
- education and professional development of staff in accordance with needs of the Bosnia and Herzegovina police bodies and the other security services and agencies;
- forensic examination and expertise.

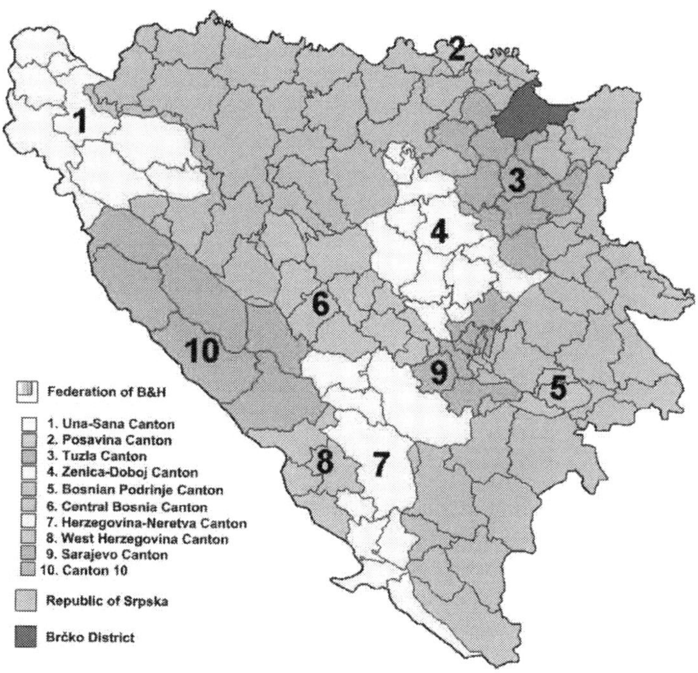

Figure 1. The territorial organization of Bosnia and Herzegovina

Constituent parts of the Ministry of Security of Bosnia and Herzegovina are also the following administrative organizations: Directorate for Coordination of Police Bodies of Bosnia and Herzegovina [11], Border Police of Bosnia and Herzegovina [12], State Investigation and Protection Agency [13], Forensic Examination and Expertise Agency, Personnel Education and Professional Development Agency [14], Police Support

Agency, and Service for Foreigners' Affairs [15]. Each of these agencies has corresponding competences on the state level.

In addition to these state level security management organizations, there exist two on entity level: Federal Police Administration [16] and Ministry of Interior of Republic of Srpska [17]. In Federation of Bosnia and Herzegovina, due to existence of 10 cantons, security issues are in the jurisdiction of 10 corresponding ministries of internal affairs in: Una-Sana Canton, Posavina Canton, Tuzla Canton, Zenica-Doboj Canton, Bosnian Podrinje Canton, Central Bosnia Canton, Herzegovina-Neretva Canton, West Herzegovina Canton, Sarajevo Canton, Canton 10. Additionally, Police of Brčko District operates on the territory of Brčko District. Each of these institutions has operational competence on their corresponding territorial unit.

Given the complexity of the security management structure and the country itself, but mainly due to the opposite political stances and goals within Bosnia and Herzegovina, one may comprehend why it is so challenging and slow to perform activities in this sector such as initiation of the conduction of strategic activities, decision making, taking over responsibility, and many others that would benefit the country and its citizens.

1.2. Bosnia and Herzegovina's Legislation in Terms of Cyber Security

In accordance with international and comparative law, Bosnia and Herzegovina has not adequately followed progress in the information security field and thereby not in cyber security as well. There exists no law on information security or cyber security on the state level. The existing legislation such as: the Law on the protection of classified information [18], Law on the protection of personal information [19], Law on Agency for identification documents, registers and data exchange of Bosnia and Herzegovina [19], Law on communications [21], Law on electronic signature [22], and Law on ministries and other administrative bodies in Bosnia and Herzegovina [9] only partially cover these hot issues. However, the Ministry of Communications and Transport of Bosnia and Herzegovina has initiated the activities on drafting the amendments on the existing Law on communications, and it is expected that certain issues in this area will be regulated in a more effective manner. On the entity level, the Federation of Bosnia and Herzegovina has not adopted laws on information security and lacks the corresponding institutions to deal with ensuring the security of information, while the Republic of Srpska has adopted the regulations regarding this topic and the Agency for Information Society shall implement them.

Regarding the international documents, Bosnia and Herzegovina has signed several agreements and conventions whose regulations are relevant for the information and cyber security. The most important are:

- Stabilisation and Association Agreement (SAA) [23], and
- Convention on Cybercrime [24].

Stabilisation and Association Agreement between European communities, and their member states, and Bosnia and Herzegovina has been signed on June 16th 2008 in Luxembourg. This agreement specifies 25 cooperation policies, where the most important in the area of information and cyber security are the ones defined by Article 103. "Information society":

> "*Cooperation shall primarily focus on priority areas related to the Community acquis (acquis communautaire) regarding the information society. It shall mainly*

support Bosnia and Herzegovina's gradual alignment of its policies and legislation in this sector with those of the Community. The Parties shall also cooperate with a view to further developing the Information Society in Bosnia and Herzegovina. Global objectives will include preparing society as a whole for the digital age, attracting investments and ensuring the interoperability of networks and services."

Article 104. "Electronic communication networks and services":

"*Cooperation shall primarily focus on priority areas related to the Community acquis in this field. The Parties shall, in particular, strengthen cooperation in the area of electronic communications networks and electronic communications services, with the ultimate objective of the adoption by Bosnia and Herzegovina of the Community acquis in the sector one year after the entry into force of this Agreement.* "

and Article 105. "Information and communication":

"*The Community and Bosnia and Herzegovina shall take the measures necessary to stimulate the mutual exchange of information. Priority shall be given to programmes aimed at providing the general public with basic information about the Community and professional circles in Bosnia and Herzegovina with more specialized information.*"

By this agreement Bosnia and Herzegovina has undertook the obligation to align its legislation regarding the information and cyber security and to establish mechanisms for ensuring ones. Further on, Convention on Cybercrime has been signed by Bosnia and Herzegovina on November 23rd 2001 in Budapest, while the Presidency of Bosnia and Herzegovina has reached the decision on ratifying the document at its 89th session held on March 25th 2006. Thereby, Bosnia and Herzegovina has obliged to adopt legislation and other necessary measures for combating cyber crime in order to harmonize them with other signers of the Convention in terms of felony treatment, and data acquisition, processing and storage.

The scarcity and disharmony of legal regulations in the field of information and cyber security in Bosnia and Herzegovina indicates that there is a need for systematic approach from the government at the state level in treating these matters. Each postponement of new adoptions and harmonization additionally complicates the situation, distorts the application of European Union (EU) recommendations, supports the technology lag of the country and exposes all information systems in Bosnia and Herzegovina to great security risk. In addition, since one of the main foreign policy objectives of Bosnia and Herzegovina is its accession to full membership to EU, consequently Bosnia and Herzegovina will inevitably have to adopt new and harmonize its current legislation regarding cyber security to the EU's, and reorganize existing or establish corresponding bodies for the enforcement of the subject legislation. Specifically, this refers on the requirements of the new Cybersecurity Strategy of the European Union: An Open, Safe and Secure Cyberspace [6] and the proposed Directive of the European Parliament and of the Council Concerning Measures to Ensure a High Common Level of Network and Information Security Across the Union [25] that are about to be adopted on the EU level.

Therefore, being aware of previously mentioned facts, the Ministry of Security according to its competences stated in the previous subsection, has created The Strategy for Establishment of CERT in Bosnia and Herzegovina [26] (hereinafter: The Strategy).

The Strategy has been adopted by the Council of Ministers of Bosnia and Herzegovina at its 156th session held on July 28th 2011, thereby becoming the first document on the state level that is dealing concretely with cyber security issues. This document shall be addressed in detail further throughout this paper, since it is the basis for all the activities regarding the BIH CERT establishment.

1.3. Internal and International Cooperation on Cyber Security

In the context of internal cooperation in the field of cyber security, one may identify four types: between public and private sector, between public and academic, between private and academic, and among the three of them. In general, the cooperation among public, private and academic sector in Bosnia and Herzegovina is not satisfying. There exists some minor and necessary level of cooperation between public and private sector, i.e., between law enforcement agencies on different levels and currently existing 76 Internet Service Providers (ISPs). This cooperation is based on the purpose of the investigation, and it differs from agency to agency. Security agencies in the Republic of Srpska have Memorandums of Understanding with several ISPs, while the agencies in the Federation of Bosnia and Herzegovina have made effort to establish or to raise the cooperation with ISPs on a higher level. The lack of adequate legal regulations has been identified as the main cause of poor cooperation, together with the lack of will and initiative to train police servants and employees of ISPs.

When it comes to cooperation between the public and academic sector, it may be characterised as dissatisfying as well. There are many possibilities to gain large grants relating to projects for strengthening cyber security capabilities in Bosnia and Herzegovina with no expected investments from the country. However, the need for a central contact point on the state level has been recognized as a single prerequisite when applying for these funds. Namely, due to the lack of the central point and lack of cooperation between institutions and universities, the funds remain unused. Regarding the private and academic relations, one may state that there is a lack of cooperation.

In the context of international cooperation in the field of cyber security, several contacts with relevant international organizations have been established, but it is impossible for Bosnia and Herzegovina to become their members until the country's legislation is harmonized and corresponding bodies are established (not necessarily operational).

1.4. Qualification Level of Institutions in Bosnia and Herzegovina

Technical qualification level of institutions in Bosnia and Herzegovina in terms of cyber security may be rated as acceptable. That is the area where the institutions in Bosnia and Herzegovina stand the best when compared to legal regulations or level of staff training. Of course, this area also needs improvement, but in the context of cyber security capacities development, great investments have been made, they are well beyond the stage of starting from scratch.

When it comes to qualification levels of the corresponding staff in police and judicial and prosecutorial institutions, it can be characterized as not sufficient. Namely, several servants from the police institutions that work on cyber security issues have been trained by international specialists, but that is still not enough. In general, training on cyber security topics should be increased and structurally distributed to the lowest level of police servants. In the context of judicial and prosecutorial institutions, there exist plans for cyber security training of the corresponding staff. However, it has been noticed that employees that had been educated in the field of cyber security have changed their positions. Thereby, invested efforts and resources are wasted and the government should in the future elect the trainees more carefully.

2. The Establishment of Computer Emergency Response Team in Bosnia and Herzegovina

Taking into account the serious repercussions for individuals, business and society that the previously described situation in Bosnia and Herzegovina could cause and additionally motivated by EU recommendations, the Ministry of Security of Bosnia and Herzegovina in accordance with its competences, as previously stated, has proposed The Strategy for Establishment of CERT in Bosnia and Herzegovina [26] thereby initiating the formation of BIH CERT body. This section describes the motives of BIH CERT formation together with its mission, vision and activities. Also, the activities that have been conducted towards the BIH CERT establishment and the ones yet to be done will be given, together with the short explanation of the structure and goals of this body.

2.1. Motives for Establishment of BIH CERT

Before going deeper into the motives, the CERT notion must be defined. Namely, CERT is a team for prevention, support and response to cyber attacks on computerized and automated systems of general social importance. The CERT team is comprised of experts who, in case of a problem or an attack on computer security, manage and coordinate response to an attack, in order to protect material assets and human lives. The main role of CERT is coordination and information sharing with interested parties and target groups in public and private sector and international partners. Currently, there are over 250 organizations in the world that use title or derivate of a title "CERT" [26].

The main motive for establishment of BIH CERT is enhancing the security in terms of prevention, as well as the prevention of catastrophic situation and consequences. Initiation of establishment of CERT should not be view in the political sense, since this project has no political dimension whatsoever, and it is generally known that cyber crime goes beyond all geographical and political borders. An additional motive for establishment of BIH CERT also derives from the EU recommendations on formation of the CERT bodies in all member countries, as well as in the potential member countries. EU recommendations that directly or indirectly suggest the establishment of CERT organizations are based on the following documents:

- Communication on Creating Safer Information Society by Improving the Security of Information Infrastructures and Combating Computer-related Crime [COM (2000) 890] [27];
- Communication on Network and Information Security: Proposal for A European Policy Approach (COM (2001) 298 final) [28];
- Council Framework Decision on Attacks Against Information Systems [2005/222/JHA] [29];
- Action Plan "e-Europe 2005" [30];

- A Strategy for a Secure Information Society - "Dialogue, Partnership and Empowerment" (COM (2006) 251 final) - Impact Assessment - annex to "A Strategy for Secure Information Society - Dialogue, Partnership and Empowerment"- SEC(2006) 656 [31];
- Council Resolution on a Strategy for a Secure Information Society in Europe (2007/C 68/01) [32];
- Digital Agenda: Commission Reviews Member States' Protection Against Cyber Attacks [33];
- Communication on Critical Information Infrastructure Protection "Achievements and Next Steps: Towards Global Cyber-security" (COM (2011) 163 final) [34];
- Cybersecurity Strategy of the European Union: An Open, Safe and Secure Cyberspace [6];
- Proposed Directive of the European Parliament and of the Council Concerning Measures to Ensure a High Common Level of Network and Information Security Across the Union [25].

Namely, according to the last two documents from the list, each EU member country should establish minimum requirements for network and information security at a national level, i.e., to designate national competent authorities for network and information security, set up a well-functioning CERT, and adopt a national network and information strategy and cooperation plan.

Further on, the regulations of a ratified Convention on Cybersecurity encourage the establishment of BIH CERT throughout the Article 16. "Expedited preservation of stored computer data" that, besides treating the legal and other measures needed for fast preservation of special electronic data, opens the issue of who should/could in an effective and expeditious manner distribute the information on necessity for expeditious preservation. The continuous communication and coordination role that BIH CERT is supposed to have with relevant institutions via its help desk call centre, makes it the body that can coordinate the activities in cases of expeditious preservation of stored computer data.

Also, Article 17. "Expedited preservation and partial disclosure of traffic data" of the Convention recognizes the need for organization that will ensure the expeditious disclosure of a sufficient amount of traffic data to a competent authority in order to identify the service providers and the path through which the communication was transmitted. BIH CERT, if established, may play that role.

In addition, according to Article 35. "24/7 Network", BIH CERT is expected to facilitate, or if permitted by domestic laws and practice, directly carry out the following measures: the provision of technical advice, preservation of data pursuant to incidents and solutions, collection of evidence, provision of legal information, and location of suspects. By establishing BIH CERT, Bosnia and Herzegovina will catch up with all other EU and non EU neighbour countries that have and have not formed the roof CERTs (Figure 2).

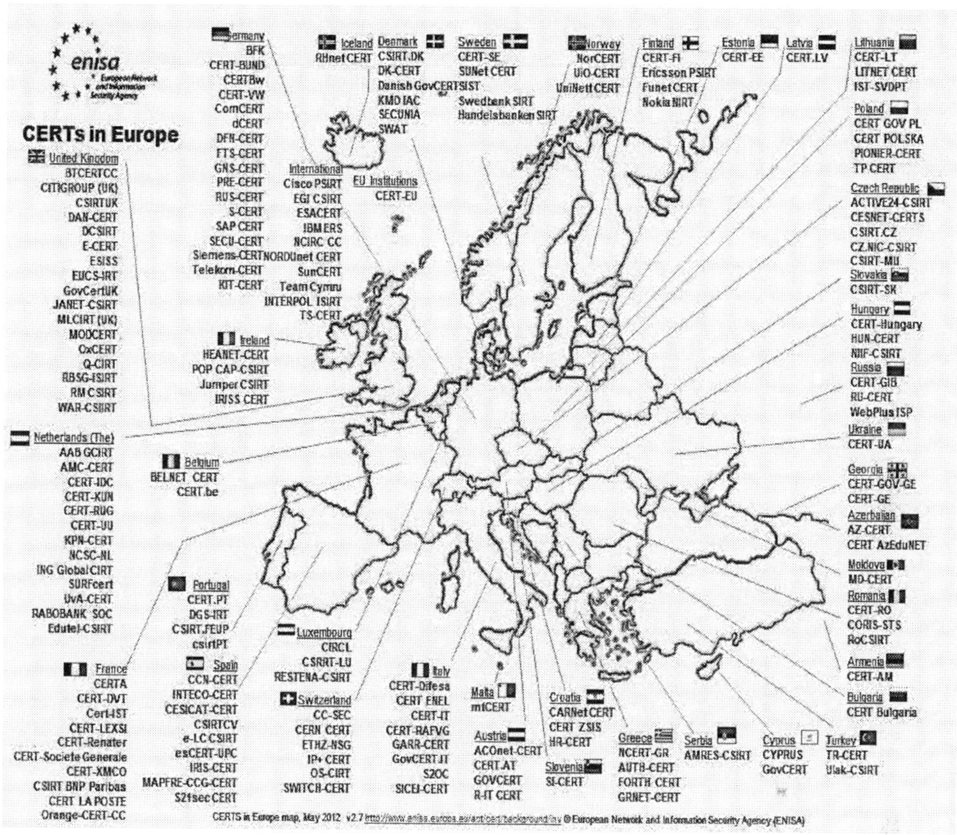

Figure 2. CERTs in Europe [35]

In addition, an image of Bosnia and Herzegovina as a country of high risk in terms of investments shall be improved, for the reason that nowadays all processes and records are computerized and connected to the Internet, and are inter-linked, which creates a basis for doing business of any enterprise at this time.

2.2. BIH CERT Vision, Mission and Activities

The BIH CERT has been envisioned as a preventive body which gives recommendation for the application and improvement of the security measures for protection of the information systems of Bosnia and Herzegovina's governmental institutions. Hence, BIH CERT does not include operational problem solving. Although it is not yet established, the vision of BIH CERT is based on fulfilment of several assumptions:

- BIH CERT shall achieve adequate coordination and cooperation between the relevant bodies in Bosnia and Herzegovina;
- The scope of cooperation will also be expanded into the fields of industry, education and development, through coordination with the manufacturing companies, higher education institutions and research centres;

- The activity of the BIH CERT will be expanded outside the borders of Bosnia and Herzegovina by cooperating with the international CERTs, and organisations such as European Union Agency for Network and Information Security (ENISA) and Task Force Collaboration Security Incident Response Teams (TF-CSIR), and international computer manufacturing companies (hardware and software); all for the purpose of mitigating or eliminating the consequences of security emergency.

The mission of BIH CERT will be to increase the reliability of the critical infrastructure through a constant dedication, work on prevention and minimization of possibilities for occurrence of a security emergency together with the provision of the assistance to the administrators of the critical infrastructure in application for the proactive measures for risk reduction from a security emergency, as well as a provision of the assistance in prevention of consequences of security emergency. Although it will not include operational activities, BIH CERT will be authorized to assist in solving all ICT security emergencies that occurred or could happen within the area of activity of the BIH CERT. It will make its resources available in solving significant emergencies that are defined according to the following priorities:

- An emergency that potentially endanger lives;
- An emergency that includes the Internet structure in Bosnia and Herzegovina;
- An emergency of a significant scope;
- New types of computer security endangerment;
- Other information security emergency.

According to The Strategy [26], the activities of BIH CERT will be proactive and reactive. Namely, in a proactive sense, BIH CERT will act before emergency or other events that may endanger the security of the information systems, for the purpose of prevention or mitigation of possible damage. In addition, proactive measures will be published. Those proactive measures are:

- Security warnings: The BIH CERT will prepare and publish the security warnings for the purpose of adequate preparation for the prevention or mitigation of damages based on the monitoring of the situations and events in the field of ICT security, analysis of the available data and prediction of trends;
- Monitoring of the ICT security technologies: The BIH CERT will regularly monitor the field of the ICT security technologies and incorporate the collected findings into the disseminated information;
- Dissemination of information from the field of ICT security: The BIH CERT will collect, aggregate, produce and disseminate relevant information, documents, recommendations and instructions in the field of ICT security;
- Promotion of awareness of the importance of ICT security: The BIH CERT will work on education of the wider public and raise awareness on the importance of the ICT security throughout the public activity;
- ICT security education and training: The BIH CERT will prepare and implement the educational actions for the target user groups through the educational materials.

On the other hand, reactive activities include support in processing the ICT security emergencies in several aspects such as: (i) determination of an emergency, which includes determination of whether an observed emergency could be classified as an ICT security emergency and the scope of the emergency, together with development and distribution of security warnings; (ii) coordination of emergency solving, which includes cooperation and coordination with CERTs or other relevant bodies in Bosnia and Herzegovina; and (iii) emergency resolution, which covers security warnings and coordination in solving the emergency.

2.3. Activities Towards the Establishment of BIH CERT Body

Among previously mentioned issues, The Strategy provides the formation of a Working Group for the establishment of CERT in Bosnia and Herzegovina. The Ministry of Security of Bosnia and Herzegovina, upon the proposal of the Sector for Informatics and Telecommunication Systems and the Sector for Secret Data Protection – State Security Body, has submitted to the Council of Ministers of Bosnia and Herzegovina a draft Decision on establishing and appointing the Expert Working Group. The subject Working Group was formed by the Council of Ministers of Bosnia and Herzegovina on their 168th session held on December 7th 2011 [36].

The Working Group was composed of civil servants who were proven experts in different fields. The membership of the Working Group were the civil servants who are experts in the ICT as well as civil servants who are experts in the field of the information systems security. Besides technical experts, civil servants who are experts in other fields, with an international experience and/or solid knowledge of world trends regarding the cyber crime were the members of the Working Group as well.

The main task of the Working Group was to conduct all necessary preparations for establishing the BIH CERT within a twelve-month mandate. That included the conduction of a detailed analysis of the existing regulations defining the area of cyber security and the proposal for the necessary modifications to existing regulations in order to establish the BIH CERT. If it were not possible to incorporate BIH CERT in some of the existing regulations, the Working Group would had to propose a new regulation for establishing the BIH CERT. Therefore, in addition to obligatory reports to the Council of Ministers of Bosnia and Herzegovina, the Working Group, as required, developed the Action Plan for establishing the BIH CERT, and thereby proposed the necessary dynamics for implementation of the Action Plan.

During its mandate, the Working Group has established a number of international connections with relevant organizations such as the North Atlantic Treaty Organization (NATO) or Organization for Security and Cooperation in Europe (OSCE), but with other CERTs in Europe, ENISA; TF-CSIRT, etc. as well, since it has been authorized to represent Bosnia and Herzegovina in CERT matters. In addition, its members have organized several study visits for the purpose of collecting experiences of other countries more experienced in CERT matters. However, even more important is the fact that the first two of three four-month reports of the Working Group have been adopted by the Council of Ministers of Bosnia and Herzegovina on its 12th and 44th session, while the final report together with the Action Plan is still pending adoption, although it was submitted in December 2012. The next subsection gives a brief summary of the subject Action Plan and provides an overview of the structure of BIH CERT body that is about to be established.

2.4. The Proposed Structure of BIH CERT Body to be Established

Considering the models for BIH CERT establishment, the Working Group took into account all previously described aspects, beginning with the complex security organization, lack of legislation, light technological lag of the country, as well as the financial crisis that is present in Bosnia and Herzegovina as well, and proposed two models:

- Model 1: BIH CERT as independent administrative organization or special body of the corresponding ministry;
- Model 2: BIH CERT as a constituent of the corresponding ministry.

The first model includes the adoption of the state law on BIH CERT that would arrange all aspects of the BIH CERT functioning, beginning with the establishment, definition, financing, competencies, organization and management. However, it is not EU practice to adopt regulations on CERTs, but to adopt the law on information security and thereby in a broader context define rights and obligations of all counterparts in the subject filed. CERTs in EU are usually established by government decision. As previously recognized, the necessity of adopting the law on information security in Bosnia and Herzegovina is not questionable, and BIH CERT establishment contributes to actualization and acceleration of the adoption of the subject law. On the other hand, the establishment efficacy of this model is questionable, since one cannot estimate the time required for regulation adoption. As well, the financial and human resources in the context of this model are difficult to plan or even gain in this period of crisis, since everything must be built from scratch. In that situation, the quality of BIH CERT information system and communication will be strongly affected.

The second model may use the existing Law on ministries and other administrative bodies in Bosnia and Herzegovina for BIH CERT establishment [9]. Namely, according to competences defined by Articles 10. and 14. of the subject Law, BIH CERT may be incorporated within the Ministry of Transport and Communication of Bosnia and Herzegovina and Ministry of Security of Bosnia and Herzegovina. In this case, the structure of BIH CERT may be regulated by the decision of Council of Ministers of Bosnia and Herzegovina on which basis one may estimate the implementation time, i.e., establishment efficacy. In this case, BIH CERT would receive financial and administrative support from the existing resources of the corresponding ministry.

In addition to BIH CERT establishment, the Action Plan suggests the formation of a Council of Minister's coordination body whose primary task would be to solve and mitigate existing problems through recommendations and support in realization of the BIH CERT establishment and the establishment of other CERTs in Bosnia and Herzegovina. The body would also publish the mandatory recommendations to the parties of interest, suggest adoption of regulations harmonized with EU and NATO standards and recommendations, insist on harmonization of existing laws, coordinate the activities between the ministries and law enforcement agencies regarding the cyber security issues, suggest and initiate the media campaigns and similar activities with the aim of raising awareness, and in general perform activities related to BIH CERT.

Further on, the Action Plan elaborates the short-, mid-, and long-term strategic goals defined in The Strategy. BIH CERT will immediately upon the establishment submit the request for registration/accreditation by the relevant international institutions and establish the direct communication and cooperation with ENISA, TF-CSIRT, and national CERTs from the region as well as the most significant CERTs in the Europe and world. Also, BIH CERT will identify the critical infrastructure in Bosnia and Herzegovina that needs the protection and establish the contacts and define the rules for information exchange with the administrators of the subject infrastructure. Besides the advisory role, another goal of BIH CERT is education. In that context, BIH CERT will publish bulletins with the latest information regarding the security and proactive measures for risk decrease on a continuous basis. Educational initiatives also include the organization of workshops for security administrators for the critical infrastructure on a regular basis. With the realization of its mid-term goals, BIH CERT will identify other information systems which require assistance in security issues and expand its activities towards them. This, together with the continuous evaluation of the security state of the critical infrastructure and critical infrastructure administrators' education will in general improve the state of security. The long-term goal is to support the establishment of CERTs on different state levels as well as ones in the private and academic sector.

3. Conclusion

This paper has aimed to give the overview of the current situation in the field of cyber security in Bosnia and Herzegovina and to describe the activities of the Ministry of Security of Bosnia and Herzegovina on the establishment of the preventive BIH CERT body. The procedure of institutional establishment of BIH CERT has not yet started, since opposite political interests and stances in Bosnia and Herzegovina that bridle countries' progress in many other fields, found the way to affect the adoption of the previously described Action Plan and halt the progress in this important field that is apolitical in nature.

However, it is only a question of time when the subject documents will be adopted and activities towards ensuring cyber security in Bosnia and Herzegovina reinitiated. That will be accomplished firstly due to EU recommendations and prerequisites that Bosnia and Herzegovina will have to fulfil in order to access a full membership to EU, given the fact that it is the main foreign policy objective of the country. Those prerequisites include, as previously stated, the adoption of new and harmonization of the current legislation regarding the cyber security to the EU's, and reorganization of the existing or the establishment of the corresponding bodies for the enforcement of the subject legislation. Secondly, this project has no political dimension and the proposed structure of BIH CERT, together with its mission, activities and goals, is flexible and acceptable for all parties in Bosnia and Herzegovina. BIH CERT is envisioned as an expert body that has an advisory and coordinating character. Moreover, in an international context, the establishment of such a body in Bosnia and Herzegovina is desirable, since cyber threats know no geographical and political borders.

There are many benefits for establishing the BIH CERT, but the main one is that Bosnia and Herzegovina will have an ICT security team that assists organizations in reducing and prevention of major incidents and in protection of valuable property. Additionally, it will provide the coordination for the ICT security issues within an organization, the permanent expertise for support and assistance to users for fast recovery from security incidents and the service of a root point for coordinative and specialized management and response to ICT incidents. Also, BIH CERT will follow developments and advancements in the area of ICT security.

In a broader context, in the current institutional crisis in Bosnia and Herzegovina, the establishment of such a body on the state level will send out a positive signal to citizens and the international community. Thereby, government's commitment to EU and NATO integration would be confirmed and characterized as not only declarative. In addition, it will strengthen Bosnia and Herzegovina in many fields and boost economic activity, since this country will be represented as a safe country for business investment.

Ensuring cyber security will not stop with BIH CERT formation. On the contrary, it will start. It is of great importance to set the development of cyber security capabilities on the top of Bosnia and Herzegovina's priorities in the context of EU and NATO integrations.

References

[1] Digital Europe Cyber Security Paper. Digital Europe, December 2011. Available at: http://www.digitaleurope.org/SearchResults?categoryID=16.
[2] W. Krag Brotby, Information Security Management Metrics. CRC Press, Auerbach, 2009.
[3] International Organization for Standardization / International Electrotechnical Commission - ISO/IEC 27001:2013 – Information Security Management Systems. October 2013.
[4] The Law on Information Security of Republic of Croatia. Available at: http://www.zakon.hr/z/218/Zakon-o-informacijskoj-sigurnosti.
[5] International Telecommunication Union - ITU, WSIS Thematic Meeting on Cybersecurity, A comparative Analysis of Cybersecurity Initiatives Worldwide. June 2005. Available at: http://www.itu.int/osg/spu/cybersecurity/docs/Background_Paper_Comparative_Analysis_Cybersecurity_Initiatives_Worldwide.pdf.
[6] Cybersecurity Strategy of the European Union: An Open, Safe and Secure Cyberspace, February 2013. Available at: http://www.eeas.europa.eu/policies/eu-cyber-security/cybsec_comm_en.pdf.
[7] Finland's Cyber Security Strategy. Secretariat of the Security and Defense Committee, January 2013. Available at: http://www.yhteiskunnanturvallisuus.fi/en.
[8] The Constitution of Bosnia and Herzegovina. Available at: http://www.ads.gov.ba/v2/attachments/1951_USTAV_BOSNE_I_HERCEGOVINE_bos.pdf.
[9] The Law on Ministries and Other Administrative Bodies in Bosnia and Herzegovina. Official Gazette of Bosnia and Herzegovina, 2/03, 26/04, 42/04, 45/06, 88/07, 35/09, 59/09, 103/09. Available at: http://www.ads.gov.ba/v2/attachments/1978_ZAKON_O_MINISTARSTVIMA_INTEGRALNI.pdf.
[10] Official Website of the Ministry of Security of Bosnia and Herzegovina. Available at: http://www.msb.gov.ba.
[11] Official Website of the Directorate for Coordination of Police Bodies of Bosnia and Herzegovina. Available at: http://www.dkpt.gov.ba.
[12] Official Website of the Border Police of Bosnia and Herzegovina. Available at: http://www.granpol.gov.ba.
[13] Official Website of the State Investigation and Protection Agency. Available at: http://www.sipa.gov.ba.
[14] Official Website of the Personnel Education and Professional Development Agency. Available at: http://www.aeptm.gov.ba.
[15] Official Website of the Service for Foreigners' Affairs. Available at: http://www.sps.gov.ba.
[16] Official Website of the Federal Police Administration. Available at: http://www.fup.gov.ba.
[17] Official Website of the Ministry of Interior of Republic of Srpska. Available at: http://www.mup.vladars.net.
[18] The Law on Protection of Classified Information. Official Gazette of Bosnia and Herzegovina, 54/05. Available at: http://www.msb.gov.ba/Zakoni/zakoni/default.aspx?id=3403&langTag=bs-BA.
[19] The Law on Protection of Personal Information. Official Gazette of Bosnia and Herzegovina, 32/01, 49/06. Available at: http://cesi.fpn.unsa.ba/wp-content/uploads/2012/12/Zakon-o-zastiti-osobnih-podataka.pdf.
[20] The Law on Agency for Identification Documents, Registers and Data Exchange. Official Gazette of Bosnia and Herzegovina, 56/08. Available at: http://www.iddeea.gov.ba/.
[21] The Law on Communications in Bosnia and Herzegovina. Official Gazette of Bosnia and Herzegovina, 31/03, 75/06. Available at: http://rak.ba/bih/index.php?uid=1269443180.
[22] The Law on Electronic Signature. Official Gazette of Bosnia and Herzegovina, 91/06. Available at: http://www.advokat-prnjavorac.com/zakoni/Zakon_o_elektronskom_potpisu_BiH.pdf.
[23] Stabilisation and Association Agreement. June 2008, Luxembourg. Available at: http://www.dei.gov.ba/bih_i_eu/ssp/default.aspx?id=1172&langTag=en-US.

[24] Convention on Cybercrime. November 2001, Budapest. Available at: http://conventions.coe.int/Treaty/Commun/QueVoulezVous.asp?NT=185&CL=ENG.

[25] Directive of the European Parliament and of the Council Concerning Measures to Ensure a High Common Level of Network and Information Security Across the Union, February 2013. Available at: http://eur-lex.europa.eu/LexUriServ/LexUriServ.do?uri=COM:2013:0048:FIN:EN:PDF.

[26] The Strategy for Establishment of CERT (Computer Emergency Response Team) in Bosnia and Herzegovina. Council of Ministers of Bosnia and Herzegovina, July 2011. Available at: http://www.msb.gov.ba/dokumenti/strateski/default.aspx?id=6248&langTag=bs-BA.

[27] Communication on Creating Safer Information Society by Improving the Security of Information Infrastructures and Combating Computer-related Crime, January 2001. Available at: http://eur-lex.europa.eu/LexUriServ/LexUriServ.do?uri=COM:2000:0890:FIN:EN:PDF.

[28] Communication on Network and Information Security: Proposal for A European Policy Approach, June 2001. Available at: http://eur-lex.europa.eu/LexUriServ/site/en/com/2001/com2001_0298en01.pdf.

[29] Council Framework Decision on Attacks Against Information Systems, February 2005. Available at: http://eur-lex.europa.eu/LexUriServ/LexUriServ.do?uri=OJ:L:2005:069:0067:0071:EN:PDF.

[30] Action Plan "eEurope 2005", Available at: http://europa.eu/legislation_summaries/information_society/strategies/l24226_en.htm.

[31] A Strategy for a Secure Information Society - "Dialogue, Partnership and Empowerment", May 2006. Available at: http://ec.europa.eu/information_society/doc/com2006251.pdf.

[32] Council Resolution on a Strategy for a Secure Information Society in Europe, March 2007. Available at: http://eur-lex.europa.eu/LexUriServ/LexUriServ.do?uri=OJ:C:2007:068:0001:0004:EN:PDF.

[33] Digital Agenda: Commission Reviews Member States' Protection Against Cyber Attacks, April 2011. Available at: http://europa.eu/rapid/press-release_IP-11-395_en.htm?locale=en.

[34] Communication on Critical Information Infrastructure Protection "Achievements and Next Steps: Towards Global Cyber-security", March 2011. Available at: http://eur-lex.europa.eu/LexUriServ/LexUriServ.do?uri=COM:2011:0163:FIN:EN:PDF.

[35] European Union Agency for Network and Information Security. Available at: http://www.enisa.europa.eu/activities/cert.

[36] Decision on Establishment and Appointment of Expert Working Group for Conduction of All Necessary Preparations for the Formation of CERT Body in Bosnia and Herzegovina, December 2011. Available at: http://www.sluzbenilist.ba/Sluzbeni%20dio/Sluzbeni%20glasnik%20Bih/2012/broj6/Broj006.pdf.

Cyber Security and Resiliency Policy Framework
A. Vaseashta et al. (Eds.)
IOS Press, 2014

doi:10.3233/978-1-61499-446-6-82

Turkey's Approaches on Cyber Security Policy Framework

Nazife BAYKAL[1]
Middle East Technical University
Ankara, TURKEY

Abstract: Advanced and sophisticated cyber-attacks pose a serious risk to economic and national security. The solutions for cyber security problems necessitate initiatives from all legal, institutional, scientific and technical domains, and the cooperation of governments, universities, industry and civil societies. The global nature of the problem also puts a special emphasis on international cooperation. Therefore, countries need to develop strategies on both national and international scales in a holistic approach. Today, most strategies developed by countries share the holistic, integrated, comprehensive approach supported by strong leadership, enhanced governmental co-ordination at policy and operational levels, reinforced public-private co-operation, and improved international co-operation. Cyber security strategies generally include action plans. Since Turkey has a critical and important geopolitical position due to its location in the Middle East; cyber security has an immanent importance to our country. Studies in this scope resulted in the June 2013 National Cyber Security Strategy document and 2013-2014 Action Plan. In this strategy document, cyber security risks and measures, 7 major topics, 29 key actions and 30 governmental organizations responsible of these actions are identified. In the 2013-2014 Action Plan, 29 actions in the scope of the major topics, sub-actions and organizations responsible of these actions are identified. According to these documents, cyber security activities in Turkey include government, Turkish Armed Forces, universities, industry and non-governmental organizations (NGOs). Studies for legal regulations are also in progress. There have been various laws, draft laws, and regulations in cyber security. Cyber Security activities require national cooperation of governmental organizations, universities, industry and non-governmental organizations. In this paper, we will first briefly present the general headlines and commonalities of national strategies of various countries. Then we will chronologically summarize the cyber security studies in Turkey, and focus on the National Cyber Security Strategy and Action Plan, stakeholders and their studies, legal regulations, awareness and educational studies, and national and international collaborations. Lastly, we will further elucidate a brief evaluation of cyber security studies in Turkey.

Keywords: *cyber-security, policy framework, national strategy, legal, Turke*

Introduction

It is well known that cyber security and defense has been the focus of extensive debates since the end of 1990s when cyber-attacks began to be widely used to threaten

[1] Email: baykal@metu.edu.tr

governments and nationwide institutions. However, the earliest reports of cyber-attacks date to the 1970s when cyber-attacks were launched against the information systems of various organizations such as companies or banks. Now, cyber space has become a critical area of national security with the ever increasing amount of information transferred through and contained within digital environments. Attacks over the last couple of years reveal the severity of the threat regarding both the target and the number of the attacks. Recent cyber-attacks target all sectors of economies and global entities from strategic governmental institutions such as ministries of foreign affairs, internal affairs, defense, military organizations, to political parties, airlines, internet service providers, even to information security companies, social network websites, and search engines like Google.

Many governments and large multi-national institutions have been targeted. Cyber wars occurred in Estonia (2007), Georgia (2008), during the Israeli–Palestinian conflict (2000 and 2008), Kyrgyzstan (2009), Kosovo (2010), and the Jasmine Revolution in Tunisia (2011). Forty-four (44) million attacks were directed against the governmental websites of Israel after its army force operations in Gaza (2013), and the attacks that Thai hackers launched against Philippine governmental organizations during the Thailand-Philippine conflict (2013) reveal that there is now a new "front" in international wars. Finally, cyber-attacks were directed against Aramco Company that provides the 40% of world's oil demand (2012).

In recent years, serious cyber attacks have occurred in Turkey. Several institutions including the Ministry of Internal Affairs, the Turkish National Police, the Land Forces Command, the council of higher education, Turkish Airlines and TTNet which is one of the main internet service providers in Turkey were targeted by cyber-attacks. In the light of these examples it is clear that the austerity of cyber warfare will keep increasing and calls for assuring the sustainable security of cyber-space in near future. Future cyber-attacks will be even more detrimental. As evidenced by the 2011 attack affecting Dutch DigiNotar, hackers can acquire rogue digital certificates, which then enable them to impersonate significant domains. Also, WikiLeaks-like attacks that compromise masses of private information conflated with false information are among the most damaging ones. The complexity and damage of these attacks point that the agents of the attacks are states rather than individual hackers (12). Therefore, countries need to develop strategies on both national and international scales. Also, cyber security necessitates the cooperation of governments, universities, industry and civil societies. The solutions of cyber security problems also necessitate initiatives from all legal, institutional, scientific and technical domains. The global nature of the problem also put a special emphasis on international cooperation.

1. National Cyber Security Strategies in the World

When strategic researches on cyber security and defense are considered, it can be seen that these type of research has increased since 2010. The EU and NATO also undertake important initiatives on this particular problem of our age. NATO made new arrangements to increase its capability of facing this problem in 2010 'Strategic Concept'. In this scope partner countries engaged in revising their cyber security policies. The crucial point of this revision is centralization (12). The ever increasing complicatedness of cyber-attacks results in the discussions on concepts that can lead the strategic studies.

Active Cyber Defense **(ACD)**, that is defined as "a range of proactive actions that engage the adversary before and during a cyber incident" aims to increase the capacity to deal with cyber attacks. Detection and forensics, deception and attack termination are the key concepts of ACD. Although these concepts are technologically realizable, their legality is questionable (9). Therefore, ethical and legal studies on cyber security must be simultaneously undertaken with technological studies.

Although there are commonalities between the cyber security strategies of different countries, there are also some differences due to the particular structure and properties of individual countries. For US and UK, the critical components are the leading role of the private sector, a well-trained workforce, outreach and diplomacy. The EU gives more importance to the soundness of legal and regulatory structure, and advocates the Council of Europe (Budapest) Convention of Cybercrime as the guideline of legal regulations and cooperation between countries. The Baltic Countries are closely connected to NATO in the determination of their strategies. The post-Soviet bloc, concentrates more on internal security, less emphasis on international court decisions, and supports a similar international cooperation structure guided by the UN. Most of these strategies are different with respect to the particular importance that they attach to private and governmental organizations. They also differ in their promotion of profit or non-profit cyber security organizations, policy, and enforcement (10).
As stated in (9), the most common cyber security challenges are:

- International nature of cyberspace
- Municipal nature of law
- The challenge of combating cybercrime in the context of a wider cyber-security strategy is that law enforcement is limited in reach.
- Human factor

As stated in an OECD analysis (16 Nov 2012), most countries put a special emphasis on cyber security strategies in the determination of national policies. These strategies are developed to be wide-ranging and integrated where they range over economy, social life, educational regulations, law, technology, diplomacy, and military forces. Two critical points that a cyber security strategy must meet are to promote economic and social wealth on one hand, and to secure society against cyber crimes on the other. So, any strategy must deal with the conflict between satisfying these two points and maintaining the openness of the internet as an innovative medium (6). These strategies mostly focus on the followings:

- Holistic, integrated, comprehensive approach supported by strong leadership
- Enhanced governmental co-ordination at policy and operational levels.
- Reinforced public-private co-operation
- Improved international co-operation
- Respect for fundamental values

Sovereignty in security, intelligence and military force is one of the most important concerns when determining a cyber security policy. Some of these strategies also focus on the flexibility, the economical aspects, and the interaction with non-governmental actors.

Following is the chronological list of countries pursuing a cyber security strategy:

Table 1: Publication year of National Cyber Security Strategies of European Union countries

European Union	
Slovak Republic	(2008)
Germany	(2011)
France	(2011)
Luxembourg	(2011)
Poland	(2011)
Austria	(2013)
Finland	(2013)
Estonia	(2008)
United Kingdom	(2009)
Czech Republic	(2011)
Lithuania	(2011)
The Netherlands	(2011)
Romania	(2011)
Belgium	(2013)
Hungary	(2013)

Table 2: Publication year of National Cyber Security Strategies of other countries

Other Countries	
Russia	(2000)
Japan	(2010)
Canada	(2010)
South Africa	(2010)
United States of America	(2011)
Australia	(2011)
New Zealand	(2011)
Switzerland	(2012)
Norway	(2012)
India	(2013)
Singapore	(to be published)
Turkey	(2013)
Kenya	(Announced 2013 - to be published)
Montenegro	(Announced 2013 - to be published in October 2013)
Uganda	(Announced 2013 - to be published)

Research and development activities are among the crucial components of new cyber security strategies. Most of these activities put special emphasis on strong cooperation with private sector. Although strategies include the maintenance of the critical infrastructure, the global nature of this issue is still missing. There are also some strategically aspects that are offered by non-governmental organizations. These organizations mostly focus on the necessity of flexible and sound policies, and collaboration between stakeholders due to global accessibility of the Internet as a collaboration promoting medium. Business world and technology communities also call attention to an international dimension for ensuring cyber security.

When the above points are considered, it is clear that many countries must extend their cooperation to the international domain, and governments must pursue organizational and international cooperation simultaneously with strong centralization.

When the above mentioned points are considered, it can be seen that most cyber security strategies include:

- Protection of critical information infrastructures
- Government security
- Awareness raising
- Education
- Response
- Fight against cybercrime.

2. Short History of Cyber Security Activities in Turkey

Cyber security and defense has been the focus of extensive debate since the late 1990s when cyber-attacks were started to be widely used to threaten governments and nationwide institutions. Since Turkey has a critical and important geopolitical position due to its location in the Middle East; cyber security has an eminent importance to our country. In 2002 both the e-turkey project and information security studies came to the forefront in Turkey. Like most countries, Turkey recognized the significance of these studies because of the increase in cyber attacks. These studies can be listed chronologically as follows:

- "**Information Society Strategy and its Annex, Action Plan**" that was prepared by State Planning Organization in 2006 includes headlines concerning cyber security.
- Several governmental organizations collaborate on the document titled "**National Cyberspace Security Policy"** in 2008 to be presented to the Office of Prime Minister in 2009.
- **2010-2014 Strategic Plan of the Ministry of Health** includes headlines on cyber security.
- At **Cyber Security Strategy Workshop** (June, 2012) organized by **Turkish Information Security Association** a draft strategy document was prepared with the participation of more than 80 IT security professionals from public and private sectors. This document was presented to the Ministry of Transport, Maritime Affairs and Communications.
- Cabinet decision (Nr. 2012/3842, 20 October 2012) determines the responsibilities for the Turkish national cyber security activities. According to this decision, the responsible authority is The **Ministry of Transport, Maritime**

Affairs and Communications. Previously the responsible authority was the **TUBITAK** agency. Also, the **National Cyber Security Board** is founded in the scope of this decision.

- In June 2013, the National Cyber Security Strategy and 2013-2014 Action Plan was published.

3. Stakeholders and Structure of Cyber Security in Turkey

The regulations of cyber security responsibilities in Turkey are determined by the decree of the Council of Ministers in October 2012. According to this decree, the main authority is The Ministry of Transport, Maritime Affairs and Communications. The Cyber Security Council was also founded in the scope of this decree. In general, the cyber security structure in Turkey includes government, Turkish Armed Forces, universities, industry and non-governmental organizations (NGOs). This structure is shown in Schema 1:

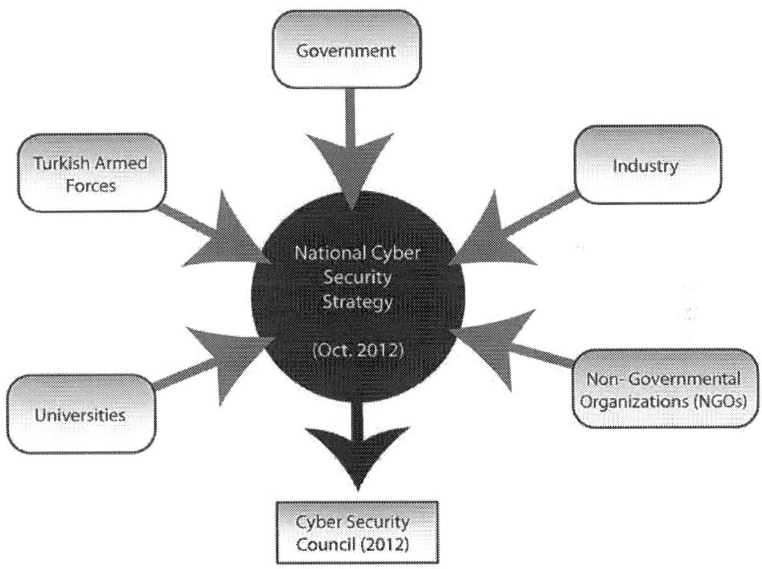

Schema 1*:* Cyber security structure in Turkey.

The members of the Cyber Security Council that are responsible for cyber security activities are as follows:

1. Minister of Transportation, Maritime Affairs and Communications (President)
2. Undersecretary of Ministry of Foreign Affairs,
3. Undersecretary of Ministry of Internal Affairs,
4. Undersecretary of Ministry of National Defence,
5. Undersecretary of Ministry of Transportation, Maritime Affairs and Communications,
6. Undersecretary of Public Order and Security,

7. Undersecretary of National Intelligence,
8. President of Turkish Armed Forces Information and Communication Systems,
9. President of Information and Communication Technologies Authority,
10. President of The Scientific and Technological Research Council of Turkey,
11. President of Financial Crime Investigation Board,
12. President of Telecommunication Communication,
13. Senior managers of governmental and financial organizations that are to be determined by the Minister of Transportation, Maritime Affairs and Communications.

The responsibilities of the Cyber Security Council are as follows:

1. Policy, strategy, action plan preparation for cyber security
2. Procedures and principles preparation for protecting digital assets of the government organizations
3. Track and assess technical security controls built within the government organizations
4. Promote and support development of national IT security systems and its usage among the government organizations.
5. Plan, coordinate and execute training of required number and skilled staff for the critical organizations
6. Collaborate with other countries and international organizations
7. Execute awareness and training activities about national cyber security
8. Defining procedures and principles for contractors giving training, testing and solution development services for government organizations
9. Executing the secretariat role within the Cyber Security Council.

1.1 Government

Governmental organizations that are responsible for cyber security activities in Turkey are the Ministry of Transport, Maritime Affairs and Communications, The Ministry of Science, Industry and Technology, The Ministry of National Defense, The Ministry of Development (former State Planning Organization), The Ministry of Internal Affairs.

The particular departments that are devoted to cyber security in these organizations are *Information Technologies and Communication Foundation* (in Turkish abbreviation BTK) that was founded under the Ministry of Transport, Maritime Affairs and Communications in 2008, *Internet Improvement Board* (that constitutes *Cyber Security Initiation*) that was founded in 2011 and *Cyber Security Department* that is founded in 2012; *Cyber Security Institute* that was founded in 2012 under The Scientific and Technological Research Council of Turkey (in Turkish abbreviation TÜBİTAK) that is under the Ministry of Science, Industry and Technology; *Under secretariat for Defense Industry* under the Ministry of National Defense; *IT Crime Department* (2011) under the Ministry of Internal Affairs. The name of this department was changed to *Cyber Crime Department* in 2013.

This structure is shown in Schema 2:

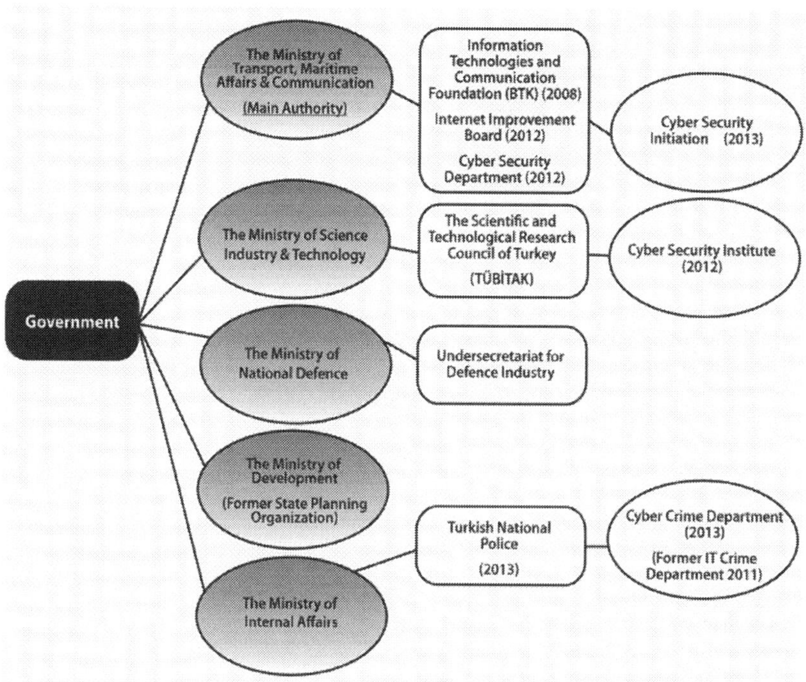

Schema 2: The formal cyber security structure in Turkey.

1.2 Turkish Armed Forces

Cyber space is considered as a separate force domain and this point results in the foundation of the Cyber Defense Command. In 2013, the Cyber Defense Center was founded to engage in cyber security activities with an aim to "prevent cyber threats by gaining a sound centralized capability of improved warning and reaction systems."

The cyber security structure in the Turkish Armed Forces is as follows:

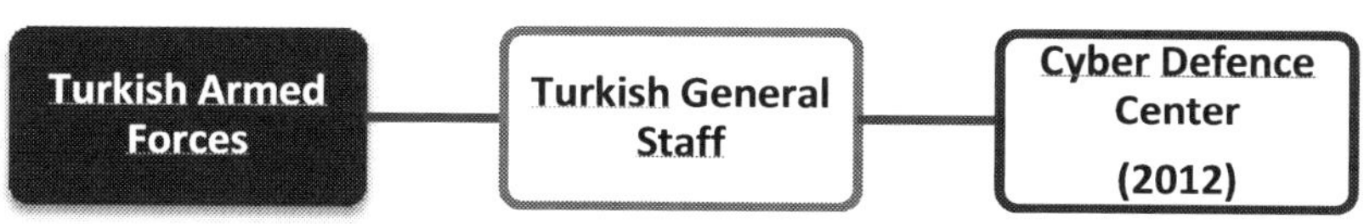

Schema 3: The cyber security structure in Turkish Armed Forces

The Cyber Defense Center pursues its activities in cooperation with the ministry of Transportation, Maritime Affairs and Communications, TÜBİTAK and other governmental organizations.

1.3 Universities, Industry and Non-Governmental Organizations

As stated earlier, cyber security activities require national cooperation of governmental organizations, universities, industry and non-governmental organizations which has taken place in Turkey. The Cyber Security Association and Turkish Information Security Association are two voluntary organizations in this area. There are also cyber security companies in industry and collaboration between academy and industry.

Below schema shows these organizations:

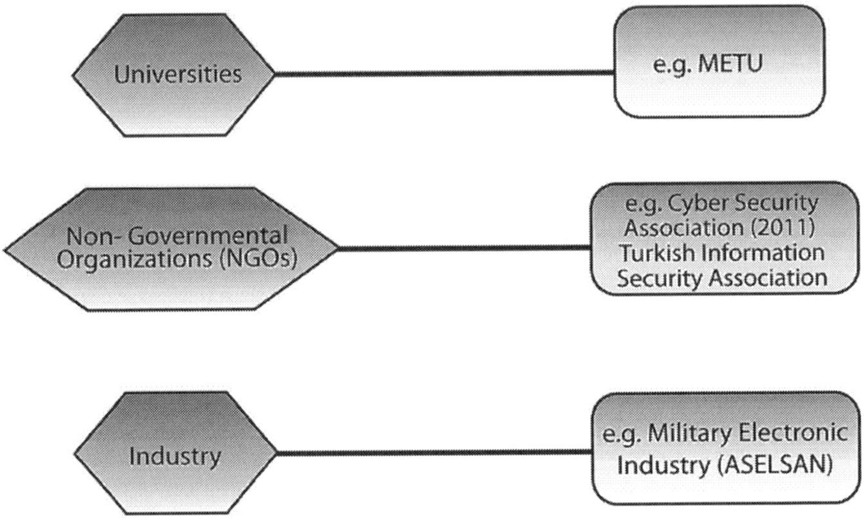

Schema 4: Universities, Industry and Non-Governmental Organizations that involves in cyber security activities in Turkey

4. National Cyber Security Strategy of Turkey

Cyber defense poses legal, technical and organizational challenges. To face with these challenges countries must to develop strategies on both the *national* and *international* scale. In Turkey, the 2008 "National Cyberspace Security Policy" document presented to the prime minister's office pins the preparation of a National Cyber Security Strategy as the first mission. To this aim, the studies started in 2013 and "National Cyber Security Strategy and 2013-2014 Action Plan" was published in June 2013.

The objectives of the strategy document are as follows:

- Providing the security of information technology infrastructure, systems and services offered by governmental institutions and organizations;
- Providing the security of information systems of governmental or private critical infrastructures;
- Creating the capability to minimize the damages of cyber attacks, to determine cyber security strategies to provide quick recovery after cyber attacks, and to ensure the efficient legal investigations.

In the strategy document, cyber security risks are listed in the *Cyber Security Risks chapter*; and principles are determined in *Principles* chapter. In the *Strategic Cyber Security Actions* chapter 7 major topic, 29 key action and 30 governmental organizations responsible for these actions are determined. Seven major topics are as follows:

- Legal regulations
- Activities to support legal procedures
- Development of national cyber security incident response organization
- Reinforcing national cyber security infrastructure
- Increase number of cyber security trained personnel
- Development of national cyber security products and technologies
- Extending the scope of national cyber security mechanisms

4.1 Action Plan

As stated earlier, seven major topics are determined under the *Strategic Cyber Security Actions* headline in the National Cyber Security Strategy and 2013-2014 Action Plan document. In 2013-2014 Action Plan, 29 actions and their sub-actions under these topics, and organizations responsible for these actions were identified.

Some points that are considered in this action plan are collecting evidence for cyber events, founding a national cyber security agency, and establishing a National Cyber Event Response Center (abbreviated as USOM in Turkish) and Cyber Event Response Teams (abbreviated as SOME in Turkish) under this center that respond to cyber events 24 hours a day 7 days a week. Strengthening the cyber security infrastructure of organizations, regulating the human-resource allocation for cyber security, and organizing International Cyber Security Exercises leaded by Turkey to test the cyber security measures and infrastructure are also included in this plan.

In the plan, there are also several points that focus on creating competent human resources in the medium and long term. Including cyber security courses within the primary, secondary, and higher education curriculum, and offering graduate and doctoral scholarships for cyber security programs are among these points.

5. Related Laws and Regulations

In Turkey, there are continuous studies towards the cyber security legal regulations. There are various laws, law drafts and regulations in this scope. These laws and organizations that are authorized in the scope of them are as follows:

5.1 Laws:

- 5070 law number Electronic Signature Act (2004): With this law secure electronic signature and wet signature are considered to be equivalent and to result in same legal consequences. National Information and Communication Technologies Authority is identified as the regulatory and supervisory agency.
- 5809 law number Electronic Communications Act (2008): Identifies the regulatory and supervisory principles in electronic communication sector. There are information security measures among these principles. National Information

and Communication Technologies Authority is identified as the regulatory and supervisory agency.

- 5651 law number Regulation of Publications on the Internet and Combating Crimes Committed by means of Such Publication (2007): This law identifies the obligations and liabilities of content, hosting, and access providers, and measures against cyber crimes. The Telecommunication Communications Department of the National Information and Communication Technologies Authority is identified as the regulatory and supervisory agency.

5.2 Draft Laws:

- Draft Law on Regulation of Electronic Commerce (2011): Regulates the obligations and regulations in business communication, electronic communications and information disclosure in electronic trade.
- Draft Law on National Information Security Organization and Its Duties: Regulates the protection of national security information, improvement of information security activities, identification of security policies, and measures to found an organization to support and supervise cooperation in information security.
- Draft Law on Regulation of Processing of Personal Information and Protection of Privacy in the Telecommunications Sector (2012): Regulates the confidentiality of correspondence, processing of traffic data, and detection of location.

5.3 Draft Regulations and Procedures:

- Draft regulation regarding Unsolicited Electronic Messages.
- Draft Principles and Procedures for the Secure Use of the Internet (2011)

5.4 Turkish Penal Code:

In the Turkish Penal Code 10, specifically below three crimes are defined:

- Breach to the IT system (Item 243).
- Denial of service, system disruption, data modification and destruction (Item 244).
- Offense of misuse of debit and credit cards (Item 245).

In 2010, Turkey signed the Convention of Cyber Crime of Council of Europe which is the most significant convention with the broadest participation.

6. Cyber Security Activities in Turkey

6.1 National Cyber Security Exercises

In 2008 a Cyber Security Exercise was conducted with the participation of 8 governmental organizations. Since 2011, National Cyber Security Exercises have been conducted by the collaboration of Turkish Information and Communication Technologies Authority (BTK) and The Scientific and Technological Research Council of Turkey (TUBITAK) under the supervision of the Turkish Ministry of Transportation, Maritime Affairs and Communications. The first of these exercises was conducted with the participation of 41 governmental and private organizations from several sectors including education, finance, and security and defense. In the scope of exercises, several cyber security scenarios were tested. 2. National Cyber Security Exercise was conducted between December 25 2012 – January 11 2013 with the participation of 61 governmental, private sector and non-governmental organizations (*for more information please visit* http://www.tubitak.gov.tr/tr/haber/).

Table 3: Information on National Cyber Security Exercises.

	2011	2012
# of participants	**41**	**61**
Who is participating?	Public privates and NGO's including judicial and law enforcement agencies and various ministries as well as finance, ICT, education, defense, health sector companies.	
Duration	3+2 days	12+2 days
Scenarios	4 real attacks and 14 written scenarios	6 real attacks, 6 written scenarios and Capture the Flag competition

6.2 *Cyber Shield Exercise*

In 2012 BTK organized "Cyber Shield Exercises 2012" with participation of 12 companies from electronic communication sector. Access provider companies with the biggest market share and 3 generation (3G) mobile internet provider companies participated in these exercises. In this respect, these exercises are significant examples of governmental and private sector collaboration in cyber security (13).

6.3 Cyber Security University Competition

TUBITAK Cyber Security Institute organizes cyber security competitions for universities with aim of promoting the awareness of and improving the technological capabilities on cyber security in the scope of the National Cyber Security Strategy and Action Plan.

6.4 Conferences and Symposiums

Various cyber security conferences, symposiums, and workshops are organized in Turkey. Some examples of these are as follows:

- The International Conference on Information Security and Cryptology (ISC) (The fifth organization in May 2012 with the main theme of Cyber Security and Defense)
- Information Technology Security Conference for Public Institutions.
- National Cyber Security Workshop

- Cyber Security Law Workshop
- Cyber Security Conference
- International Cyber Warfare & Security Conference B2B Meetings.
- "International Cyber War and Security Conference and Exhibition" (2013) organized by the collaboration of Defense And Aerospace Industry Manufacturer Association, Journal of Defense Turkey, and METU Techno park Defense Industry Cluster under the supervision of Under secretariat of Defense Industry.
- Cyber security panels are organized in the scope of annual Information Summit.

6.5 Cyber Security Education in Universities

The Turkish Higher Education Council is promoting cyber security departments within the universities. Currently there are graduate programs in 3 universities (Gazi University, İstanbul Şehir University, Yaşar University). Two universities (METU and Bahçeşehir University) announced their Cyber Security MSc program to be started within this year. Numerous universities provide information security and cyber security courses within related departments.

6.6 Training Activities

There are a large number of cyber security training programs provided by private educational institutions. A Cyber Security Summer Camp is organized by the collaboration of TÜBİTAK BİLGEM Cyber Security Institute and Information Security Academia educates cyber security experts and training university students about cyber security. Undergraduate, master and doctoral students participate and are educated on information systems security in the Cyber Security Summer Camps that aim to overcome the cyber security expert deficiencies.

In addition to trainings, the students who participate in camps meet with the information security experienced academicians, and managers of governmental and private organizations. The students are informed on cyber world threats, required precautions, and career opportunities. Also, the competitions through the camps enable students to improve their team work capabilities, and solidify the knowledge that they acquire in camps (15).

6.7 Cyber Security Awareness Raising Portal

www.bilgimikoruyorum.org.tr
www.bilgiguvenligi.gov.tr

Table 4: Cyber Security Awareness Raising Portal publications.

Published	Feb 2008 (start date)
Authors	161
Voluntary Authors	67
Articles	297
Voluntary Articles	140
Guides	32
Security Bulletin	846

6.8 Activities of Armed Forces

The TAF Cyber Defense Center, engages in national and international cyber security activities in collaboration with NATO. This center is responsible for the defense of all cyber systems of TAF, 7/24 management of cyber activities, participation to national and NATO supervised defense exercises, pursuing the awareness increasing and education events, and auditing the TAF networks. Also, there are several projects are underway for the Turkish General Staff and other forces and the TAF personnel participate to several symposium and conferences.

6.9 National and International Cooperation

The global nature of cyber security challenges can only be addressed through international cooperation and partnership. Therefore, countries must develop new models for international cooperation and partnership, and promote a global culture of cyber security. Turkey attaches particular importance to national and international collaborations in cyber security and conduct joint projects with several organizations. The 2009 project of BTK is an example of these projects that focus on preventing spam e-mail with the participation of various governmental and private organizations. This project provides a decline both in the IP address count that spread spam mails and in the daily spam mail number (1).The Internet Improvement Board under the Ministry of Transport, Maritime Affairs and Communications created the *Cyber Security Initiation.* The responsibilities of the Cyber Security Initiation are defined as organizing projects with the participation of stakeholders to promote collaboration and intellectual communication among them, and present the results of these projects to the ministry of Transportation, Maritime Affairs and Communications. This initiative includes the Cyber Security Association and other non-governmental organizations, Internet Service Providers, consultant companies, technology companies, and various service providers. Cyber Security Exercises and Summer Camps are organized through the collaboration of various national organizations. On the international level there is cooperation between the Turkish Armed Forces (TAF) and NATO. Also, the METU Informatics Institute has been organizing cyber security training courses by the support of and collaboration with NATO. This course is an example both of the cyber security education activities and international collaboration.

6.10 Related Protocols and Contracts

Various cyber security protocols and contracts are signed by several organizations. These are;

1. Ministry of Transport, Maritime Affairs and Communications and Ministry of Science, Industry and Technology signed 2 cooperation protocols in 2012.

2. Ministry of Transport, Maritime Affairs and Communications and The Scientific and Technological Research Council of Turkey signed "National Cyber Security Technology Development Consultant Service Procurement Protocol" in 2012. This protocol includes the following work packages.

a. National Cyber Security Management
b. Cyber Threat Detection and Prevention System Development
c. Sophisticated Cyber Spying Threat (APT) Analysis
d. Malware Analysis and Management Center
e. National Internet Sustainability Project

3. Under secretariat for Defense Industry under the ministry of National Defense and STM A.Ş. signed the "Integrated Cyber Security System" feasibility study protocol aiming at gaining information security and defense capabilities. In the scope of this protocol, a prototype functioning in the test medium will be developed for concept verification, and cyber security systems, software, and processes that can be used for ADY will be reported (16).

Necessary protocols were signed by related organizations.

6.11 R&D Activities Conducted by Government

In Turkey, there are various cyber security government projects. These projects include:

- Cyber Security Threat Monitoring and Prevention Center
- APT Analysis System
- Honeypot System
- Data Leakage Prevention System
- Malware Analysis Center

The projects that are conducted by Information Technologies and Communication Foundation are as follows:

- Prevention of Cyber Threat Project (STOP): Project includes the creation of honeypots for cyber threat detection, construction and development of cyber attack logging systems, cyber threat data production, and construction of required cyber threat prevention mechanisms.
- Management of Spam E-Mail Project: In 2009 a BTK led pilot project was conducted with the participation of internet service providers and hosting providers. The project focuses on the prevention of unwanted e-mails that threaten the cyber security and use resources unnecessarily. Upon the success of the pilot project, the solution is applied through country in 3 phases. After the project, the number of IP transmitting spam reduces to % 99 (17).

6.12 Evaluation

In recent years, Turkey made significant progress in Cyber Security. The publication of the National Cyber Security Strategy and Action Plan, identification of main authorities and authorities that are responsible for the execution of main and sub activities in the action plan are important steps for the Turkish Cyber Security Policy. These points highlight the fact that Turkey addresses cyber security on the broadest level. If one asses the cyber security in Turkey, it can be seen that the most important problem is the deficiency in competent cyber security personnel. Even though necessary steps to solve this problem are identified in the strategy document and two universities announced the launching of cyber security graduate programs, competent human resources can be considered still as the most important problem since the results of these improvements will become evident only in future. There is also a deficiency in the number of companies that conduct research and development (R&D) studies, or develop cyber security software.

Another problem is that mostly governmental organizations are responsible for the process since internet service providers, hosting providers are not among the responsible organizations identified by the strategy document and the action plan, and non-governmental organizations are not considered as the principal actors.

7. Conclusions

Cyber space is a critical area of national security. Countries need to develop strategies on both the national and international scale. Also, cyber security necessitates the cooperation of governments, universities, industry and civil societies. The solutions of cyber security problems also necessitate initiatives from all legal, institutional, scientific and technical domains. The global nature of the problem also put a special emphasis on international cooperation. Educating the competent cyber security human resources is among the most important problems of countries. Global information sharing has a great impact on the improvement of cyber security capabilities of countries. Also, sharing negative experiences is as important as sharing the positive ones. Today active cyber defense approaches that focus on proactive actions for the detection and prevention of attacks have become more prominent in cyber security. It is evident that these actions have an important role in the prevention of cyber attacks. Therefore, it is a must for countries to include these actions within their cyber security policies.

References

[1]. Cyber Security Analysis of Turkey, *International Journal of Information Security Science*, Hakan Şentürk, C. Zaim Çil, Şeref Sağıroğlu, *Vol.1, No. 4.*

[2]. *Ulusal Siber Güvenlik Stratejisi ve Yürütülen Çalışmalar*, Türköz, T., TÜBİTAK BİLGEM, Siber Güvenlik Enstitüsü.

[3]. National Cyber Security Document, Ministry of Transport, Maritime Affairs and Communications, 2013.

[4]. http://www.tk.gov.tr/bilgi_teknolojileri/siber_guvenlik/usgt2013.php

[5]. http://www.tk.gov.tr/bilgi_teknolojileri/siber_guvenlik/usgt2011.php

[6]. Cybersecurity Policy Making at a Turning Point, Analysing a New Generation of National Cybersecurity Strategies for the Internet Economy, OECD, 16 Nov 2012, No: 211, Pages 57, DOI 10.1787/5k8zq92vdgtl-en.

[7]. http://www.ata-sac.org/subory/file/CEPI/TPB%20Cyber%20Terlikowski%20Vysko%C4%8D(1).pdf

[8]. A Framework for Policymakers, Policy Brief, Irving Lachow, Center for a New American Security, February 2013.

[9]. Securing Cyberspace: A Comparative Review of Strategies Worldwide, Avner Levin, Paul Goodrick & Daria Ilkina.

[10]. http://www.enisa.europa.eu/media/news-items/new-cyber-security-strategy-hungary-and-worldwide

[11]. Telekomünikasyon Şebekelerinin Güvenliği, Atila Çelik (Communication General Director in Ministry of Transport, Maritime Affairs and Communications), (presentation).
[12]. Coming to Terms with a New Threat: NATO and Cyber-Security. http://www.cepolicy.org/publications/coming-terms-new-threat-nato-and-cyber-security
[13]. http://www.tk.gov.tr/bilgi_teknolojileri/siber_guvenlik/uskt2012.php
[14]. http://www.elektrikport.com/universite/universiteler-arasi-siber-savunma-yarismasi-kayitlari-basladi/9039#ad-image-0
[15]. http://www.siberkamp.org/
[16]. http://www.ssm.gov.tr/anasayfa/hizli/duyurular/etkinlikler/torenler/arsiv/2012/Sayfalar/20122507ButSbrGuvSist.aspx
[17]. http://www.telekomunikasyonkurumu.gov.tr/bilgi_teknolojileri/siber_guvenlik/calismalar.php

Cyber Security and Resiliency Policy Framework
A. Vaseashta et al. (Eds.)
IOS Press, 2014

doi:10.3233/978-1-61499-446-6-99

Cyber Security Challenges in Smart Homes

Luben BOYANOV[1] and Zlatogor MINCHEV
Institute for Information and Communication Technologies
Bulgarian Academy of Sciences
Sofia, BULGARIA

Abstract. This chapter addresses cyber security issues related to smart homes. With the introduction of smart devices and systems in our homes, the risks and threats linked to them, and respectively to the smart home inhabitants is growing. The digital world has gradually developed standards, protocols, interfaces, operating systems, programming models and architectures, making both computing and networking a type of plug-and-play environment. The smart house and its services, as we know them at present, form a highly heterogeneous environment, which presents a significant challenge for future users and manufacturers. Healthcare services contain unknown danger for human's life and present real vulnerabilities in interconnected medical devices. The chapter discusses details of cyber security risks, available technologies and methodologies to minimize and mitigate threat vectors.

Keywords: smart homes, threat vectors, medical devices, interconnectedness, Modeling

Introduction

Smart homes have emerged because people want to improve and optimize the comfort in their homes, while minimizing daily home responsibilities. The first automated home systems were presented at the Chicago and New York World Fairs in 1934 and 1939. Introducing more wires in the home was carried out by some hobbyists in the 1960s but at the time, technologies did not offer too many options for optimization and efficiency in the house. The expression "smart house" was first used by the American Association of House builders in 1984 [1].

Despite the growth and advances in electronics – namely the appearance of microcontrollers, microprocessors, RAM and ROM memory, and also the emergence of smaller and less expensive household appliance, smart homes have been built only by the very rich and technologically savvy "geeks" until the late 1990s. At the same time, home security systems offering intruder and fire detection capabilities became more widespread. Since the start of the 21st century, with the penetration of personal computers, Internet, cell phones, and wireless networks in every home, technologies advanced. In addition, the emergence of cheap, autonomous wireless sensors, passive and active identification tags – RFID also drove smart home technologies. It is now common to introduce and implement technological advances in the home.

[1] Email: lb@acad.bg

1. Smart Homes Today

Nowadays, the term "smart home" is used for a house with technological equipment for control, monitoring, automation and optimization of:

- Home environment – temperature, humidity, air purity, house light, etc.
- Home security and safety – burglary, fire, smoke, carbon monoxide, gas, etc.
- Inhabitants and their health – children, elderly people, disabled, etc.
- Household appliances – air conditioning, gas or electric cooker, refrigerator, TV, video and audio systems, etc.
- Energy efficiency – electricity, gas, water, etc.

Examples of smart homes are most common in countries with advanced economies like the USA [2], [3], [4], Japan [5], [6], [7] and EU [8], [9], [10]. In addition to the advances in various technologies mentioned above, another factor influencing the wider implementation of smart homes is that energy use in residential and commercial buildings, in developed countries is between 20 and 40% [11]. Smart home energy saving features may allow the average household to reduce its carbon emissions by 71% and annual energy cost – by 105% [12]. Some 1.5 million automation systems have been installed in the USA in 2012, doubling the shipments from the previous year, with estimates that this number will raise to 8 million per year in 2017 [13].

2. Smart Homes Features

As mentioned earlier, the term "smart home" is used for dwellings equipped with technologies that allow monitoring of its environment and inhabitants. The equipment can actively react to the occurrence of an event. A simple example of an active reaction is when somebody enters the house and does not enter the correct security alarm code or when there is fire or smoke and it is detected by the monitoring system and an alarm is set or the owner is informed by a prerecorded message sent over the phone (cell or landline). Another example of the "simple" behavior of smart devices is when somebody enters a room and the light goes on. Such situations and use of automation in homes are rather popular but they do not require much intelligent data processing. However, if we look at a situation when one must find out if an elderly person or a child is home alone, or whether they feel comfortable and need no attention, or if someone has fallen on the floor and/or does not feel well, much more intelligence is required by the smart home system to assure the safety and welfare of the inhabitants.

This is how we move to a higher level of "smart" processing of data – indications that suggest that the safety and welfare of the inhabitants is at risk are detected by sensors or multimedia sources in the smart home, possibly saved, and then treated by an intelligent system (a computerized one). The last action is likely to include some assessment in regard to data or a scenario, given in advance, and on the basis of thresholds specified in the system. It is also possible that in terms of energy efficiency optimization, monitoring and control of devices and appliances can be carried out in the house. Such activities are possible because of electronic advances in sensor devices, video and audio surveillance, computers, and various types of networks that connect all modules in the house.

Different examples on the state and varieties of a smart home are presented in [14] and [15]. Summarizing the applications, a smart home contains:

- Various sensors in rooms and other house areas with some activity– including on the floor, where they can detect whether a person or an object has fallen
- Systems for monitoring the health of the inhabitants of the home
- Sensors and systems for home safety monitoring
- Systems for monitoring pets, appliances or the state of an object
- Devices that control lighting and temperature
- Systems that monitor and control entertainment, or outdoor (e.g. garden) equipment

This can be categorized as the lowest, ***first level*** – the ***detection*** level. All those sensors, systems and devices actively react to certain events, which sends an input to the ***second level*** that can be either an inhabitant of the house or a control and monitoring system – the ***perception*** level. The second level may or may not actively react to events from the first level. In case the house has a specialized control and monitoring system, it is usually connected to the sensors and detecting devices via some communication network. The connections may also lead to an integrated intelligent center in cases when no direct reaction is expected. A simple example of such a system is a home security system that records the area of intrusion, sets up a siren and dials a phone number to transmit a warning. This can be viewed as a ***third level – the intelligent integration*** level. It is possible that a reaction from outside to certain events in the house might be needed – so there must be communication from the intelligent integrating center to the outside world. This can be regarded as the last, ***fourth level – the outdoor*** level. External communication can be via cell-phone services or the Internet and can pass data to home owners or inhabitants, social and medical staff, or security services. A smart home architecture is depicted in Figure 1.

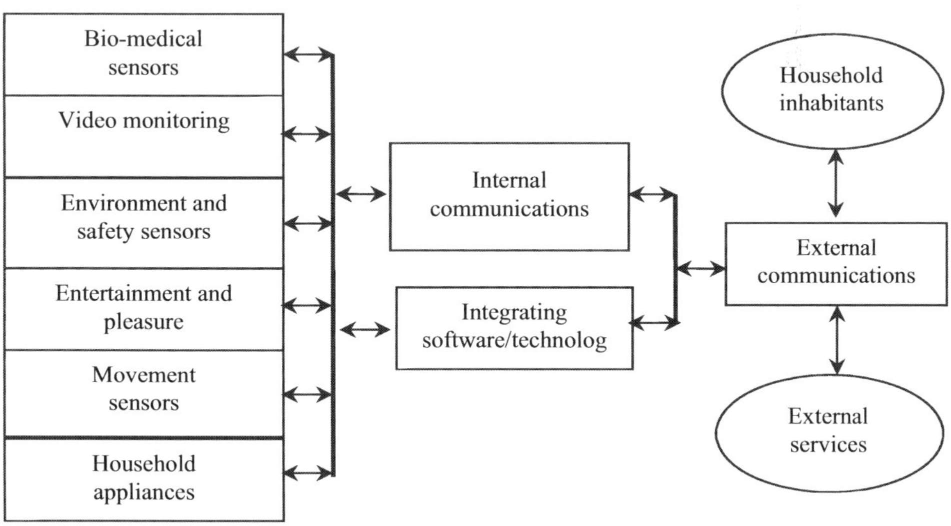

Figure 1. Smart home architecture.

The most important features that differentiate smart homes from other linked and controlled systems like the global Internet, Municipal Area Networks (MAN) and office networks are:

- Lack of professional network or system administrator,
- The big heterogeneity of connected equipment – sensors, appliance, machines,
- The very high requirements for privacy, robustness, availability of services and denial of unauthorized access.

While it is common to think of smart home users as those persons who are very rich and/or technologically savvy (geeky), many other smart home users that do not fall into these stereotypes are

- People who live on their own and may be not capable of handling emergency situations by themselves,
- People with physical or medical problems – diabetics, cancer, asthma, Alzheimer, dementia, etc.,
- People living in remote or isolated areas, or places with no proper health care,
- Children.

3. Technologies

Sensor technology is the most important technology used in smart homes. Recent advances in this field, including the emergence of low-cost and low-weight electronic circuits, novel manufacturing technologies and signal processing methods, allow their effective and efficient intrusion in the domain of smart homes [16]. Sensors work on optical, acoustic, thermoresistive, piezoresistive, capacitive, electromagnetic, piezoelectric principles. In the field of medicine, the micro-electromechanical systems (MEMS) can detect triglycerides, c-reactive protein, and glucose, measure tissue softness during surgical procedures; count blood cells; measure intramuscular pressure, etc. [17]. Such advances allow data, gathered from sensors not only to monitor the home environment but also the activities and health status of smart home inhabitants.

In addition to the use of sensor technologies, home monitoring, can also be implemented using video surveillance and RFID technology. A high-quality digital video IP camera with Internet network connectivity can provide the required clear video and images in both daylight and night, to be used by humans or processed by computer system. Until a decade ago, major obstacles included the price of memory and the lack of proper technology for fetching critical information from the bulk of collected data, as such was only available for expensive, high-end computer systems. However, technologies have become less expensive and more sophisticated and will continue these trends as time goes on. Another unresolved issue that hinders the benefits of video surveillance is privacy protection.

Another important technology is RFID - Radio Frequency Identification, which is a wireless non-contact use technology that uses radio-frequency to transfer data to and from tags attached to objects. Since 2004, many hospitals in the USA implant RFID tags to identify and track patients [18] and this technology is used for healthcare in smart homes [19]. RFID tags can be implanted within pets and even people. The fact that the implant carries personal identification, contact information and medical history, raises some security and privacy concerns [20].

4. Products, Communication and Integration

The most common products in regard to comfort, control and security are remote control devices, intrusion detection and home monitoring systems (security alarms, motion sensors, security cameras), and more recently – sensors and devices for biometric monitoring that can be attached or implanted in people, who require automated health care. Also very popular are mobile or stationary products and systems for control of physical (lighting, heating, cooling, and noise) or chemical (gas, smoke) features and components.

The most common communication products at home at present are wired (Ethernet) and wireless (Wi-Fi) networks, devices and systems linked via infrared transceivers and Bluetooth. Other promising communication protocols are Z-Wave, ZigBee and HomePlug. ZigBee is an open wireless IEEE standard, which can be used in direct communications but is most often applied on a star or tree topology mesh network. It operates in the 2.4-GHz band with maximum data rate of 250 kbits/s. It has a typical power of 1 mW and free space range to about 10 meters. Z-Wave is a proprietary wireless standard with wireless mesh networking technology. It operates at 908.42 MHz in North America but uses other frequencies in other countries depending on the regulations. Data rates are 9.6 kbits/s and 40 kbits/s. Output power is 1 mW covering a range of up to 30 meter. Z-Wave and ZigBee are low power, short range wireless protocols that carry small messages to/from sensors and are likely to become the dominant communication technologies for Home Area Networks (HANs).

Integration systems consist of computers or similar intelligent systems that can "read" data, issued by sensors and monitoring devices. On the basis of the received data, these systems must be able to take decisions. So far there is no widespread integrating software for such systems but a promising approach is being taken by Microsoft since 2010 with its HomeOS. Its version has been used in 12 actual households for periods of 4-8 months [21]. The operating system is designed to control the lighting, video surveillance, kitchen appliance, computers, interact with various sensors and entertainment devices. HomeOS has a four layer architecture – the top of which is application layer, next is management layer, then follows the device functionality layer and at the bottom stands the device connectivity layer. The HomeOS unifies various interface modules of the different devices and uses the C # language of the Microsoft.Net Framework 4.0 platform. There are also applications developed by Apple and Android phones and tablets that are used in home automation. Based on the forecast that this market will grow rapidly in the years to come, one can expect serious advances in home integration systems, devices and software.

5. Impact on Society and Challenges

Bearing in mind the presence of aging societies in the developed countries, it is very likely that one of the most important features of smart homes and factor that will push for their development and demand on the market is e-health/telehealth. Health services can become more efficient and responsive when using advanced smart home features and implementations. Smart homes can improve the quality of life for elderly and people with chronic conditions or disabilities, who wish to remain at home or do not have the opportunities to move to a specialized institution. Even simple automation like turning on/off lights when getting out of bed can facilitate better safety for those people. Meal intake, general activity, temperature, blood pressure, social interaction, communications and environmental hazards such as fire or gas leak are of paramount importance not only for the above mentioned categories for senior people but also for those with disabilities and for small children.

Major challenges with smart homes are the reliability of the sensors and surveillance systems, their calibration, provision of reliable communication from and to smart homes, granting security and integrity of data, provision of action plan or scenario in case of system failure or denial of services, security for the integration systems, including devices and decision making software. In addition to the danger, related to the reliability and security, which are of technological and architectural design nature, there are also social dangers. For example, smart home inhabitants might feel social isolation from family and friends, or may trouble an elderly person who may feel unsafe with technologies [22].

6. Smart Homes Cyber Security Challenges

The introduction of smart devices and systems in our homes comes with associated risks and threats for the home itself and habitants therein. The digital world as we know it now has gradually developed standards, protocols, interfaces, operating systems, programming models and architectures during the last 50 decades, making both computing and networking a type of plug-and-play environment. The smart house and its services, as we know them at present, form a highly heterogeneous environment, which presents a significant challenge for future users and manufacturers. Healthcare services may have system vulnerabilities that endanger the patient's life. The scenario of a villain causing a heart attack by remote intervention in a pacemaker or shutting down an insulin pump on a diabetic can occur from real vulnerabilities that exist in connected medical devices [23]. These are rather worrying facts, bearing in mind that between 1993 and 2009, 2.9 million patients received permanent pacemakers in the United States with this number constantly increasing [24].

One definition of a cyber threat is "any identified effort directed toward access to, exfiltration of, manipulation of, or impairment to the integrity, confidentiality, security, or availability of data, an application, or a federal system, without lawful authority" [25]. In our daily lives, a threat for our home can be an open window or unlocked door, a clothes iron or cooking device that is not turned off or water running from an open tap. In future smart homes, in addition to the threats related to the household appliance, those with malicious intent can endanger the health or life of the inhabitants.

Modern research shows that online cyber threats have not only grown and evolved considerably but have also expanded of traditional threats into new forums – social media, mobile devices and cloud computing [26], [27]. This territory will inevitably extend in the near future to smart homes.

7. Cyber Threats Related to Smart Homes

The consequences of cyber attacks can lead to serious problems like misinformation, cripple tactical services, access sensitive information, espionage, data theft, financial losses, and other. The nature, complexity and severity of the cyber threats are increasing in time, which makes it difficult to build a good classification framework.

Cyber threats can be classified in several directions:

- According to the intention – unintentional and intentional. The cause of the former is due to lack of training, software upgrade, equipment failures or software upgrades that unintentionally disturb the functioning of computers or corrupt data. The latter can be either targeted or non-targeted.
  - A targeted attack aims to harm a person, institution or critical infrastructure system. Such may include the energy, finance, telecommunication, military, transportation or water sectors. They originate from spies, criminals, hackers, virus and malware programmers, or employees ("insiders") within an organization.
  - Non-targeted attacks have no particular aim but are intended to do harm to as many digital systems as possible. Example of non-targeted attacks are viruses, worms, and malware released on the Internet.
- According to the effect of the attack – critical, non-critical and non-critical but dangerous. Critical attacks can block or phase out entire systems, including infrastructural or certain modules, leaving them in limited or fully non-functional state. Non-critical attacks do not harm or modify the system or its elements. For example – classified information may be fetched; information to be used for marketing or advertisement purposes may be gathered. Non-critical but dangerous attacks are such that they do not cause immediate harm (no effect on the system or its elements) but may have a critical effect at a later moment. For example – stealing passwords, identity theft, misuse of personal or confidential information, etc.
- According to utilization – syntactic and semantic. Syntactic attacks are direct – insert viruses, worms, malware, etc. Semantic attacks modify and/or disseminate information. Modified information can be used for covering tracks of crime, or setting somebody to a wrong track.

The recently published Red book - A Roadmap for Systems Security Research [28] presents the cyber security landscape of our society and lists the assets that are target of cyber attacks. The top four of them, which people feel are the most important are:

- Life – human's most valuable asset, which can be the target of cyber attacks. Such attacks can target medical systems, transport systems, emergency response systems all of which may lead to a loss of life, even at some occasions – on a mass scale;
- Health – the widespread use of technologies within healthcare systems leads also to increased probabilities of attacks;
- The Environment – water systems and ecosystems are of paramount importance for the survival and health of humans and all living species and increased monitoring and control of systems by technologies also introduce a level of vulnerabilities to the systems. Attacks on the ecosystem or the inability of the monitoring system to respond to attacks may worsen damages resulting from large scale pollutions, fires, or floods and have devastating effects on communities
- Privacy –is challenged at present and appears to be even more threatened in the near future, as people are taking more and more actions online, their data and activities are being recorded without their knowledge and control.

Security is fundamental in these four areas in order for future expansion of smart homes to be in line with people's most valued assets. Much time and money has been paid to securing communication protocols over Internet and for computer systems, but little is done in this respect for sensor technologies, integrated systems and smart home environment. Table 1 below presents the main services, dangers, critical attack points and consequences of cyber attacks in smart homes:

Table 1. Services, dangers, attack points and consequences in smart homes.

Smart home services	Possible threats	Critical attack points	Possible consequences from the attack
Health care	Irregular doses of medicine, pacemaker malfunctioning, etc.	Sensors, video surveillance, communication system, integrating system, external communications	Critical
Care for children or people with disabilities	Lack of monitoring or response	Sensors, video surveillance, communication system, integrating system, external communications	Critical
Security and safety	Undetected Intrusion	Sensors, video surveillance, communication system, integrating system, external communications	Critical
Home environment	Fire, flooding, gas leakage	Sensors, video surveillance, communication system, integrating system, external communications	Critical
Smart home appliance	Does not turn off, turns on/off at wrong time	Sensors, video surveillance, communication system, integrating system	Non-critical, but dangerous
Privacy	Violation of privacy, data gathering	Video surveillance, communication system, integrating system, external communications	Non-critical but dangerous
Entertainment and pleasure	System Malfunction	Sensors, communication system, integrating system	Non-critical

Possible consequences from cyber-attacks can be:

- Denial of service (DoS) – targeting the sensors, video surveillance or communication systems,
- Data integrity violation or data modification in communication media;
- System breach with unauthorized access to network resources or system integration resources.

To deal with the attack, it is necessary:

- to have an operating intrusion detection system;
- to have an attack prevention system;
- to maintain reliable identification, authentication and access control;
- to support leakage monitoring information;
- to employ reliable and effective communication protocols;
- to operate secure integrating systems and external communication systems.

8. Cyber Threats Modelling and Identification

The identification of cyber threats using expert elicitation can be performed in different ways, like: q-based surveys, discussions, morphological analysis, scenarios contextualization, etc.; we have tried to find a more comprehensive method by implementing system modeling and analysis. This allows different data sources and analysis results integration and at the same time provides an understanding of the threat's possible origin, thus marking the entities of interest. As presented in the Figure 2 model, we have tried to integrate a q-based generated dimensions from a morphological analysis [29] into an E-R system model that is outlining the entities of interest of real/potential cyber threats.

Briefly, this methodological approach is based on the utilization of the well-known General Systems Theory, and thus concerns the studied system building elements in-between nonlinear interactions. An assumption for a smart home complex dynamic system approximation is made. It is built of entities and time-dependent weighted relations together with an improved graphical visualization of the entities' resulting sensitivity [30]. A more detailed description of the implemented software environment and resulting identified model entities classification is given in the next paragraph.

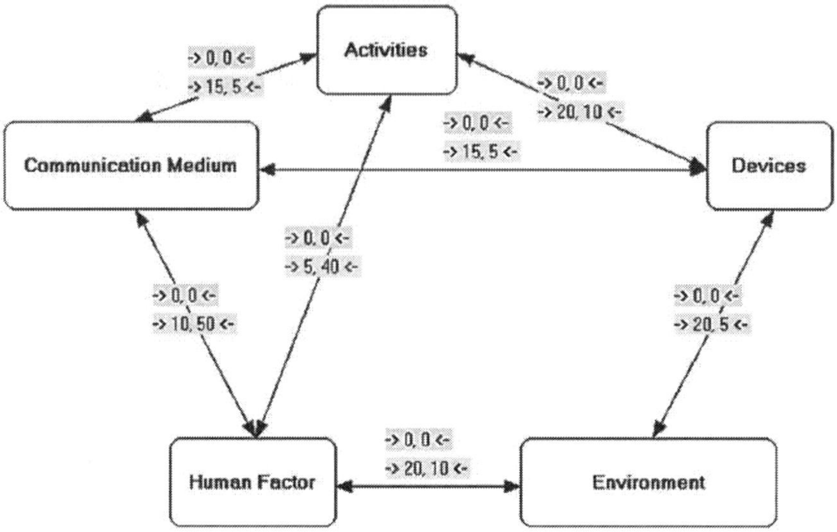

Figure 2. A smart home general system modeling for cyberthreats entities of interest identification.

9. Software Implementation

The software environment model implementation is based on I-SCIP-SA v.2.0 [30]. Briefly, I-SCIP-SA allows model building by using "entities" (also noted as 'elements' or 'objects', interpreted as rectangles, squares or circles), which are connected with "bonds" ("relations") that are interpreted as headed weighted arrows – uni- and bi-directional. The arrows' weights are marked as yellow labels over the arrows and are expressed in percentages from the interval [0, 1] using the following scale: low [0-30], middle [30-50] and high [50-100].

The relations weights' generalization produce a Sensitivity Diagram (SD) that encompasses and extends the ideas of Vester's sensitivity model [31], allowing model entities' zone classification and system sensitivity analysis as follows: Red zone ('Communication Medium', active elements, Influence/Dependence Maximum Ratio (IDMR) =100/50, SE (South-East) part of SD cube), Blue zone ('Devices', 'Activities', passive elements IDMR=50/100, NW (North-West) part of SD cube), Yellow zone ('Human Factor', critical elements, IDMR=100/100, NE (North-East) part of the SD cube) and Green zone ('Environment', buffering elements, IDMR=50/50, SW (South-West) part of SD cube). Additionally, the 3D SD gives a possibility for direct sensitivity (z-coordinate, marked with red arrow in Figure 3) calculation of a given object from the system as an absolute difference between the influence (x-coordinate, marked with green arrow in Figure 3), and dependence (y-coordinate, marked with blue arrow in Figure 3) values, concerning a certain object from the system of interest. When this difference is negative the object in the SD is classified as passive (producing a decreased system sensitivity in its SD zone, 'Devices' and 'Activities') and is colored in light grey, otherwise it is active (producing an increased system sensitivity in its SD zone, all other model entities) and is colored in white.

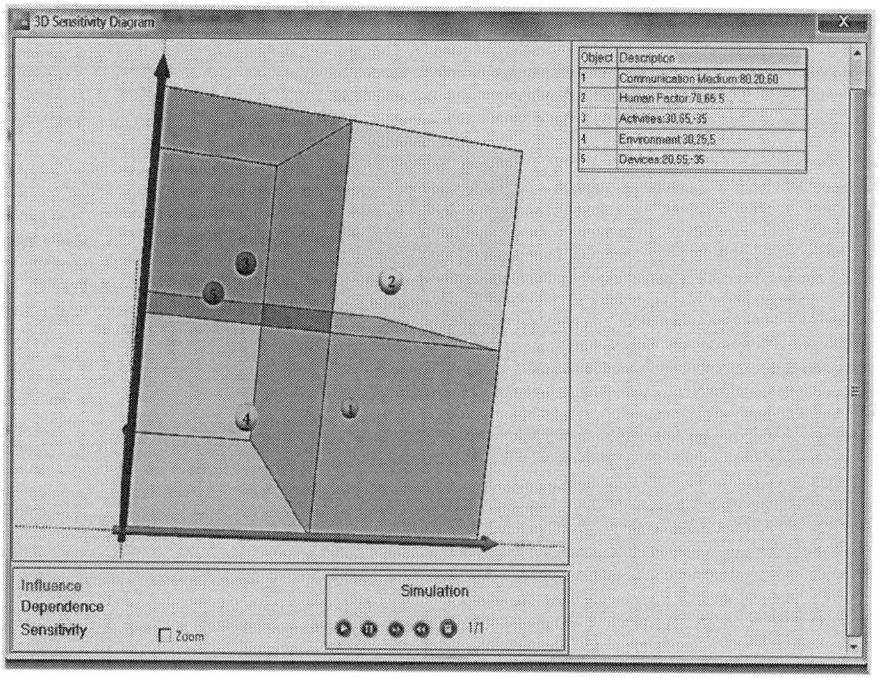

Figure 3. A smart home general system modelsensitivity diagram.

The resulting SD from Figure 3 is giving a profitable classification for further analysis, outlining the 'Human Factor'(noted in Figure 3 with indexed ball '2' with coordinates {x=70, y=65, z=5}) as a critical entity together with the potential hidden cyber threats passive entities: 'Devices'(indexed ball '5' with coordinates {x=20, y=55, z = -35}), 'Activities'(indexed ball '3' with coordinates {x=30, y=65, z= -35})and real active one: 'Communication Medium'(indexed ball '1' with coordinates {x=80, y=20, z=60}). This expert' based classification, though quite general, is in line with a recently outlined comprehensive EU study of cyber security trends, developed by the SysSec international consortium [28]. As far as these results are based only on experts' data and analysis we have also decided to add a practical validation through a constructive smart home test bed simulation.

10. Results Validation

A suitable approach for experts' believes validation is the usage of a cyber-attacks simulation in a smart-home test-bed environment and monitoring human (smart homes' inhabitants) psychophysiological responses, as well as behavior dynamics to these attacks.

10.1 Agent-Based Modelling Framework

Generally, the idea for interactive agent-based simulation could be summarized in Figure 4:

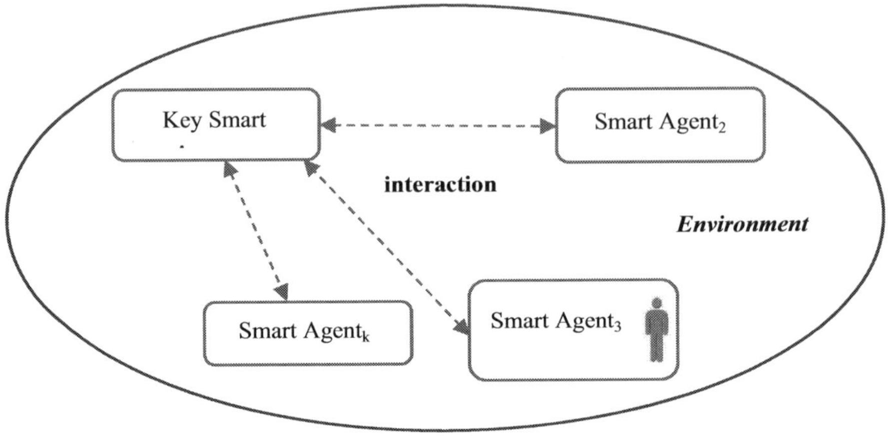

Figure 4. A general concept for interactive prominence agent-based simulation of cyber attacks in a smart home test-bed environment.

Figure 4 outlines the heterogeneous agent-based simulation concept with human-in-the-loop participation. As in general, no global organization of the model elements is required, two different swarm techniques could be used for autonomous multi-agent-based interaction modelling: *prominence* and *negotiation* based organization [32]. For simplicity and fast practical smart home implementation, an assumption for prominence agent organization [33] is made, following the idea that each agent has two basic components: 'Properties' and 'Activities'. The 'Properties' set includes {*agent **role***, ***interaction channel***, *agent **state***, ***other** additional agent peculiarities*}. The subset ***other*** incorporates colour, weight, size, technical and environmental characteristics. When the agent role is presented by a human, physiological properties are examined - heart rate variability, body temperature, galvanic skin response dynamics. When the agent role is given by a smart room environment, physical parameters like environment temperature, humidity, CO concentration are monitored. The 'Activities' set covers the agent's behavior dynamics {**role dynamics**, **interaction events**, **state dynamics**}. As the *prominence* swarm organization was chosen, the 'Key agent' is responsible for simulation running following a preliminary defined script of activities (noted in the 'Properties' and 'Activities' sets) covering different cyberattacks scenarios. More complex simulation configurations are also possible but require a busier communication channel and smarter agents.

10.2 Experimental Test-Bed

Recently, a smart home test-bed environment equipped with a number of smart devices, including: 3D TV/monitors, X-box game console, entertainment and cleaning robots, programmed tablet remote control, IP video omnidirectional monitoring system and digital assistant voice control for lighting, multimedia and heating with holo-like projection avatar. In addition, an environment embedded Xbee sensor barometer system and wearable human factor bio headband are being developed. The sensor barometer system will be extended with CO/CO2 concentration measurement, radiation, electromagnetic fields and dust particles sensors [34]. The bio headband is for ECG and body temperature monitoring [35]. All data from sensors and video monitoring is stored in data base storage. The above described test-bed has been organized for practical agent-based interactive experiments (see Figure 4) in the framework of DFNI T01/4 project [36].

Figure 5. A photo of experimental activities in smart home test-bed environment.

The simulation is currently based on a virtual agents' roles classification. A 'Key attacks agent' that is organizing cyber-attacks following a scenario script of events in cooperation with the 'Connectivity agent' is practically responsible for the simulation running. The other agents could be grouped according to their roles as follows: 'Data storage agent' (responsible for all exchanged data storing, encompassing at present environment and human biometrics sensors), 'Entertainment agent' (responsible for multimedia entertainments with audio-visual effects, social robots, intra/internet), 'Digital assistant agent' (providing voice, IR, Bluetooth remote control of smart room equipment), 'Monitoring agent' (encompassing all embedded sensor systems in the smart room), 'Connectivity agent' (organizing different communication channels routing and protection) and 'Human-in-the-loop agent' (a real human factor participant). All connections are organized via the 'Connectivity agent' through different protocols: Wi-Fi, LAN, Bluetooth, LAN, Xbee, IR and for the 'Human-in-the-loop agent' - audio-visual and multimodal biometric ones.

11. Conclusion and Discussion

Modern smart homes have advanced significantly compared to those from the first half of the 20th century. This progress, however, has opened not only great opportunities and benefits, but also a number of threats to their inhabitants. Whilst some of these threats (classified in Table 1) look quite obvious, other related to entertainment, privacy and appliances (by means of emerging technologies) are hiding a number of unexplored domains. Examples for such new cyber threat areas are digital drugs (addiction to technologies) and social engineering that are especially important for the future generations of inhabitants of smart homes.

A suitable and promising framework approach for studying these problems is to combine experts' data, analysis, modelling, inhabitants and environment monitoring as well as practical validation through real experiments. This does not assure comprehensiveness, but at least provides plausibility of the near future technological progress and outlines measures to be taken it to account for their users.

References

[1] Harper, R. (Ed), Inside the smart home, Springer-Verlag Publ., 264p., 2003, ISBN 978-1-85233-688-2.

[2] Kidd C, Orr R, Abowd G, et al., The aware home: a living laboratory for ubiquitous computing research. CoBuild'99, Proceedings of the 2nd international workshop on cooperative buildings, integrating Information, Organization, and Architecture, Springer-Verlag Publ., 191-198, 1999.

[3] Intille S, Larson K, Tapia M, et al.. Using a live-in laboratory for ubiquitous computing research, Fishkin KP, Schiele B, Nixon P, Quiley A, editors. Proceedings of the 4th international conference on Pervasive Computing, PERVASIVE 2006, vol. LNCS, Berlin, Heidelberg, Springer-Verlag Publ., 349–365, 2006.

[4] Helal S, Mann W, et al., The Gator Tech Smart House: a programmable pervasive space, Computer, vol. 38, issue 3, 50–60, 2005.

[5] Tamura T, Togawa T, Ogawa M, Yoda M., Fully automated health monitoring system in the home. Medical Engineering & Physics, vol. 20, No 8, 573–579, 1998.

[6] Matsuoka K., Aware home understanding life activities. Towards a humanfriendly assistive environment, ICOST'2004, Proceedings of the international conference on smart homes and health telematics, IOS Press, 186–193, 2004.

[7] Yamazaki T., Beyond the smart home, ICHIT'06, Proceedings of the international conference on hybrid information technology, 350–355, 2006.

[8] Bonner S., Assisted interactive dwelling house, Assistive Technology Research series, 6, IOS Press, Amsterdam, 524-533, 1999, ISBN: 1586030019.

[9] Cerni M, Penhaker M., Circadian rhythm monitoring in homecare systems, Proceedings of the 13th International conference on biomedical engineering, Vol. 23, 950-953, 2009.

[10] Chan M, Campo E, Esteve D., Assessment of activity of elderly people using a home monitoring system. International Journal of Rehabilitation Research, March, Vol. 28, No. 1, 69–76, 2005.

[11] Perez-Lombard L, Ortiz J, Pout C. A review on buildings energy consumption information. Energy and Buildings. s.l. : Elsevier Publ., Vol. 40, 394-398, 2008.

[12] A, Bae. www.navigantresearch.com/blog/articles/smart-house-in-japan. [Online]

[13] Research, ABI, https://www.abiresearch.com/press/15-million-home-automation-systems-installed-in-th. [Online]

[14] Chan M, Esteve D, Escriba C, Campo E. A review of smart homes - present state and future challenges. Computer methods and programs in biomedicine. s.l. : Elsevier, Vol. 91, 55-81, 2008.
[15] De Silva L, Morikawa C, Petra I. State of the art of smart homes, Engineering Applications of Artificial Intelligence, Volume 25, Issue 7, 1313-1321, October, 2012.
[16] Trankler H, Kanoun O, Recent advances in sensor technology, Instrumentation and Measurement Technology Conference, IMTC 2001, 309-316, 2001.
[17] Khoshnoud, F, De Silva, C, Recent advances in MEMS sensor technology – biomedical applications, Instrumentation and Measurement, Vol 15, no 1, 8-14, 2012.
[18] Fisher, J, 2006. Indoor Positioning and Digital Management: Emerging Surveillance Regimes in Hospitals. , Surveillance and Security: Technological Politics and Power in Everyday Life, New York: Routledge, 77–88, 2006.
[19] Hanshen G, Wang D., A Content-aware Fridge based on RFID in smart home for home-healthcare , 11th International Conference on Advanced Communication Technology ICACT 2009, Vol. 2, 987-990, 2009.
[20] Newitz A., The RFID Hacking Underground, http://www.wired.com/wired/archive/14.05/rfid.html [Online]
[21] Dixon C, Mahajan R, Agarwal S, Brush A, Bongshin L, Saroiu S, Bahl V, An Operating System for the Home, Microsoft Research – Publications, Microsoft, April, 2012.
[22] Borges I, Smart home: Independence or isolation for older people? http://www.age-platform.eu/images/stories/EN/pdf_AGE_Presentation__Senior_project.pdf [Online]
[23] Computerworld, October 2012, http://www.computerworld.com/s/article/9232477/Pacemaker_hack_can_deliver_deadly_830_volt_jolt [Online]
[24] Greenspon A., et al, Trends in Permanent Pacemaker Implantation in the United States from 1993 to 2009, Journal of the American College of Cardiology, vol. 60, issue 16, 1540-1545, October, 2012.
[25] U.S. Department of Homeland Security, Privacy Impact Assessment for the Initiative Three Exercise 3, March 2010, http://www.dhs.gov/xlibrary/assets/privacy/privacy_pia_nppd_initiative3exercise.pdf [Online]
[26] Symantec Corp., Internet Security Threat Report 2013, Volume 18, http://www.symantec.com/content/en/us/enterprise/other_resources/b-istr_main_report_v18_2012_21291018.en-us.pdf [Online]
[27] Sophos, Security Threat Report 2013, http://www.sophos.com/en-us/medialibrary/PDFs/other/sophossecuritythreatreport2013.pdf [Online]
[28] The Red Book. The SysSec Roadmap for Systems Security Research, The SysSec Consortium, 2013, http://www.red-book.eu/m/documents/syssec_red_book.pdf [Online]
[29] Minchev, Z., Boyanov, L., Georgiev, S. Security of Future Smart Homes. Cyber-Physical Threats Identification Perspectives, In Proceedings of National conference with international participation in realization of the EU project 'Development of Tools Needed to Coordinate Inter-sectorial Power and Transport CIP Activities at a Situation of Multilateral Terrorist Threat. Increase of the Capacity of Key CIP Objects in Bulgaria', at Grand Hotel "Sofia", Sofia city, Bulgaria, June 4, 165-169, 2013.
[30] Minchev, Z., Shalamanov, V., Scenario Generation and Assessment Framework Solution in Support of the Comprehensive Approach, In Proceedings of SAS-081 Symposium on "Analytical Support to Defence Transformation", RTO-MP-SAS-081, Sofia, Boyana, April 26 – 28, 22-1 – 22-16, 2010.
[31] Vester, F. The Art of Interconnected Thinking, MCB Verlag GmbH, Munich, 2007.
[32] Minchev, Z. Generalized Nets Representation of Biological Inspired Multi-Agent Based Modelling, In Proceedings of BIOPS'05, Sofia, Bulgaria, October 25-26, III.81-III.94, 2005.
[33] A Conceptual Generalized Nets Immunological Model for Agent based Exploration of Unknown Environment, International Journal BIOAUTOMATION, 14(1), 49-60, 2010.

[34] Georgiev, S., Kolev, H., Obreshkov, N., Lalev, E. Security System for Future Smart Homes, In Proceedings of National conference with international participation in realization of the EU project 'Development of Tools Needed to Coordinate Inter-sectorial Power and Transport CIP Activities at a Situation of Multilateral Terrorist Threat. Increase of the Capacity of Key CIP Objects in Bulgaria', at Grand Hotel “Sofia”, Sofia city, Bulgaria, June 4, 91-100, 2013.

[35] Georgiev, S., Minchev, Z. An Evolutionary Prototyping for Smart Home Inhabitants Wearable Biomonitoring, In Proceedings of Conjoint Scientific Seminar ‘Modelling and Control of Information Processes’, Institute of Mathematics and Informatics, Sofia, Bulgaria, November 19, 2013 (in press)

[36] DFNI T01/4 Project Web Page, www.smarthomesbg.com. [Online]

Cyber Security and Resiliency Policy Framework
A. Vaseashta et al. (Eds.)
IOS Press, 2014

doi:10.3233/978-1-61499-446-6-115

Development of Defense-Oriented Application Software under Fire: The Case of Israel

Galit M. BEN-ISRAEL (Fixler)[1]
Beit-Berl Academic College
Beit Berl 4490500, ISRAEL

Abstract. This paper presents an analysis of the efforts to develop new application software under fire by innovators of the Israeli start-up nation. The applications were developed voluntarily by Israeli civilians living in Tel Aviv during Operation Pillar of Defense in November 2012. At the time when the IDF (Israel Defense Forces) was engaged in a military attack on Gaza, codenamed "Pillar of Defense", the armed Palestinian militant groups Hamas and Palestinian Islamic Jihad were firing Grad and Kassam rockets at civilians in the State of Israel's home front. The new applications were designated to mark and map the locations of public shelters during emergencies in Israeli cities and towns for the benefit of civilians regularly using smartphones and applications. These applications were the brainchildren of Israeli home front civilians who wanted to help themselves as well as others who could find themselves trapped under rocket fire in the "City of Tel Aviv" for the first time in their lives (apart from Iraqi missiles in the winter of 1991 during the "Gulf War"). This article originated in and was written as a result of the personal experiences of this writer on the home front of the State of Israel in the physical and digital expanses (social media, Web 2.0) during "Operation Pillar of Defense", in November 2012.

Keywords: Operation "Pillar of Defense", application software, innovators, start-up nation, rockets, developers, Tel Aviv, Hamas, shelters, emergencies, smartphones, missiles, home front, (social media, Web 2.0)

1. Introduction: The Web 2.0 Era

The world has changed completely: first, at the end of the 20th Century, the internet (Web 1.0) entered into people's everyday life; second, at the beginning of the 21st Century, Google and the social media revolution (Web 2.0) together with the invention of the smartphone, iPhone, Android, tablets and apps (application software) became life itself. Nowadays 85% of the people in the world have internet access and nearly 25% of the people in the world use social media [1]. The Web 2.0 Era [2] is one of users who fill the empty platforms with information and know-how by means of Google searches and by uploading statuses, posts, photographs, video clips, films and music, tweeting tweets as well as location updates on social media (Facebook, Twitter, Instagram, Pinterest, YouTube, Reddit, Waze, etc.).

[1]E-mail: galitbif@gmail.com

In the modern "Old World", knowledge and information was held by the authorities and the media [3]. In the postmodern-global-digital "New World", knowledge is concurrently distributed, diffused and accessible to the authorities and the media as well as to the masses ("wisdom of crowds", "crowdsourcing") and the digital entrepreneurs [4]. The latter two groups are in most cases more agile, faster and better skilled than the institutional ones, and are active and unwilling to wait for orders or for procedures that are delayed by institutional bureaucracy. They require innovations, assistance, and the fastest and most efficient and easiest form of help and support. They want simultaneous replies to their queries. The internet world and even more the social media have turned us all into clients, and if we do not receive the service we want to our satisfaction, we will disconnect ourselves from the authorities. As a result, the hierarchies between the authorities and the masses have become destabilized and the requirements have to be rapidly adapted to suit the digital time of the Web 2.0 Era.

2. The Age of Smartphones - The Era of Applications (Apps)

The majority of people in the Western world, and especially the younger ones among them, experience the world and its inhabitants through and by means of their mobile dashboard/icons/apps, which lead us all to communicate differently among ourselves, to do business differently, to act differently during crises, and at the end of the day – to live differently. Smartphones are our personal friends. We peek at them the last thing before going to bed at night and the moment we wake up and open our eyes in the morning. "In the U.S.A, 25% of smartphone owners aged 18–44 say they can't recall the last time their smartphone wasn't next to them" [5]. You can reach people almost anytime, since they have their smartphones with them almost always. We live in a riveting era in which we are all permanently interconnected.

The mobile revolution has enabled billions of people to communicate with each other. By 2014 there will be 7.3 billion mobiles in the world. The mobile has tipped the balance of power, transferring it from a mere handful of people – to almost everyone. The prices of smartphones are falling and more than a billion units have been sold in 2013. Millions of people don't have a desktop or laptop and their main source of communication is the mobile smartphone [6].

It is an established fact that the smartphone, tablet and phablet have taken over our lives. These devices have become enjoyable, informative and especially effective for their owners because of the enormous amount of apps available today on the market. According to Gartner's market survey in 2013, 102 billion apps have been downloaded, 91% of which were reported to be freeware downloads that have created incomes to the value of $26 billion (though each app is measured by its frequency of usage and extent of its coverage rather than by the number of people who have downloaded it) [7]. Studies published by the Global WebIndex research center in November 2013 have shown a steady decline in the usage by youngsters in 30 countries throughout the world of Facebook, the worldwide popular social network [8]. And what have the adolescents who abandoned Facebook replaced it with? Unsurprisingly, they are chiefly using apps, mostly correspondence apps, which they can surf on their smartphones.

As well as all the social media apps, Google Maps is the most frequently used mobile app in the world, according to GlobalWebIndex data on global smartphone users in Q2 of 2013 (969.49 million users). 54% of all smartphone owners used Google Maps during 2013. The top three apps after Google's popular mapping tool are

Facebook (44% of smartphone users), YouTube (35% of users) and Google+ (30% of users). Others are WeChat, Twitter, Skype, Facebook messenger, WhatsApp and Instagram [9].

The most popular Israeli app is Waze, a freeware GPS community-based traffic navigation app for smartphones developed by the Israeli start-up Waze Mobile and sold to Google in June 2013. As of then, approximately 51 million drivers have used this app. Waze provides turn-by-turn information and user-submitted travel times and route details, downloading location-dependent information over the mobile telephone network [10]. The program works co-operatively and is updated by the community of users (crowdsourcing) [11]. Information provided by each user is transferred to all the other program users in order to update roads, landmarks and house numbers as well as to send warnings regarding heavy traffic, police patrol cars, and obstacles on the road. Furthermore, information regarding speed and location is sent anonymously from each user and this enables the app to plan smart routes. The program also enables all its active users to track their individual location on the map and to communicate with one another by a "ping" (sending a request to chat).

3. Disaster Management in the Age of the Smartphone

The steadily increasing use, by young people as well as by others all over the world, of smartphones and apps – especially of apps for correspondence, location/check in, and maps – suits to a T successful conduct during emergencies. At such times, you need a smartphone and several important lifesaving apps: a shelters app, a maps app, a location app, an emergency force app and a message/correspondence app [12].

Because Waze is an app that is applicable for every smartphone and is based on wisdom of crowds/crowdsourcing to build its own map, it could be a perfect app during or after a disaster. It is an app that warns of obstacles on roads, directs and navigates, and also gathers data on overloads and obstacles, etc. Furthermore, it can function as a social network forwarding notices of disasters, reassurances and resilience. At present, the Waze app also enables public authorities to send warnings of hazards and approaching dangers. This is an example of how private initiative has succeeded in combining the wisdom of the driver-masses in order to bestow meaningful significance to an empty platform. It also enables the governmental authorities to succeed in giving assistance, especially in emergencies and within the private platform, in the form of knowledge that only they possess [13].

Location-based apps are the hottest thing going in the mobile world from the economic aspect of the innovators, Waze Location, Facebook Places, Foursquare, Location-Based Social Media, and they are just the tool for coping with disaster episodes, enabling people to receive reports on places that can save them during a disaster. Location Based Service (LBS), an app for mobile communication equipment, pinpoints the geographical location of the equipment and utilizes this ability to supply the user with essential information. A component common to the majority of location-based social networks is the ability to perform an act known as "check in" that notifies the user's friends of his/her whereabouts, for example, in disaster and resilience situations, using applications like: “Lost and Found People” tracking, “Situational Awareness” applications, and “Asset and Need” tracking applications" [14, 12]. A few hours before hurricane Sandy (October 2012) struck, 5 apps were suggested in the East

Coast: American Red Cross: Disaster Readiness, iMapWeather Radio, Disaster Alert and Red Panic Button [15].

4. Operation Pillar of Defense in the Age of the Smartphone

The case study for this article deals with the shelters apps that were developed during the IDF Operation Pillar of Defense in November 2012. After rockets were fired on Tel Aviv during the IDF Operation Pillar of Defense, messages could not be sent on most of the cellular networks, but the internet continued to function. The Home Front Digital Media segmented contents, segmented surfers and maintained an ongoing, mostly infographic, multi-channel dialogue with surfers, but this did not satisfy "the young and the restless" and consequently the most interesting activity in the digital sphere was the development of Defense-Oriented Application software by civilian volunteers.

5. Operation Pillar of Defense, November 2012

Operation Pillar of Defense (Hebrew: Amúd Anán, literally: Pillar of Cloud) was an eight-day IDF operation in the Hamas-governed Gaza Strip. It was officially launched on 14 November 2012 with the killing of Ahmed Jabari, chief of the Gaza military wing of Hamas. The Israel government stated that the aims of the military operation were to halt rocket attacks, originating from the Gaza Strip, against civilian targets and to disrupt the capabilities of militant organizations. During the course of the operation the IDF struck more than 1,500 sites in the Gaza Strip, including rocket launch pads, arms depots, government facilities and apartment blocks [16].

Throughout the operation, Hamas, the al-Qassam Brigades and the Palestinian Islamic Jihad further intensified their rocket attacks on Israeli cities and towns, in an operation code named Operation Stones of Baked Clay (Arabic: حجارة سجيل, ḥijārat sajīl) by the al-Qassam Brigades, firing over 1,456 rockets (Fajr 5, Grad rockets, Qassams) and mortars into Israel, and an additional 142 which fell inside Gaza itself. Some of these weapons were fired into Rishon LeZion, Beersheba, Ashdod, Ashkelon and other population centers; Tel Aviv was hit for the first time since the 1991 Gulf War, and rockets were fired at Jerusalem! The rockets killed three Israeli civilians in a direct hit on a home in Kiryat Malachi. By the end of the operation, six Israelis had been killed, 240 were injured, and more than 200 had been treated for shock by Magen David Adom. Israel's Iron Dome missile defense system intercepted about 421 rockets, another 142 rockets fell on Gaza itself, 875 rockets fell in open areas, and 58 rockets hit urban areas in Israel [17].

Operation Pillar of Defense, as well as the rounds of escalation that preceded it, proved that the Iron Dome, one of the systems of the defense doctrine against high-trajectory fire that Israel developed over the years, does not provide complete defense despite its interception successes. Rockets penetrated the defense system causing property damage and personal injuries. These incidents also brought home the realization that the real problem was not the physical damage that the rockets caused – damage that was ultimately negligible, as also was the loss of lives as unfortunate as it happened to be – but rather the fact that in each separate event about one million Israeli civilians were forced to remain in shelters. Schools and other educational institutions were closed down by order of the Home Front Command, and in consequence numerous workers did not attend their workplaces – because parents had to stay home with their children [18].

The rocket attack on Israel did not come as a big surprise because Israel has been under attack by rocket fire for many years. The first instance of rocket fire against Israel was on 16 September 1968, when rockets were fired from the direction of Jordan toward Beit She'an [19]. Especially remembered are the periods during which the communities of the Galilee Panhandle were shelled during the nineteen seventies; the Second Lebanese War in 2006, during which Israel was hit by over 4000 rockets in a single month; and the incessant firing from the Gaza Strip over the last decade [20]. However, the rocket attack on Tel Aviv and Gush Dan (the Dan Region) was a huge surprise and shocked civilians in the home front even though such an escalation had been widely discussed in the public domain.

6. Rockets Falling on Tel-Aviv

Citizens of the Israeli home front or the "State of Tel-Aviv", living the good life of the Western world in the global postmodern 21st century, were made to face a modern attack of rockets from the previous century, which threatened their erstwhile relatively peaceful civilian lives. Such a situation had not occurred in Israel since 1991 (the Gulf War), during which missiles were fired at Tel Aviv and the surroundings as well as at other regions in Israel. The peripheral rear in Israel – but not Tel Aviv – usually suffers such blows routinely.

As citizens of one of the most connected countries in the world, Israelis have become accustomed to using cutting edge technology. Since the start of Operation Pillar of Defense they have come to rely on their smartphones, with new apps and sites keeping them safe and informed. But not everyone in Tel Aviv was on the ball when the first siren alert went off in the city. According to residents in some parts of the city, the sound of the sirens was very faint and people indoors where music was playing did not hear any alarm.

A useful tool for tracking attack locations is the Red Alert warning app, which lists where the latest siren alerts are taking place. The app warns users when a missile is on the way, enabling them to immediately run for cover. The app users are able to delimit the alerts to specific areas, and are also able to send comments and messages of encouragement to those under attack. Meanwhile, the Home Front Defense Ministry's maps show how long residents of each area have to get to a safe place before the missile hits the area. Secure Spaces will tell you where to hide, while Google Maps pages also list the protected spaces in the city [21].

7. Development of Defense-Oriented Application Software by Civilian Volunteers Under Fire During Operation Pillar of Defense, November 2012

At the time, the sources offered by the authorities apparently failed to satisfy the young innovators and in consequence the values of resourcefulness, initiative and volunteerism under defensive environmental hardship served as the catalyst for the development of apps showing the map locations of shelters. The apps were all freeware and invented under fire within a day or two by Tel Aviv's Israeli high-tech innovators – men who, for the first time in their lives, had to face an atypical situation for Israelis, and especially for Israelis of their kind. They were not doing military service under fire, nor were they doing military reserve service under fire (as do most Israeli men and also, to a lesser extent, do women). They were not residents of the (northern and southern) peripheral towns but rather residents of Tel Aviv (in the Dan Region), a place that has been unaccustomed to suffering under war/enemy fire. They found themselves involved willy-nilly in a state of emergency in a civilian home front under attack – a civilian rear in the center of the country, not on its periphery. They therefore retaliated by inventing apps that would enable them, their families, their friends and the entire civilian environment under attack, to find shelter from rocket fire as quickly as possible.

All the developed apps were free, shared and open sourced in order to enable other people in other areas to adapt the app to their particular situation and location at the time. The first of these developers was Lior Si'on, the CTO of the start-up GetTaxi, an app for taxi drivers and taxi bookers based on smartphone and location. Si'on was taking a walk with his young son on the day the first rockets landed in Tel Aviv. "I realized that I had no idea where the nearest shelter was", he recalls. This understanding led him to acquire the data base listing all the shelters located throughout Tel Aviv, which he placed on a map. He then developed an application that could be installed in any smartphone for the purpose of informing users of the nearest shelter according to their actual location. Si'on describes how he creates his Shelter Finder [22], in a slideshare presentation [23], and on YouTube [24], both social media tools, and also on his blog:

Several months ago, during the short war that struck Tel Aviv (after the long war in the South...) I decided to take some spare time in order to write a Shelter Finder app – something simple that could show in real time where the nearest shelter is relative to your own location. There were a number of basic requirements: a): Could be done quickly – what with the war and little Nebo, especially at the week-end, I did not have much time to spare. b): Could be rapidly distributed – iPhone app, for example, is out of the question because approving it takes at least a week. c): Should be interesting – in order to enable me to learn something new while being easily updated – even though I created the app for Tel Aviv shelters, I wanted to enable easy updating of information on shelters in other towns. d) Should be efficient and easily amended. I decided to utilize the Tel Aviv municipality free data banks (with listed shelters) – and with the courteous assistance of Eitan Schwarz who helped me find them – I soon had access to the information I required. In order to make distribution easy I decided to go for html5, which afforded me information on locality on new computers and smartphones. I thought it would be nice, as a bonus, to enable the app to be executed client-side.

I have to admit that I spent most of my time on the api (application programming interface) and the Tel Aviv municipality data banks. They were unclear, inconvenient, and I was finally almost completely unable to utilize them. They perhaps subsequently helped me implement several more of the aims of the app (chiefly learning something new and providing efficiency and agility in making amendments) – but in real time they only engendered a great deal of frustration. I subsequently conceded and simply took all the data bank. I wanted initially to enter it inside the app page, which would thereby be enabled to become very fast as well as totally independent server wise – not bad at all! But eventually, and mainly because of the problems of Hebrew conversion in my Mac of data that I received (in Excel...) – I chose something slightly different.

I thought it would be a nice bonus to make the entire app executed client side. Google tools are good at working with themselves – and a new (beta) service called

Fusion enables data from a Google doc to be combined with Google maps – perfect. All that I needed was a list of addresses, enter them in a Google doc and undergo geocoding in a Google map – and from that moment on everything contained in the doc appears on the map. As simple as that! [25]

The second developer was Omri Baumer, the national strength Hackathon initiator who organized a Hackathon meeting of initiators and developers under the sponsorship of Google Tel Aviv during the attack on civilians in the Israeli home front. According to Baumer, he noticed at the time that "there are numerous people with ability, such as graduates of the 8200 (the elite IDF intelligence unit) as well as all kinds of developers who are willing to assist in bolstering the home front." He decided to organize them as a group on a Facebook page. Within a single day, 400 such innovators were organized on a Facebook group and together they developed the following apps: 1). A Mobile App for Eran (Voluntary humanitarian assistance). 2). An App designated for chats with civilians in enemy countries. 3). A family app for contacting family members during or after a rocket fall in order to ascertain that they are alright [26].

The third developer was Ori Segal of **"Secure Spaces"**, iApps Technologies. His company initiated an app named Secure Spaces for the benefit of State of Israel civilians who are unable to hear (due to deafness, double glazing, etc.) the siren alert for a nearby rocket fall on the home front. This is an app functioning in cooperation with local municipalities and showing all the protected spaces located around the spot where the person is presently located or intends to go to. The app aspires to help people anywhere find the protected spaces nearest to them. The developer company works in cooperation with the municipality security officers during regular times as well as during crises. The app has an additional important function, namely broadcasting information to the emergency authorities regarding your whereabouts should you become injured or trapped in a building that has been destroyed in a disaster. Segal maintains that he works hand in glove with the municipalities and that they supply him with all the required information [27].

The fourth developer was Yuval Tissona, CEO of Zebrapps, is the developer of The Next War app [28]. He began to develop this app close to the critical situation of Operation Pillar of Defense. At the time of the crisis he came to realize the extent of the necessity of his app and continued to develop it further during and also after the operation. The app enables access to all the public shelters in Israel. It indicates the location of the nearest public shelter when you happen to be in the public domain during a rockets falling alert. The app contains a flashlight, access to Galei Zahal (the IDF radio station) and another two items. Like Si'on, Tissona claims that the municipalities find it difficult or do not want to supply the required information in the correct format. The data regarding the list of shelters is inaccessible and that is why he developed his app [29].

8. What Caused the Flowering of Freeware Emergency Apps in the Minds of the Digitals?

1. Shelters in the State of Israel are a must in every home/building, street, and neighborhood. All of them have shelters; all the buildings that have been built during the past 20 years have, in addition to a communal shelter in the building, also a security room ("mamad") in each apartment [30]. There are also urban/neighborhood public shelters that remain open. When you are

under fire and there is a sudden alert and you are in the middle of the street, shopping, going to school, or whatever, you could become panic stricken, hysterical, and bewildered. One click on the shelters app on your smartphone solves everything. A map of the shelters opens up showing you, by means of the GPS on your smartphone, the location of the shelter nearest to you, enabling you to run immediately to it for lifesaving protection.

2. The feeling of entrapment, of the inability to respond to the missile attack by civilians at home motivated Israeli developers and New Media actors to invest material and intellectual capital in ventures that would benefit the home front and Israeli information services. In addition, civilians volunteered their help in numerous initiatives.
3. Over most of the years of its existence the State of Israel has been termed "A Nation in Uniform" (that maintains a "civilian military") and "Democracy of the Barracks" [31]. However, most of the researchers and other participants in the public discourse tended to define Israel "positively" as a "mobilized nation whose civilians serve as soldiers called up to defend their homeland in times of need and take off their uniforms when the danger has passed, without affecting the standing of the military in society." According to this argument, the military has no influence "beyond the requirement" on the political, economic and cultural domains [32] and therefore it is not a country under direct military rule with decisive influence on the political institutions [33], or a country-cum- military base [34]. Consequently, when the Tel Aviv Israeli men who had all completed their full military service (combat or noncombat) found themselves in a security emergency in the civilian rear, they felt that they should "do something" and their contribution was to develop freeware apps for the benefit of civilians. It therefore follows that Israel is also a 21st Century Hi-tech Digital country though it is also a nation in uniform that maintains a military comprising civilians who are ready to volunteer at critical times. It's in the "DNA" (metaphorically speaking) of the Israelis.
4. The directions to run to the public shelter or to the security room in your home, or to go into the stairwell and stand between two walls and wait for the successful interception of the rocket or for it to fall in a desolate region or, worse than that, for it to fall near you, are helpful and lifesaving but they also weaken you psychologically and morally and instill fear in your heart. As opposed to that, a smartphone app is something that strengthens both your personal and your family's psychological security. It enables you to click on the app icon and then run to the nearest shelter, which are active procedures that have an intensification and enhancement effect on the civilian.
5. In their bestselling book *Start-up Nation*, Dan Senor and Saul Singer attempt to unravel the special connection between the State of Israel and the innumerable start-up companies born within its unique environment. Senor and Singer assign that success to, among other things, difficult constraints factors (e.g. limited natural resources, unfriendly neighbors), and argue that these have positioned Israel with "its back to the wall". This pressure, which has motivated the taking of personal and national responsibility, has provoked the unprecedented creativity that has been translated into national survival. Evidence of the success of this innovativeness – and confirmation of the Senor and Singer thesis – can be found in technological developments of applications [35].

6. In addition to being a Start-up Nation, Israel is also an Application Nation. Israelis are world leaders in the utilization and development of apps. There are 1500 apps developers in the country and they are responsible for one out of every 200 app implementations worldwide and to approximately 5000 apps marketed to date. The amount of time that Israelis spend using apps is the longest recorded. The Israeli is the heaviest app user in the world, spending on the average 80 minutes of app utilization per day. Israelis also stand high, relative to other nationals, on the index of scope of downloading apps [36].
7. Today digital people throughout the world as well as in Israel want digital solutions for their distress situations. The need comes from below, from the masses, and this obligates the authorities. The possibility of updating the municipality website/home front network as to the location of the shelter nearest to your home before the crisis occurs is not interesting, challenging, or user friendly in the eyes of the digital person in the Web 2.0 era. People, especially those who are young, want to have the instrument, the means of obtaining solutions/assistance and the management of the crisis, all in one downloads on their smartphone. They want to update by means of a tweet or status or uploaded picture, or by tracking the crisis situation around them. For example: an Israeli application called "Emergency Situation" offers the possibility of dialing quickly to all the emergency numbers of the authorities and private companies. It also includes first aid instructions in the case of a crisis such as an outbreak of fire, etc. [37].
8. Nowadays the public, and especially the younger set, prefer data rather than voice messages. 86% of smartphone owners regularly use only immediate correspondence apps, but only 75% do this by texting SMSs while 73% of them send proper word messages on their smartphones [38]. That is why they prefer to click on a map app for shelters or on an announcement regarding the emergency situation they are in rather than to dial the emergency numbers supplied by the authorities. Throughout the world there is a sharp decrease among youngsters in dialing to the authorities' emergency numbers during crises and a rise in uploading on social media informatory statuses regarding emergencies on your personal profile (for your friends) as well as, but to smaller extent, on the wall of the emergency authorities page in the social networks. And on top of all this, another problem arises when the line (the Voice) of the emergency number usually fails and there is no connection. In such a situation how could citizens possibly call in and report? Again data and an app will solve the problem.

9. Summary:

1. While the communications infrastructure (line and cellular) collapses, either because of physical damage incurred during the event or because of overloading due to pressure by callers, the internet has proved to be an infrastructure that survives.
2. The cell phone, and especially the smartphone, has become the most important means of communication in times of emergency, both for searching for information and for processing it, but chiefly for publicizing and disseminating information. This technology has almost become the sole

communication channel that continues working and remains readily available under all conditions.
3. There is an increase in data over the world – data in preference to voice.
4. Smartphones, phablets and tablets are being used in preference to computers, mobiles and stationary phones.
5. Correspondence and text messaging apps, disaster apps, social networks apps and location apps are in use in preference to all other methods.
6. Today people, and especially young ones, like those discussed in the case study in this article, are initiators, high tech careerists, gadget and applications lovers ready to co-operate freely and eager for free co-operation, especially in times of emergencies. Today, private companies and the public are ahead of the authorities. People love to help and want to do so by means of the wisdom of crowds and co-operation between crowds and with the authorities.
7. Technology can help play its part in preventing further casualties in times of disaster.
8. The stories of these inventors provide inspiration and models for emulation for people caught in the midst of emergencies and other crises (e.g., earthquakes, tsunamis, and mega terror attacks) throughout the world.

10. Conclusions: What should the authorities do?

1. In a global and digital world; the future is very brittle, fragile and unforeseen. With all the half-yearly fast technological inventions it has become difficult to impossible to forecast forthcoming events. In the future, the authorities will have to incorporate Telephone for adults and Web 2.0 and apps for youngsters.
2. The authorities should be attentive to digital technological inventions, in accordance with the wishes of their citizens.
3. Smartphones, mobiles and social media will replace emergency services. The state should offer these services because that is what numerous citizens want.
4. The authorities, especially the emergency forces, should engage in crowdsourcing.
5. The authorities should incorporate young entrepreneurship in times of emergency.

References:

[1] I. Ahmad, "Global Internet, Mobile and Social Media Engagement and Usage Stats and Facts", Socialmedia today, December 11, 2013, URL: http://socialmediatoday.com/irfan-ahmad/1993606/global-overview-internet-mobile-and-social-media-engagement-and-usage-infographi [Accessed: 20 January 2014].

[2] P. Anderson, "What is Web 2.0? - Ideas, technologies and implications for education", *JISC Technology and Standards Watch*, (Feb. 2007). 2-64, URL: http://www.jisc.ac.uk/media/documents/techwatch/tsw0701b.pdf [Accessed: 20 January 2014].

[3] D. Bell, "The Third Technological Revolution", *Dissent*, **Vol. 36**, No. 2, (Spring 1989), 164-176.

[4] J. Surowiecki, *The Wisdom of Crowds*. Anchor Books, New York, 2005.
[5] B. B. Cooper, "10 Surprising Social Media Statistics That Might Make You Rethink Your Social Strategy", buffer blog, July 16th, 2013, URL: http://blog.bufferapp.com/10-surprising-social-media-statistics-that-will-make-you-rethink-your-strategy [Accessed: 25 December 2013].
[6] J. Pramis, "Number of mobile phones to exceed world population by 2014", Digital Trends, February 28, 2013, URL: http://www.digitaltrends.com/mobile/mobile-phone-world-population-2014/#!D37Fv [Accessed: 25 December 2013].
[7] "Technology, media and telecommunications predictions 2013", Deloitte, URL:https://www.deloitte.com/assets/Dcom-Shared%20Assets/Documents/TMT%20Predictions%202013%20PDFs/dttl_TMT_Predictions2013_Final.pdf [Accessed: 20 February 2014].
[8] D. Maeve & A. Smith, "Social Media Update 2013 - 42% of online adults use multiple social networking sites, but Facebook remains the platform of choice", Pew Research Internet Project, December 30, 2013, URL: http://www.pewinternet.org/2013/12/30/social-media-update-2013/ [Accessed: 20 February 2014].
[9] Z. Fox, "The 10 Most Frequently Used Smartphone Apps", Mashable, August 5, 2013, URL: http://mashable.com/2013/08/05/most-used-smartphone-apps/ [Accessed: 20 February 2014].
[10] A. Maierbrugger, "Google buys map-software provider Waze for $1b". Inside Investor, 13 June 2013, URL: http://investvine.com/google-buys-map-software-provider-waze-for-1b/ [Accessed: 20 February 2014].
[11] D. Hardawar, "Waze revs up crowdsourced driving app with $25M", VB NEWS, December 7, 2010, URL: http://venturebeat.com/2010/12/07/waze-revs-up-crowdsourced-driving-app-with-25m/
[Accessed: 25 December 2013].
[12] N. O. Palmer, Smartphones: A Platform For Disaster Management, A thesis submitted for the degree of Doctor of Philosophy, VRIJE University, 2012, URL: http://www.cs.vu.nl/~bal/NickPalmer-PhD-thesis.pdf [Accessed: 25 December 2013].
[13] R. Kim, "How Waze's crowd-sourced data helped FEMA deliver the gas after Sandy", Gigaom, November. 6, 2012, URL: http://gigaom.com/2012/11/06/how-wazes-crowd-sourced-data-helped-fema-deliver-the-gas-after-sandy/ [Accessed: 24 December 2012].
[14] See (12).
[15] "Five apps to get you through a natural disaster", FoxNews.com, October 29, 2012, URL: http://www.foxnews.com/tech/2012/10/29/apps-to-get-through-natural-disaster [Accessed: 24 December 2012].
[16] "Operation Pillar of Defense", Israel Security Agency, URL: http://www.shabak.gov.il/English/EnTerrorData/Reviews/Pages/OperationPillarofDefense.aspx [Accessed: 24 November 2013].
[17] "Operation Pillar of Defense: Summary of Events", Israel Defense Forces, URL: http://www.idfblog.com/2012/11/22/operation-pillar-of-defense-summary-of-events/
[Accessed: 24 November 2013].
[18] A. Harel & A. Issacharoff, "Lessons of the Escalation in the South – The Iron Dome has granted the political leadership an important but limited achievement, Israel's wakeup call", *"Haaretz"*, March 16, 2012. [Hebrew].
[19] The "Davar" correspondent, "For the first time the terrorists have triggered heavy weapons when bombarding Beit She'an", *"Davar"*, September 18, 1968. [Hebrew].
[20] Y. Shafir, "Lessons from the Iron Dome", *Army and Strategic*, **Vol 5**, No. 1, (April 2013), 1. [Hebrew].
[21] Apps and websites help Israelis stay safe, Jewish News One, November 19, 2012, URL: http://jn1.tv/video/israel?media_id=74720 [Accessed: 20 February 2014].
[22] Shelter Finder, URL: https://s3-eu-west-1.amazonaws.com/findshelters/index.html) [Accessed: 20 February 2014]. [Hebrew].

[23] L. Si'on, Development and new media under fire, February 15, 2013, URL: http://www.youtube.com/watch?v=YoO8HqYJvCU [Accessed: 20 February 2014]. [Hebrew].

[24] L. Si'on, ShelterFinder's presentation, Slideshare, Feb 17, 2013, URL:http://www.slideshare.net/ISOCIL/ss-16581100 [Accessed: 2 February 2014].

[25] L. Si'on, ShelterFinder app, February 2013, URL: http://lior.sion.co.il/ [Accessed: 2 February 2014]. [Hebrew].

[26] O. Baumer, Development and new media under fire, February 15, 2013, URL: https://www.youtube.com/watch?v=qO53mkj_slI [Accessed: 14 February 2014].

[27] O. Segal Development and new media under fire, February 15, 2013, URL: https://www.youtube.com/watch?v=irrWZrhS-80 [Accessed: 14 February 2014]. [Hebrew].

[28] Y. Tissona, The Next War app's presentation, Slideshare, URL: http://www.slideshare.net/ISOCIL/ss-16580950 [Accessed: 8 February 2014]. [Hebrew].

[29] Y. Tissona, Development and new media under fire, February 15, 2013, URL: https://www.youtube.com/watch?v=vH1h7siwGac [Accessed: 8 February 2014]. [Hebrew].

[30] 'Mamad' or shelter - Home front Regulations", Architecture and construction in Israel, URL: http://www.architecture.org.il/info_hokim_haga.php [Accessed: 20 February 2014]. [Hebrew].

[31] G. Ben-Dor, "Politics and the Military in Israel in the Seventies", In: M. Lisk & E. Gutmann (eds.) *Israeli Political System*, Am Oved, Tel Aviv, 1979, 411- 432. [Hebrew].

[32] R. Luckham, "A Comparative Typology of Civil-Military Relations", *Government and Opposition*, **Vol. 6**, No 1, (1971), 24-25.

[33] H. Lasswell, "The Garrison State", *American Journal of Sociology*, **Vol. 46**, No. 4, (1941), 455-468.

[34] D. Rapoport, "A Comparative Theory of Military and Political Types", In: Samuel Huntington (ed.), *Changing Patterns of Military Politics*, The Free Press, New York, 1962, 71-101.

[35] D. Senor and S. Singer, *Start-up Nation: The Story of Israel's Economic Miracle*, Twelve Hachette Book Group, New York, 2009.

[36] M. Orbach, "The Israelis are World Leaders in the Utilization and Development of Applications", *"Calcalist"*, October 2, 2013, URL: http://www.calcalist.co.il/articles/0,7340,L-3613346,00.html [Accessed: 20 January 2014]. [Hebrew].

[37] M. Matzliach, "Closest public shelter smartphone app for southern residents", No Fryers, November 19, 2012, URL: http://nofryers.com/closest-public-shelter-smartphone-app-for-southern-residents-in-israel/ [Accessed: 20 January 2014].

[38] A. Tsinakos & M. Ally, "Global Mobile Learning Implementations and Trends", China Central Radio & TV University Press, 2013, URL: http://www.crtvup.com.cn/ad/top_gg/image/globalMobileLearning.pdf, [Accessed: 20 January 2014].

Cyber Security and Resiliency Policy Framework
A. Vaseashta et al. (Eds.)
IOS Press, 2014

doi:10.3233/978-1-61499-446-6-127

Education as a Long-Term Strategy for Cyber Security

P. PALE[1]
Faculty of Electrical Engineering and Computing
University of Zagreb, CROATIA

Abstract. Most strategies and policies for cyber security are in essence reactive since they devise (counter) measures for known problems or quantitative forecasts of known problems. A long term strategy should predict new problems qualitatively. The problem with cyber security stems from the fact that cyberspace will invade physical space almost completely, including human bodies. The speed of changes in the way people live and work; as well as the emergence of new, related security problems, is accelerating while legislative and technical counter measures merely react on detected problems. Moreover, that critical mass of humans which should recognize risks, dangers and attacks in cyberspace does not, and does not have required knowledge and skills. In addition the general population is at risk for cyber security incidents due to his/her ignorance or to the mere statistical probability that he/she will make a mistake given the huge number of human-machine interactions in a unit of time and human nature being unsuitable for multiple, simultaneous routine tasks. While short term strategies have to rely on development and deployment of technical means for supervision and protection of systems, for (re)defining the legal framework and creating and nurturing the (new) body of cyber law enforcement, a long term strategy is also needed. It has to focus on accelerated and prompt education and increased awareness in all age groups, literally from kindergarten to retirement. This education has to be mandatory in all school systems and within the working environment in the framework of occupational safety. It has to be a major component of everyone's continuous, lifelong education. In order to support this strategy, national centers for increased awareness and broad education should be established, strongly linked with academia both because of academia's deep insight in cyber security development and its involvement in development of educational methods and tools. The long term strategy has to evolve a new culture of self preservation as well as community (self) care and preservation providing visible and omnipresent emergency response focal points. This long term strategy needs to be devised urgently and put in operation in parallel with short term strategies.

Keywords: cyber security, long-term strategy, education, awareness, culture

Introduction

Many respectable institutions have tried to define cyber security [1, 2], one of them being: "*Cyber security, also referred to as information technology security, focuses on protecting computers, networks, programs and data from unintended or unauthorized*

[1] Email: Predrag.Pale@FER.hr

access, change or destruction" [3]. There is even a distinction between the terms "cyber security" and "cyber security" [4].

Perhaps it is better to try to explain, rather than to define, what is meant with the term "cyber security", at least in the scope of this paper: Cyber security is the property and state of legal and physical entities to receive, process, archive and disseminate information in a way that is desirable and suitable for them. The cyber security is compromised or reduced when authorized entities do not have access to information, the information they access is unreliable or altered in an unwanted way, or their information is made available to unauthorized entities or when they cannot avoid receiving huge amounts of unwanted information.

It is also compromised if their information processing capability is reduced, altered, or made available to unauthorized entities. The information processing capability assumes the ability to receive, retrieve, browse or find wanted information, to process it, to store and archive it in a secure fashion and to disseminate it to all intended recipients in desired moment of time in a secure fashion. Processing assumes transformation of information of any kind, extraction of meaning from data by any method such as comparison, mathematical processing or transformation. Cyber security relates to cyber space which is constituted of a network of information processing nodes as well as of data and information. People can be viewed either as entities interacting with cyberspace or as components of cyber space, or both.

1. Cyber Space

Again, a multitude of definitions are available [5]. In the scope of this paper cyber space is considered to be a network of information processing nodes as well as the data and information traversing the network and/or stored within. So all sorts of devices and places they are put into, the fabric interconnecting them, being material or immaterial but also processes running on and between them compose the cyber space.

Devices are no longer just (big) computers or personal devices like desktops, laptops, tablets or smart phones. Entertainment equipment like TV sets, vehicles including cars to trains to roads, production equipment and 3D printers, sensing devices from meteorological sensors to radars, medical devices in operating room to those in our home, homes to public buildings, rain forests to outer space: all sorts of devices in all sorts of places. Besides connecting people to other people or to machines, there is a strong trend of connecting machines with machines, creating the "Internet of things" [6]. The data exchange rates and quantity of interactions will soon vastly overcome those where humans are involved. The last frontier to cross is the human body. Cochlear implants and neurological stimulators are already put inside human bodies, but a true revolution will come with the advent of tiny devices implanted in multitude of places inside a healthy man for the purpose of biofeedback and disease prevention [7]. Thus, human beings are no longer just users of cyber space, we are irreversibly becoming part of it: be it for the necessity to use and process the information it contains or for being connected directly into it.

2. The Problem

This dependence on cyberspace is essential. A majority of global citizens can no longer perform their duties at work without proper functioning of cyberspace. Even private life is increasingly dependent on it. Every interaction with a financial, legal or administrative system is impossible without cyberspace. Health services can be provided only in the most basic situations without ICT. One of crucial questions today is: "How long can citizens survive in case of cashless payment services breakdown". The first estimates are at three days.

The pervasiveness of ICT is so intense that it seems impossible to resist its usage in work and life. An individual can try it, but even if they succeed it is at expense of being marginalized in many ways. The true question is: "is it scalable? How many individuals can actually be 'disconnected'?" Cyber space is also everywhere. Pristine nature is only an illusion. Forests are monitored and overwhelmed with radio waves as are the oceans.

Further complications are created by the speed of change. New possibilities, new tools, new services are emerging daily. Even worse, those we have already used for years are changing daily. If nothing else, the user interface is changed just to create impression of novelty. However, even simple, 'cosmetic' changes influence our ability to use them, and to actually to understand them fully [8]. Indeed, it is difficult to find a single user, who completely understands even one service or tool: its functionality, undocumented features, bugs, and interaction with the cyber environment. No one can be sure what data is on his/her media and which communication messages are sent to where from his device by tools used daily or occasionally. No one has the time and most people don't have competencies to study any tool or service in depth. With the speed of change it is practically impossible to gain expertise. Combined with the fact that we cannot refuse to use those tools and services, we are in fact at the mercy of events in cyberspace. Further problems arise from the fact that even the simplest of new services and tools or even the smallest changes in existing ones can have unforeseeable consequences. It is obvious that users need methods, initiative and opportunity to learn about technologies, their scientific foundations and then the practicalities and consequences of using tools and services. They also need time and opportunity to think, rethink and discuss possible short and long term consequences. Currently there are no systems in place supporting those needs.

3. Current solution

Currently, most counter measures to cyber threats are in form of technological tools, legal instruments and law enforcement. They all have substantial weaknesses. Technology does not have intelligence to respond to all threats. Current technologies are able to build defense from known attacks and only from those which are easily recognizable. Attacks using slow scans and multiple attackers, combined with social engineering are practically undefeatable.

Legal protection works only for known attacks. Legal defense and instruments can be designed only after undesirable types events are identified, analyzed and studied. This can help in reducing overall load from cyber attacks, reduce damage and cost. However it fails to protect the critical infrastructure from novel attacks. Finally, there is low enforcement those professionals trained and equipped to combat cyber attacks. Unfortunately, they have two major weaknesses: they are outnumbered and slow.

4. The Real Problem

The real problem is deeply rooted in the essence of cyberspace. First, the attacks are being performed by machines while the defense is being led by humans. Attackers, humans, can use all the time they need to construct an attack. They can do so completely isolated from cyber space. They can be fully undetectable, hidden from law enforcement and any form of surveillance and monitoring. Once they design the attack and necessary tools and test them in their detached lab; they only need a few seconds to inject them in cyber space. They can do so from any public cyber terminal, by penetrating unprotected wireless networks or by tricking some legitimate user to do so. They can be completely hidden. In some cases, once their attack is injected, cyber space alone takes over and repeats the attack over and over again. In milliseconds the attacks spread over nodes of cyber space. Law enforcement, humans, on the other hand needs to recognize the attack but they rely on systems in place capable of detecting cyber attacks. Unfortunately, novel attacks may not be detected by current technologies. Even if systems detect the attack, humans have to analyze it and devise counter measures. In the time it takes to respond to the cyber attack, machines have repeatedly spread the attack in milliseconds all over the cyber space. This is a battle that is hard to win, especially in critical situations when critical infrastructure is attacked.

Secondly, the notion of attacker has changed, as well. While there are, and probably will always be professional attackers, in cyberspace everyone is a potential attacker. Mistakes made by ordinary users or technicians running the cyber space, misunderstandings and lack of knowledge all create events equally dangerous as "true" attacks. Even more, actions and reactions taken by law enforcement may be exaggerated, misjudged, ill devised or simply wrong in light of the attack, and cause new damage, sometimes worse than the potential from the original attack. All these mistakes can also multiply rapidly within the cyber space.

5. The Real "Real" Problem

Besides being rooted in the essence of cyber space, the risks and dangers are also rooted in the essence of modern (western) society: its values and principles. Firstly, everything is allowed, unless explicitly forbidden. Even forbidden things can be done, if one cannot be caught. This means that no one is thinking about the real consequences of one's actions. Rather only about existing rules. In the environment where new tools are deployed daily with unknown side effects, action without weighing consequences creates a dangerous combination.

Secondly, ignorance for everything outside of the immediate task and goal and a narrow field of action is overwhelming. Besides the lack in breadth and depth of knowledge, there is a significant lack of care to consequences for other people and common things, and a lack of empathy and lack of loyalty. If care for some resource, process, culture or any other non-individual item is not explicitly assigned to someone, there is a slim chance that someone will take responsibility for it. An unmonitored asset is an easy target for attackers. The 'Cyber police', those professionals in charge of protection of cyber space are vastly outnumbered by potential attackers, especially if all those who create problems by making mistakes are included. They need help and assistance from every cyber citizen.

6. A Solution

The true, long term solution is obviously the empowerment of individuals and strengthening of society's ability to respond to cyber security incidents. Individuals should acquire significant competence to understand cyber space and to recognize risks, threats and incidents as well the ability to deploy personal counter measures. The sheer knowledge and skills have to be accompanied with a changed culture and climate that values the integrity of cyber space. The wellbeing of cyber space in its fullness as well as other citizens (even outside of the cyber space) has to become everyone's priority. Only understanding that no one can be secure and safe for him/herself but only in a group, jointly with his peers can we build a path to significantly higher levels of cyber security.

Every strange, odd or unusual behavior or fact should be communicated to everyone concerned, law enforcements included even when one is not personally involved. Similarly, before taking any action, especially new ones or involving new tools and services, we need to think and re-think whether they could harm someone or something and check with the authorities to see if we can proceed in a safe way.

If these two principles became the way of living for all cyber citizens, the majority of incidents caused by mistakes could be prevented. Also most of remaining incidents could be identified early on and authorities warned in a timely manner. This all would tremendously reduce the load on law enforcement allowing them to devote their resources to real threats.

However, this proposal sounds utopist. Changing a value system is a massive undertaking, even for a small community. On the global scale, it may be impossible because some cultures see placing value for others and society above oneself to be communistic in nature or reminiscent of a "hippie movement"; while other societies (particularly Asian) societies have a strong sense of social responsibility. Western societies sometimes prefer short term benefits over long term benefits. The fact that the growth of cyberspace threats outpaces the ability of societies to change poses another challenge.

Building competence is a no less challenging endeavor. It requires intense learning on the daily basis that does not improve productivity immediately. In addition, the learning outcomes on one's financial well-being are not visible immediately. On the contrary, today's learning reduces today's productivity, when work and private life are summed up.

A further problem with education is that we do not have educational resources for novel services and tools, educational resources are time consuming and costly to develop. Also education about adverse effects can be produced only after these effects are recognized. And finally, there are always multiple sources of similar educational programs and it is difficult to define which benefits the needs of a particular learner.

7. The Strategy

Regardless how utopist the proposed solution might appear, there really is no alternative to it in the long run. Technological advancement cannot be stopped. Machine intelligence that might replace humans in combat against cyber attacks is not even on the horizon and a totalitarian society which would automatically control all activities of all global citizens is also impossible in a short run. Therefore the long term strategy must focus on education, awareness and care as well as building support systems for citizens.

Education about information security, its foundations, essentials, mechanisms and procedures should be targeted at the broadest audience attempting to encompass all citizens. It should start with kindergarten and should accompany introduction of every information technology service or tool that children encounter as they grow up. This education should be an integral part of curricula throughout a child's formal education, continue throughout their active work life and should not stop in the "golden" age of retirement. As long as we are part of the cyber world, education in efficient and safe use of technologies is needed.

Education should not be limited to knowledge and skills in using cyber space and protecting oneself. Rather, awareness and care should be integral part of it. One should be aware of the broad consequences of one's actions in cyberspace as well as inactions, a failure to care and failure to mitigate our own mistakes as well as to those of others regardless of intention or target. An overarching value of good citizenship in cyber space is desperately needed.

Finally, citizens need support. Getting knowledge and skills should be simple, fast and free of charge. It should be a pleasant experience motivating for further study. Systems should be in place enabling every citizen to self assess his/her knowledge and skills in the area of cyber security, whenever they feel to do so, immediately and free of any charges. Such self assessments should be anonymous.

Reporting mistakes, attacks, and suspicious activities should be simple, fast, and free of charge and liabilities. The process of alerting authorities should be simple and quick, with a fast, professional, and tangible response. Finally, authorities should follow up with the citizen in a timely fashion until the threat is mitigated.

8. Action plan

Lifelong information security educational curriculum should be designed and become mandatory. It should cover all formal levels of education from kindergarten to university. It should be designed for in-service trainings for all workplaces and become mandatory in similar fashion to standards regarding fire safety and emergency preparedness. Education for the third age should be abundant and easily accessible.

National information security education centers /NISEC/ (and their international super structures) should be established with the sole role of raising awareness and providing life-long education. They should the primary source of trusted information and the first place to send one's own questions, sightings, and suspicions. In their operation, they have to be strongly tied with the academic community as a source for research information and as a partner to leverage academia's educational resources.

National CERTs need to be the primary coordination and response levels. Information received by NISEC should automatically be forwarded to CERT. While

NISEC will evaluate it from an educational point of view and leverage feedback received from CERT, CERT's role is to analyze information and react and/or escalate it to other levels/bodies. In case of false alarms, mistakes in reporting and other non-critical outcomes, their feedback should help NISEC to improve education in general and for the particular citizen who sent the report.

9. Conclusion

In is inevitable that cyber security will assume a larger concern within a country's overall security posture. Technological, legal and law enforcement measures cannot cope with it unless cyber citizens significantly increase their competences, awareness and responsibility and take an active approach toward their own safety and security and those of other citizens and cyber space in general.

The tremendous speed by which new services and tools are introduced and rapid change of the existing ones coupled with the values of global society may hinder the process of improving cyber security. However, there is no long term alternative to awareness and education. In order to achieve this, national and international authorities need to undertake firm and broad actions, fast and decisively: create mandatory lifelong educational curriculum related to cyber security; establish national information security educational centers, and foster and strengthen the role of national CERTs.

It is common sense that short term strategies based on technology, legislation and law enforcement need to be fostered as well and should not be replaced or in any way slowed down by the proposed long term strategy. On the contrary, they should be developed and put in operation in parallel with proposed measures. Since nothing in cyber security is permanent, it is clear that development of both short and long term strategies and their operationalization is not a single-shot project but rather an everlasting program comprised of various projects.

References

[1]. ITU. Cybersecurity [Internet]. ITU. 2014 [cited 2014 Mar 9]. Available from: http://www.itu.int/en/ITU-T/studygroups/com17/Pages/cybersecurity.aspx

[2]. ISACA. A simple definition of cybersecurity - ISACA Now [Internet]. 2014 [cited 2014 Mar 9]. Available from: http://www.isaca.org/Knowledge-Center/Blog/Lists/Posts/Post.aspx?ID=296

[3]. UMUC. What is Cyber Security? | UMUC [Internet]. 2014 [cited 2014 Mar 9]. Available from: http://www.umuc.edu/cybersecurity/about/cybersecurity-basics.cfm

[4]. InfoSecIsland. Cybersecurity vs. Cyber Security: When, Why and How to Use the Term [Internet]. 2013 [cited 2014 Mar 9]. Available from: http://www.infosecisland.com/blogview/23287-Cybersecurity-vs-Cyber-Security-When-Why-and-How-to-Use-the-Term.html

[5]. Rajnović D. Cyberspace – What is it? [Internet]. BlogsCisco - Cisco Blogs. 2012 [cited 2014 Mar 9]. Available from: https://blogs.cisco.com/security/cyberspace-what-is-it/

[6]. Carretero J, Daniel Garcia J. The Internet of Things: connecting the world. Pers Ubiquitous Comput. 2014 **18(2)**: pp. 445–7.

[7]. Rudall BH. Contemporary systems and cybernetics. Kybernetes. 1999, **28(1):**8–20.

[8]. Weir CS, Douglas G, Carruthers M, Jack M. User perceptions of security, convenience and usability for ebanking authentication tokens. Comput Secur. 2009 **28(1–2)**, 47–62.

Cyber Security and Resiliency Policy Framework
A. Vaseashta et al. (Eds.)
IOS Press, 2014

doi:10.3233/978-1-61499-446-6-135

Protecting and Preserving Ground Water with Monitoring Systems and Vulnerability Maps

Konstantin PAPATHEODOROU[1] and Konstantinos EVANGELIDIS
Technological Educational Institute of Serres
Terma Magnisias St
62124 Serres, GREECE

Abstract. As Ground Water (GW) is a natural resource of vital importance, its protection against all types of threats is an absolute necessity. GW as a natural source can be effectively protected and managed using GW monitoring systems provided that, when developing such a system for a specific area of implementation, certain conditions are met and parameters are taken into account including GW recharge conditions, hydrogeological regime, land uses and GW vulnerability from surface pollution (as GW is often hydraulically connected to surface and surface water). To assess those parameters, reliable and accurate data are needed. The acquisition of such required data, regarding their economic cost and time needed, poses obstacles sometimes difficult to overcome. At this point, contemporary technologies as Geographic Information Systems (GIS) and Remote Sensing (RS) can provide solutions. In the present paper, a combination of case studies including the identification and delineation of GW recharge areas using RS, the GW vulnerability assessment using GIS and the development of a Web based GW monitoring system that can also be used as an early warning system for GW protection, is presented. The methodologies proposed have been tested in various areas of Northern Greece providing reliable results at minimal costs. Their combined application can provide the tools to constantly monitor GW quality, to detect GW pollution at a very early stage, to select and apply remediation measures and to continuously rate them, to detect pollution sources, to support decision making regarding land uses, to help raise public awareness and overall, to ensure GW protection and sustainability.

Keywords: groundwater vulnerability, groundwater monitoring

Introduction

Ground water is a natural resource of vital importance as it is usually the main source of potable water. Conservation and enhancement of groundwater resources through land care, management, recharge preservation and protection of quality is therefore essential. Within this context, recharge area delineation, groundwater vulnerability assessment and groundwater management are key issues.

Groundwater recharge areas feed water and anything else within the aquifer towards the water abstraction facilities and have therefore to be identified and protected in order to preserve groundwater quality. Groundwater recharge can take place through

---

[1] Email: conpap@teiser.gr

inflow along aquifer boundaries among different aquifers; especially where aquifers developed in mountainous areas come in contact with permeable sediments along valley edges, thus forming primary groundwater recharge zones.

Groundwater recharge can also take place via direct rain water percolation through permeable geologic formations, and groundwater vulnerability from surface pollution is in many cases high and has to be assessed in the most accurate and reliable way. Provided that they are based on reliable and accurate data and tested and approved methodologies, vulnerability maps can then be used to help make decisions about land use planning thus preserving groundwater's integrity.

During the last decades, the continuously increasing demand in groundwater created the necessity for groundwater resources management in order to protect the quantity of groundwater and ensure a dependable and affordable supply of this resource. A management system that provides groundwater monitoring on a constant basis is therefore required. Such a System can help manage groundwater resources, fine tune exploitation parameters, indicate pollutants from a very early stage, evaluate measure effectiveness, project to future needs and over all, help make decisions about the sustainable use of this natural resource. Designing such a system is not an easy task as it is a dynamic procedure that changes both spatially and temporarily in parallel with the continuously changing demand, production and consumption conditions. Additional problems for groundwater sustainable management include the lack of a systematic source protection, not always imposed legal frameworks, the lack of reliable information and lack of public awareness.

As data availability, accuracy, reliability and costs are among the key issues in all three aforementioned problems, the use of contemporary technologies as Remote Sensing (RS) and Geographic Information Systems (GIS) to tackle these issues is demonstrated. Within this context, methodologies used and results from case studies are presented and discussed.

2. Groundwater Protection and Management. Methodologies Applied

2.1 Groundwater Recharge Area Delineation

The area of implementation is the plain of Trikala, Greece (Figure.1) where due to groundwater over-exploitation during the past decades, groundwater degradation problems emerged. As groundwater demands in the area continuously increase due to population growth and climate change, prevention and management of groundwater resources is essential for reassuring sustainable development.

There are two main aquifer systems developed in the area; one is developed in the carbonate formations of the Koziakas mountain and another, within the alluvial sediments that fill the basin of Trikala plain. Previous investigations on the groundwater regime of the area suggest [1] that there is a very small or non-existent hydraulic connection between the two aquifer systems due to the presence of an ophiolitic complex that separates them and acts as an impervious barrier (Figure.1-geologic cross section).

Groundwater recharge in the aquifers developed in Trikala basin is therefore suggested to take place directly from surface water percolation through the permeable surface formations. Based on this assumption, a number of potentially hazardous to groundwater land uses could be selected for the area where the ophiolitic formations outcrop as they are considered to be impermeable.

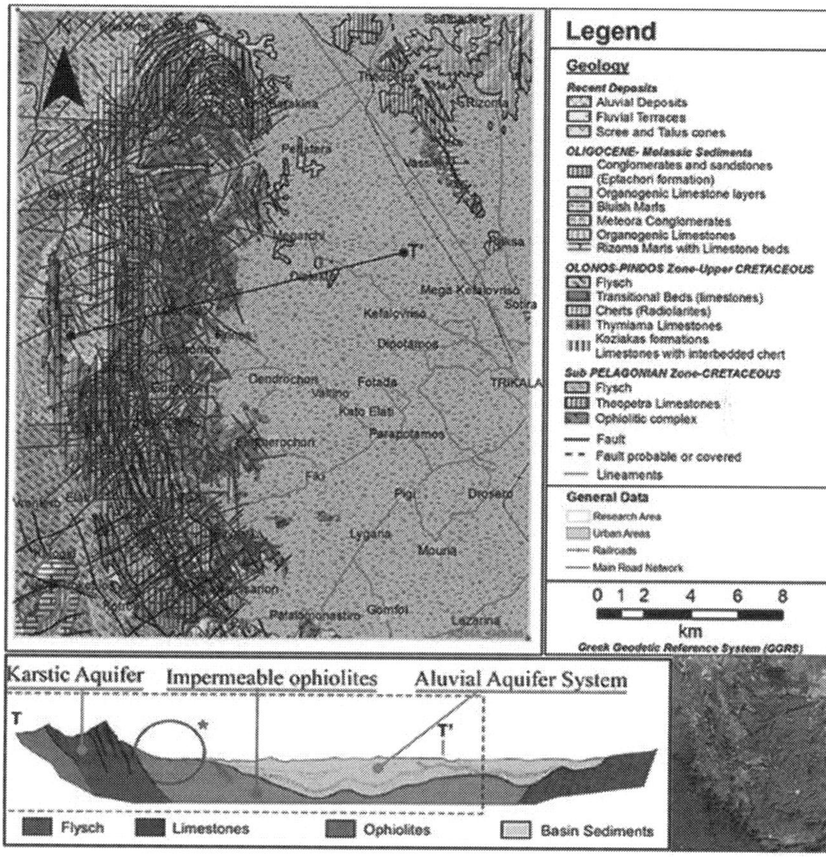

Figure 1: Geologic Map and geologic cross section of the area under investigation (red circle).

The integration of a sequence of remote sensing techniques with geologic and hydrochemical data for geological and hydrogeological assessment was used (fig. 2) to trace groundwater flow paths through the theoretically impermeable ophiolitic formations and to delineate recharge areas. Landsat TM (http://glcf.umiacs.umd.edu/) image visual interpretation was based on remote sensing techniques including band-ratioing, Principal Component Analysis (PCA), and False Color Composite creation. Lineament statistical analysis, lineament density maps, geologic maps and hydrochemical data were additionally used in order to verify remote sensing results and to indicate potential groundwater flow paths through the ophiolitic formations that outcrop in the area.

As resulted the investigation, there is a far greater number of faults than the ones already mapped in the area. Landsat TM Band Ratios (BR) and False Color Composites (FCCs) as the (R-G-B) (PC2-BR4/7-BR4/3), (BR4/7-BR4/3-TM4),

(Papatheodorou, 2010) as well as the [(BR4/3)x(BR7/4)] image [2] are suggested to be appropriate for mapping these features.

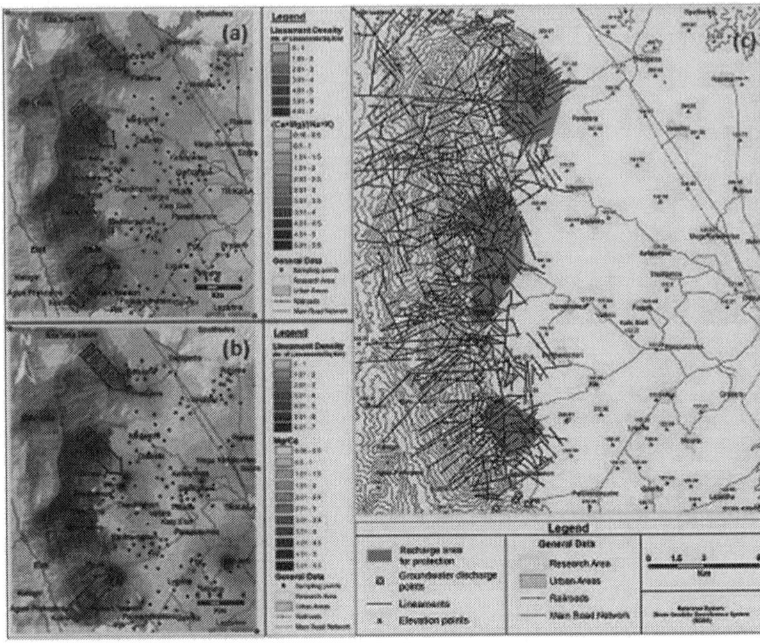

Figure 2: Ion Ratio spatial distribution in the research area as compared to lineament density maps. (2a): [(Ca+Mg)/(Na+K)] indicating groundwater residence time in the aquifer, (2b): [Mg/Ca] indicating groundwater origin and 2c: Recharge areas delineated.

To verify groundwater flow through the ophiolitic complex, groundwater chemical analyses data in the form of ion concentrations and their ratios were used as they can help indicate water origin and residence time in geologic formations [3]. Ion ratio [Mg/Ca], was used to indicate groundwater flow through limestones ([Mg/Ca] < 0.7), dolomites (0.7 - 0.9) or ophiolitic formations ([Mg/Ca] > 1.0). Ratio values in the area range from 0.1 to 5.39 and ion ratio [Mg/Ca] spatial distribution indicates groundwater inflow from the ophiolitic formations towards the plain sediments (fig. 2a). Ion ratio [(Ca+Mg)/(Na+K)] provides information about groundwater's residence time in the aquifer and indicates if a part of the aquifer is under continuous groundwater flow. Ratio values range from 0.5 towards the center of the basin, a value indicative of high residence time to 5.0 at the edge of the basin, a value that corresponds to continuous groundwater flow (fig. 2b). Concluding, ion ratios as compared to the lineament and the lineament density maps, provide strong indications of groundwater inflow towards the basin sediments so principal recharge areas that must be protected can be delineated (fig. 2c).

2.2 Groundwater Vulnerability Assessment

Groundwater is subjected to contamination from various natural and anthropogenic sources so groundwater vulnerability against pollution from ground surface must be carefully considered when planning land use on a long term. The area of implementation is located in Northern Greece and covers a large part of Emathia and Pella plains (Figure.3), forming one of the most important agricultural areas in northern Greece. In the same area, the presence of numerous industrial and other potentially hazardous installations, pose a significant hazard against groundwater preservation.

The DRASTIC method [4] and it's variations were applied to assess groundwater vulnerability in the area. DRASTIC method is considered among various groundwater vulnerability assessment methods as the one that takes into consideration most of the hydro-geological parameters. DRASTIC is in fact, the acronym of D(epth to groundwater), R(echarge rate), A(quifer media), S(oil media), T(opography), I(mpact of vadose zone) and C(onductivity of the aquifer). The method involves the calculation of DRASTIC Index (DI):

$$\textbf{DRASTIC Index}\ (DI) = Dr \times Dw + Rr \times Rw + Ar \times Aw + Sr \times Sw + Tr \times Tw + Ir \times Iw + Cr \times Cw$$

where "r" is the rating for each of the parameters and "w" the respective weighting factor which is standardized and given by respective tables (table I).

The "Pesticide DRASTIC" method incorporates a modification that takes an additional consideration on the nature of the soil media which, due to organic matter and clay minerals present, affects the pollutant reduction/retention process. An additional approach is suggested by the "Modified DRASTIC" method [5] which takes into consideration land use. The Modified Drastic Index (MDI) is calculated as MDI = DI + Lr × Lw, where DI is the typical DRASTIC Index (DI), Lr is the Land Use parameter and Lw the weighting factor (both parameters are given by respective tables provided by the methodology).

TABLE I. DRASTIC and Pesticide DRASTIC weighting factors

DRASTIC parameter	Weighting Factors	
	DRASTIC	**Pesticide DRASTIC**
D	5	5
R	4	4
A	3	3
S	2	5
T	1	3
I	5	4
C	3	2

In order to assess groundwater vulnerability, a Geographic Information System (GIS) was developed. To calculate the individual DRASTIC parameters, soil maps, digitized topographic maps of 1:5000 scale and data from more than 250 sampling points were used including bore logs, water level measurements, pumping test results and water chemical analyses results. Data available were updated with in situ measurements.

DRASTIC and Pesticide DRASTIC [6] parameters were calculated as described by the respective methodologies. Weighting factors were taken from TABLE.1 and all other parameters were classified according to the DRASTIC methodology provisions.

i. Depth to groundwater (D): Was calculated by classifying water level measurements according to the methodology's provisions.
ii. Recharge rate: Calculation was based on rainfall and on the infiltration rate of each of the geologic formations that outcrop in the area.
iii. Aquifer media (A): Characterization was based on bore log data.
iv. Soil media (S): Soil media was evaluated by available soil maps, soil analyses data and in situ observations/sampling and analyses.
v. Topography (T): Considering the low topography of the area, topographic maps at a 1:5000 scale were digitized and used to create a Digital Terrain Model which was in turn used to create a slope map of the area
vi. Impact of vadose zone (I): Calculation was based on bore log data.
vii. Hydraulic conductivity of the aquifer (C): The parameter was assessed from pumping tests carried out in the water wells of the area.

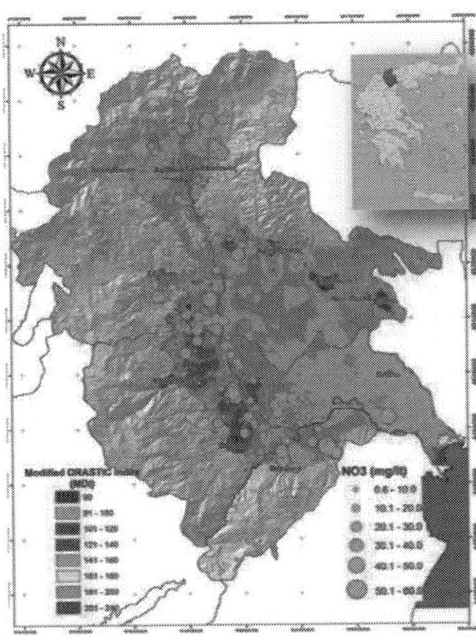

Figure 3: Nitrogen ion concentration plotted against the vulnerability map. Increased NO_3 concentrations in "High" and "Very High" vulnerability areas indicate groundwater's high vulnerability and the used method's results reliability

As a result, DI values for the entire area range from 77 to 217. These values indicate, according to the methodology, "very low" (81-100) to "Very High" (greater than 200) groundwater vulnerability.

The DRASTIC method does not take into consideration land use despite the fact that the main causes of groundwater pollution are anthropogenic so the "Modified DRASTIC" method which considers land use in assessing vulnerability was used. Modified Drastic Index (MDI) was calculated using Corine Land Cover 2000 (European Environment Agency) data and maps. As resulted, MDI values range from

81, which is considered as "Low" to 256 which is considered as "Very High", groundwater vulnerability. As is shown (Figure.3), the western part of the plain exhibits a "High" to "Very High" vulnerability whereas the eastern part a "Low" to "High" one with a part showing a "Moderate" vulnerability (green area).

To evaluate groundwater vulnerability assessment results, groundwater chemical analyses data from 114 water wells in the area were used. Nitrate concentration has been suggested as an anthropogenic pollution index and has been used to evaluate the results of groundwater vulnerability assessment methods [7]. Nitrate concentrations (as NO_3 N mg/l) in groundwater as compared to the vulnerability map created show a considerable agreement. Nitrate concentration is greater in the western part of the implementation area which exhibits "high" to "very high" vulnerability. Moreover, nitrate concentration in a number of water wells has been found to be very high indicating that pollution has advanced, especially considering the fact that water samples were pumped from the well and not taken from the shallow phreatic aquifer alone. As it therefore appears, the DRASTIC methodology based on relatively high resolution data, can provide reliable results regarding the assessment of groundwater vulnerability to contamination from ground surface. Vulnerability maps can in turn, provide reliable information and assistance to decision making regarding legislation and landscape sustainable planning.

2.3 Groundwater Protection and Management

A monitoring and early warning system for groundwater level fluctuations due to climatic condition changes or human activities as well as for water quality changes can greatly help in decision-making on water-takings, drought management and land use planning; thus providing support for groundwater sustainable management. Designing groundwater monitoring systems and networks is not a simple task because such a system strongly depends on site specific conditions and on the continuously changing demand, production and consumption conditions. Various approaches have been proposed and adopted for that matter [8,9] and any approach, in order to be effective, must depend on the objectives of the groundwater monitoring system as well as on the parameters affecting groundwater quantity and quality over the entire study area.

The presented GroundWater System's (GWIS) development was based on those concepts so it is designed in a way that selected parameters regarding groundwater quantity and/or quality can be constantly or selectively measured and data can be instantly transferred and stored in a server [2,10,11]. This is achieved either by direct input or by using telecommunications technology (i.e. commercial GPRS network). Sampling point's selection in an area is based on the conceptual site model, the data quality objectives, the existing regulatory framework and the performance monitoring requirements.

The conceptual model itself focuses in understanding the existing problems for the specific site. Factors that must be known include the scope of the monitoring procedure, the geologic and the hydro geologic regime of the area, the biological and geochemical conditions, potential pollutant transport pathways of (potential) contamination as well as historical data. GWIS implementation includes performance monitoring which aims at the progress verification towards the overall monitoring program goals; the most important being to make informed decisions regarding environmental issues as well as possible groundwater monitoring system enhancements (fig. 4).

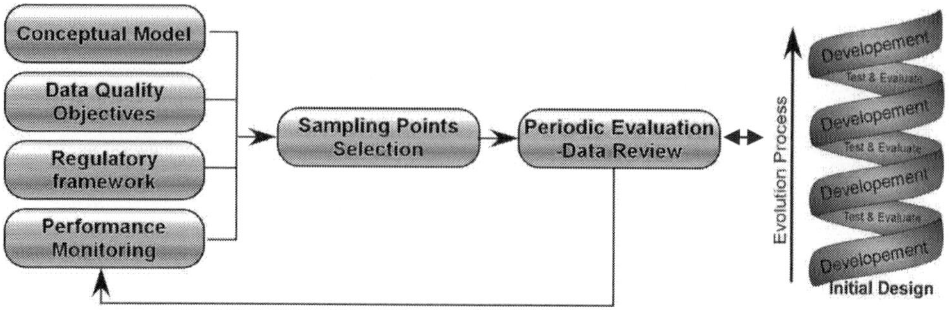

Figure 4: GroundWater Information System's (GWIS) conceptual model.

The adopted System Architecture is a typical multi-tier architecture customized to meet the proposed system requirements and is introduced through three major tiers (layers):

A. The Data Collection Layer which comprises any kind of field equipment device that is used to perform measurements related to groundwater critical factors.

B. The Data/Services/Application Layer which groups the typical data and application (business logic) layers of the 3–tier architecture along with a layer comprising the required services provided by standard software components (Web Server, Map Server and Database Sever). It also includes a number of sub-layers as:
   - Database and Assisting Services.
   - Application and Data access code that contain Web-GIS applications and groundwater simulation models.
   - User access control and content management, that ensures authorized user access built on user profiles.

C. The Presentation layer which aims at providing custom browser based applications to satisfy user interaction.

GWIS, made use of commercial software products including ESRI's Internet Map Server (v.9.3) which cooperates with specific combinations of Web Server and Servlet Engine versions of the Apache products. The test area selected for the implementation was a part of Thessaly plain (fig. 1) where data from a total number of 303 sampling points were available. Data included bore logs, water levels measured periodically as well as data regarding the physical and chemical parameters of groundwater in the area. As the data used in the pilot implementation were already available, they were imported in GWIS as standard tabular data files (Excel worksheets, comma and/or tab delimited etc.) and were used to create various types of spatial information including groundwater level maps as well as spatial distribution maps of physical properties and ion concentrations. Data retrieval and processing is done through a Web application, so authorized users can have access to the system remotely, through a web browser service (fig. 5a).

Sustainability and improvement of the GWIS is through periodic evaluation on a regular basis. Evaluation includes a review of all the data and results generated and their comparison to historical data. Data reviews can help detect major changes in the hydro geologic regime of the area sometimes indicative of contamination. It can also help reveal contaminant trends and evaluate remedial measure performance in case measures have been taken. The designed system including the monitoring network can not only adapt to local conditions but it can also be optimized. The monitoring network optimization can be based on tracking measured parameters as groundwater levels or ion concentrations and evaluating their spatial distribution changes over time. GWIS is capable of monitoring in real time, the status of critical groundwater parameters and of providing alarms and special information when a set threshold in one or more selected parameters is exceeded (fig. 5b). As all parameter values change over time, appropriate feature symbology facilitates sampling point performance control and "surveillance" capabilities.

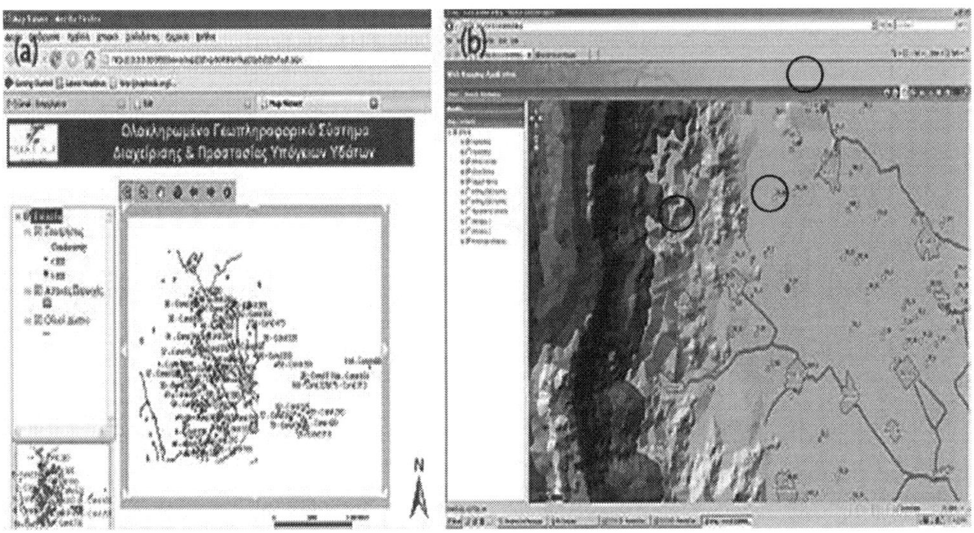

Figure 5: GWIS implementation. (a) Data input and management. (b) Alarms triggered (red dots) when set parameter thresholds are exceeded.

Concluding, the basic characteristics of the GWI system developed and implemented, include adaptability to user needs that change according to demand, production and consumption conditions, conformity with National and EU Provisions and Directives regarding the use of Geographic Information Systems and Data, ease of use for non-expert users, remote access for data updating and evaluation, integration of various types of data and information. Moreover it can incorporate various models for data processing and interpretation and it can provide results in various forms (tables, charts, maps, reports) [12]. Map and data access over the internet provides accessibility to experts according to their access rights and can also be used to inform the public thus helping raise public awareness and promote groundwater protection, conservation and management strategies.

3. Conclusions

Contemporary technologies as Remote Sensing and Geographic Information Systems can provide reliable and accurate enough information to assess important parameters necessary to protect and preserve groundwater. Vulnerability maps can be produced and used to support decisions regarding legislation and land use planning. In any case, data availability, reliability and accuracy are the main concerns. Groundwater protection and management can be based on a GroundWater Information System as the one proposed. GWIS can adapt to local conditions and to user needs even as they change over time. By tracking measured parameters as groundwater levels or ion concentrations that are above a set threshold, it can be used as an early warning system helping identify hazards at a very early stage. In any case, contaminant trends can be identified and remedial measure performance can also be evaluated. Finally, as it is Web based, it can provide information to the public, helping in this way to raise public awareness and promote groundwater conservation, protection and management strategies. Overall, contemporary technologies as remote sensing and geographic information systems can add value to scientific knowledge and strongly support decision making regarding the establishment of regulatory frameworks for groundwater sustainable exploitation, management and protection.

References

1. Kallergis Y. (1970). Hydrogeological study of the Kalabaka sub-basin (W. Thessaly) [In Greek], Ph. D Dis., National Technical University of Athens, Athens.
2. Papatheodorou K. and Evangelidis K. (2009): Ground Water Information System. A digital tool for groundwater resources protection and management. BENA Conference on "Life Quality and Capacity Building in the frame of a Safe Environment, Katerini, Greece.
3. Hounslow A.W. (1995): Water Quality data analysis and Interpretation. Lewis Publishers. pp397.
4. Aller L, Bennett T, Lehr JH, Petty RH, Hackett G (1987): DRASTIC: a standardised system for evaluating groundwater pollution potential using hydrogeologic settings. US Environmental Protection Agency, Oklahoma City, OK, pp. 622.
5. Secunda, S., Collin, M.L., Melloul, A. (1998): Groundwater vulnerability assessment using a composite model combining DRASTIC with extensive agricultural land use in Israel's Sharon region. Journal of Environmental Management 54, 3957.
6. Engel B., Navulur K. and Cooper B. (1996): Estimating groundwater vulnerability to nonpoint source pollution from nitrates and pesticides on a regional scale. Department of Agricultural and Biological Engineering, Purdue University, West Lafayette, IN 47907-1146, USA.
7. Rupert, M.G., Dace, Tana, Maupin, M.A., and Wicherski, Bruce, 1991, Ground-water vulnerability assessment, Snake River Plain, southern Idaho: Boise, Idaho Department of Health and Welfare, Division of Environmental Quality, p. 25.

8. Dutta D. Das Gupta A., Ramnarong V. (2007): Design and Optimization of a Ground Water Monitoring System Using GIS and Multi-criteria Decision Analysis, groundwater monitoring & Remediation, Wiley.
9. Environmental Agency UK, (2001): Environment Agency Framework for Groundwater Resources. Conceptual and Numerical Modelling. R&D Technical Report W214.
10. Papatheodorou, C (2010): Groundwater Flow Paths Delineation Using Remote Sensing Techniques and GIS. EARSEL Symposium Proceedings on "Remote Sensing for Science, Education and Natural and Cultural Heritage", Paris France.
11. Papatheodorou C., Theocharis D and Fountoulis G. (2012): A Remotely Sensed contribution to the Western Attica (Greece) tectonic geology. 4th International Workshop of EARSEL SIG "Geological Applications" on Remote Sensing and Geology, Myconos, Greece
12. Radian International, White Rock, New Mexico USA (2000): Guide to Optimal Groundwater Monitoring, Naval Facilities Engineering Service Center, Port Hueneme, CA, USA.

Subject Index

Author Index